T0304699

CYBER SECURITY MANAGEMENT AND STRATEGIC INTELLIGENCE

Within the organization, the cyber security manager fulfils an important and policy-oriented role. Working alongside the risk manager, the Information Technology (IT) manager, the security manager and others, the cyber security manager's role is to ensure that intelligence and security manifest in a robust cyber security awareness programme and set of security initiatives that when implemented help strengthen the organization's defences and those also of its supply chain partners.

Cyber Security Management and Strategic Intelligence emphasizes the ways in which intelligence work can be enhanced and utilized, guiding the reader on how to deal with a range of cyber threats and strategic issues. Throughout the book, the role of the cyber security manager is central, and the work undertaken is placed in context with that undertaken by other important staff, all of whom deal with aspects of risk and need to coordinate the organization's defences thus ensuring that a collectivist approach to cyber security management materializes. Real-world examples and cases highlight the nature and form that cyber-attacks may take, and reference to the growing complexity of the situation is made clear. In addition, various initiatives are outlined that can be developed further to make the organization less vulnerable to attack. Drawing on theory and practice, the authors outline proactive, and collectivist approaches to counteracting cyber-attacks that will enable organizations to put in place more resilient cyber security management systems, frameworks and planning processes.

Cyber Security Management and Strategic Intelligence references the policies, systems and procedures that will enable advanced undergraduate and postgraduate students, researchers and reflective practitioners to understand the complexity associated with cyber security management and apply a strategic intelligence perspective. It will help the cyber security manager to promote cyber security awareness to a number of stakeholders and turn cyber security management initiatives into actionable policies of a proactive nature.

Peter Trim is a Reader in Marketing and Security Management at Birkbeck Business School, Birkbeck, University of London. He has published over 50 academic articles in a range of academic journals and has produced a number of single-authored, co-authored and edited books. Peter has been Chair of the UK Cyber Security Research Network

Group and taken two delegations of UK cyber security experts to South Korea and hosted two cyber security South Korean delegations in the UK. Peter has won a number of grants and has been Principal Investigator on two research projects. He has also organized a number of conferences and workshops and has worked on a number of cyber security initiatives involving academia, government and industry.

Yang-Im Lee is a Senior Lecturer in Marketing at Westminster Business School, University of Westminster, where she teaches marketing and related subjects. She has published over 30 articles in a range of academic journals and has also been the co-author of several books. She has also worked on a number of research projects and has been a member of the UK-Korea Cyber Security Research Network and a Visiting Fellow at Birkbeck, University of London. She also provided support for the Information Assurance Advisory Council and was their Academic Liaison Panel Co-ordinator for a number of years.

CYBER SECURITY MANAGEMENT AND STRATEGIC INTELLIGENCE

Peter Trim and Yang-Im Lee

Routledge
Taylor & Francis Group

LONDON AND NEW YORK

Designed cover image: cofotoisme

First published 2025
by Routledge
4 Park Square, Milton Park, Abingdon, Oxon OX14 4RN

and by Routledge
605 Third Avenue, New York, NY 10158

Routledge is an imprint of the Taylor & Francis Group, an informa business

British Library Cataloguing-in-Publication Data
A catalogue record for this book is available from the British Library

ISBN: 978-1-032-94468-5 (hbk)
ISBN: 978-1-032-94466-1 (pbk)
ISBN: 978-1-003-57090-5 (ebk)

DOI: 10.4324/9781003570905

Typeset in Sabon
by SPi Technologies India Pvt Ltd (Straive)

Dedication
To Jeong Beim, Peter A.J., Richard, Violet and Yen Bun

CONTENTS

List of Figures   *viii*

List of Tables   *ix*

About the Authors   *x*

Preface   *xii*

1   Cyber Security Management and Strategic Intelligence   1

2   Cyber Security Management and Strategic Intelligence in Context   8

3   Cyber Security Management and Strategic Intelligence Policy
    Implementation Strategies   46

4   Artificial Intelligence and Cyber Security Management   69

5   Setting the Scene for a Cyber Security Management Conceptual
    Model and Framework   86

6   Partnership in the Context of Cyber Security   106

7   A Collectivist Enterprise Risk Management Cyber Threat Model   125

8   Theoretical and Managerial Implications   144

Index   167

FIGURES

1.1 Navigational map: The linkage between the themes and topics of cyber
     security management and strategic intelligence   3
2.1 Conceptual framework outlining the main topics underpinning cyber
     security management and strategic intelligence   30
2.2 The cyber security management and strategic intelligence process   36
3.1 Extended conceptual framework outlining the main topics underpinning
     cyber security management and strategic intelligence   59
3.2 Cyber security management and strategic intelligence continuity   64
4.1 Artificial intelligence (AI) policy and threat detection   82
5.1 Cyber security model and framework process   101
6.1 Partnership development to combat cyber security attacks   120
7.1 A collectivist enterprise risk management cyber threat model   126
7.2 A collectivist cyber threat intelligence policy and strategy framework   139
8.1 Organizational cyber security interdependency   162

TABLES

2.1 Significant cyber incidents, their categorization and risk rating from
January 2024 to June 2024   11
3.1 The usefulness and learning outcomes of selected cyber security
training videos   53
3.2 The usefulness and learning outcomes of selected cyber security
academic articles and conference papers   56
7.1 Illustrative example of a cyber security risk register   134

ABOUT THE AUTHORS

Peter Trim is a reader in Marketing and Security Management at Birkbeck Business School, Birkbeck, University of London and holds degrees from NELP/CNAA (BSc), Cranfield (MSc and PhD), City University (MBA) and the University of Cambridge (MEd). Peter is a Fellow of the Higher Education Academy and the Royal Society of Arts and was actively involved with the Information Assurance Advisory Council (IAAC) Academic Liaison Panel over a number of years. He has published over 50 academic articles in a range of journals including *Industrial Marketing Management*, the *European Journal of Marketing*, *the Journal of Business & Industrial Marketing*, *the Journal of Brand Management*, *Security Journal*, *the International Journal of Intelligence and Counter Intelligence*, *Disaster Prevention and Management*, *Cross-Cultural Management: An International Journal*, *Journal of Business Continuity & Emergency Planning*, *Simulation & Gaming: An International Journal of Theory, Practice and Research*, *Big Data and Cognitive Computing*, the *Journal of Global Scholars of Marketing Science: Bridging Asia and the World*, and the *International Journal of Retail & Distribution Management*. Peter has produced a number of single-authored, co-authored and edited books. He has co-authored with Yang-Im Lee, a book titled *Cyber Security Management: A Governance, Risk and Compliance Framework* (Farnham: Gower Publishing), and one with David Upton, titled *Cyber Security Culture: Counteracting Cyber Threats through Organizational Learning and Training* (Farnham: Gower Publishing). He has also co-edited with Yang-Im Lee, two books for MDPI (Basel, Switzerland) that originated from cyber security journal special issues. They are: *Managing Cybersecurity Threats and Increasing Organizational Resilience*, and *Advances in Cybersecurity: Challenges and Solutions*. In addition, Peter co-edited a book with Jack Caravelli titled *Strategizing Resilience and Reducing Vulnerability* (New York: Nova Science Publishers Inc.).

Peter has been Chair of the UK Cyber Security Research Network Group and taken two delegations of UK cyber security experts to South Korea and hosted two cyber security South Korean delegations in the UK. With Professor Youm, he has organized four UK and Korean cyber security workshops and co-edited two reports for the government titled *Korea-UK Initiatives in Cyber Security Research: Government, University and Industry Collaboration* (British Embassy Seoul: Republic of Korea); and *Korea-UK Collaboration in Cyber Security: From Issues and Challenges to Sustainable Partnership* (British Embassy Seoul: Republic of Korea). Prior to this, Peter contributed to the Cyber Attacks section of the University College London report *Scientific Advice and Evidence in Emergencies*, which was edited by Professor McGuire and submitted to the House of Commons Science and Technology Committee as written evidence.

Peter has won a number of grants and has been principal investigator on two research projects: One was funded by the UK's Technology Strategy Board and the other was funded by the Technology Strategy Board and South East England Development Agency (SEEDA). In addition to this, he has been involved in a number of initiatives such as the Canada-UK Partnership for Knowledge Forum, the Law Enforcement and National Security Global Forum and *Increasing Cyber Security Provision in the UK and Korea: Identifying Market Opportunities for SMEs*, which was funded by the UK's Department of Business Innovation & Skills and the Korean Government's Ministry of Science, ICT and Future Planning. Peter has also organized a large number of conferences, research workshops and has been actively involved in various professional associations.

Yang-Im Lee is a senior lecturer in Marketing at Westminster Business School, University of Westminster, where she teaches marketing and related subjects. Yang-Im has studied and worked in Korea, Japan and the UK. She undertook postgraduate studies at the School of Oriental and African Studies in London and was awarded a scholarship by Stirling University to undertake a PhD at that institution. Yang-Im has worked for both Brunel University and Royal Holloway, University of London, and provided guest lectures at Birkbeck, University of London. She has published over 30 articles in a range of academic journals including *Industrial Marketing Management*, the *European* the *Journal of Marketing*, the *Journal of Business & Industrial Marketing*, the *International Journal of Retail & Distribution Management*, the *Journal of Brand Management, Simulation & Gaming: An International Journal of Theory, Practice and Research* and *Big Data and Cognitive Computing* and also co-authored several books with Dr. Peter Trim.

Yang-Im is a fellow of the Higher Education Academy and the Royal Society of Arts and was involved in the iGRC Consortium three-year research project funded by the Technology Strategy Board and SEEDA. She also provided research input into the Technology Strategy Board Fast Track project undertaken by Peter Trim and David Upton entitled "Develop proven software system to improve emergency response exercises and extend it to develop robustness in critical information infrastructure". Yang-Im has been a member of the UK-Korea Cyber Security Research Network and a Visiting Fellow at Birkbeck, University of London. She also provided support for the IAAC and was their Academic Liaison Panel Co-ordinator for a number of years.

PREFACE

Cyber Security Management and Strategic Intelligence has been written to fill a gap in the cyber security literature. The book should appeal to a range of readers including university students, reflective practitioners, government policymakers and those without prior knowledge of cyber security management. The purpose of the book is to place cyber security management and strategic intelligence in a context that brings out the uniqueness of the subject, its importance and the role that cyber security specialists can play in ensuring that they avail themselves of relevant knowledge to undertake strategic intelligence that ensures that cyber security management is viewed as a necessary and influential component of strategic management. Taking cognizance of the fact that cyber security staff in an organization work with specialist staff within the same organization, with staff in partner organizations, and various external stakeholders, the topics covered provide insights into how cyber security management and strategic intelligence can be integrated throughout the supply chain and used to increase the resilience of the organization and the community.

The logic of the approach adopted in this book is underpinned by a commitment to improve cyber security management and to ensure that a collectivist approach is taken with regards to identifying cyber threats, ensuring that cyber-attacks are dealt with and that the lessons learned are made public. This should enable solutions to be found to unique cyber security–related problems. It should also widen the base of cyber security management and enable dialogue that provides further guidance in terms of new insights that help counter the actions of those involved in launching cyberattacks. By advocating a proactive and foresight-driven approach to what cyber security management and strategic intelligence involve, cyber security staff will be able to develop policies and strategies that help the organization to become more resilient. The emphasis placed on the use of intelligence and various aspects of analyses, will help those involved in cyber security management to interpret the subject matter and unravel the complexities associated with the cyber threat environment. The topics covered relate to both public sector and private sector organizations and the case examples should prove helpful as regards helping the reader to link theory and practice. Hence, by placing cyber security management and strategic intelligence within a strategic context, the cyber security management decision-making process will be strengthened, cyber-related vulnerabilities will be identified and eradicated and cyberattacks will be anticipated and prevented. In essence, cyber security awareness will be given greater prominence and the cyber security countermeasures highlighted will when implemented, make the organization more sustainable.

To assist the reader on their journey into cyber security management and strategic intelligence, the book has been written from the perspective of helping the reader to absorb information relating to the complexities of the subject and to help them navigate through the cyber security body of knowledge and place it in a leadership-oriented context. It is for this reason that the topics covered are given prominence and integrated in such a way as to build up the role of the cyber security manager. The reader will, as they read through the material, become aware of the type of leadership required from the cyber security manager and also the way in which the cyber security manager relates to staff and is perceived by staff. This will help the reader to gauge the role that the cyber security manager plays and, in addition, help the reader to understand the scope of the subject and how the tasks referred to can be fulfilled. Most importantly, the reader will be made aware of the uniqueness of the role played by the cyber security manager and those undertaking cyber security tasks.

One of the advantages of the book is that it contains a "reflection and questions section" that brings some of the key points covered in the chapter into focus. The "reflection and questions" section can be used as a central discussion platform to help the reader to place the main issues in context and think of how theory and practice are linked. Furthermore, the questions posed require additional thought and should provoke the reader into reading more widely and deeply into the subject matter. This should give rise to intellectual curiosity and a commitment to finding more information about the expanding topic of cyber security. The references, websites and further reading material should prove helpful in terms of finding sources of information on a variety of interlinked topics.

1

CYBER SECURITY MANAGEMENT AND STRATEGIC INTELLIGENCE

1.1 Introduction

Cyber Security Management and Strategic Intelligence is written with a number of audiences in mind and is suitable for those undertaking undergraduate business/management-related subjects and students engaged in postgraduate business/management studies. In addition, researchers who are studying aspects of cyber security and wish to know more about how cyber security is managed and what the cyber security manager needs to know and do in terms of intelligence-related work will find the book highly informative. The reader will also be encouraged to develop further their interest in social science theory as a number of theories, models and frameworks are referred to.

The book is structured in a way to place cyber security management and strategic intelligence within a holistic context and to provide guidance so that it becomes clear why the cyber security manager is considered part of the senior management team. Guidance is also provided as regards the cyber security manager identifying tasks and working with colleagues in a proactive manner that places emphasis on ensuring that cyber security is viewed as defensive. In addition, the theoretical perspectives and approaches referred to will help the cyber security manager to devise and implement cyber security management policy that is sustainable.

As well as appealing to an academic audience, the book will also appeal to reflective practitioners who want to deepen their knowledge of the subject and broaden their view of intelligence-related work. The theoretical insights and frameworks outlined will provide the reader with ways to evaluate the cyber security management process and discover ways to work with colleagues so that the cyber threats identified are managed in real time.

Cyber Security Management and Strategic Intelligence has been written in such a way as to place emphasis on how intelligence work can be enhanced and utilized. The objective is to help the reader deal with a range of cyber threats that they are able to contain and which do not get out of control or cause problems that have cascading effects. Throughout the book, reference is made to the role of the cyber security manager and

DOI: 10.4324/9781003570905-1

various other important members of staff such as the risk manager. In addition, real-world examples are provided that highlight the nature and form that cyber-attacks take. Furthermore, various initiatives are outlined that can be developed further in order to make the organization less vulnerable to attack. By drawing on various theoretical insights, cyber security management knowledge will be deepened and consequently, the proactive and collectivist approach to counteracting cyber-attacks will enable organizations to put in place more resilient cyber security management systems, frameworks and planning processes.

This chapter starts with placing the book in context (Section 1.2) and continues with adding to management knowledge (Section 1.3). The collectivist and stakeholder approach to cyber security (Section 1.4) is followed by the topics covered (Section 1.5). Next, the aims of the book (Section 1.6) are followed by the objectives of the book (Section 1.7). Learning outcomes of the book (Section 1.8) are followed by a reflection (Section 1.9) and then a conclusion is evident (Section 1.10).

1.2 Placing the Book in Context

This introductory chapter outlines the chapters that compose the book, and reference is made to a navigational map that can help the reader place the material in context. It is acknowledged that the readership represents a broad audience and people from various disciplines will find the subject matter of interest. Indeed, the theoretical underpinning provided will help the reader to develop specific insights into intelligence and security work and will also enable them to ask questions that can help focus the minds of those involved in cyber security and those seconded to work on security- and intelligence-related problems. The objective is to help those involved in or aiming to develop knowledge of cyber security management and strategic intelligence to better understand what they need to do and where they need to seek advice from. The challenges identified and the issues to be addressed will help the reader to develop solutions that make the organization more resilient, and this will be achieved through them enhancing their own learning.

It is envisaged that those already based in an organization will be aided by the organizational learning approach and will find new ways to solve the problems that they are confronted with. The examples cited have been drawn from a number of sources and are to illustrate points of interest that the reader can research into and develop a firmer appreciation of by going deeper into the subject matter. The references provided are drawn mainly from academic sources and this should enable the reader to develop their knowledge base and think in terms of cause and effect. Each chapter is crafted in a way that brings out the key points of interest and the reflection and questions sections help place in focus the main points.

Cyber Security Management and Strategic Intelligence is distinct in the sense it contains references to policies, systems and procedures that will enable university students, researchers and reflective practitioners to understand the complexity associated with cyber security management and strategic intelligence and what the cyber security manager needs to do in order to make sure that cyber security awareness is turned into actionable policy. The navigational map, Figure 1.1, illustrates how the reader is to be guided through the material and how the main themes and topics are linked with the subtopics covered. The main objective of the book is to make the reader aware of how the cyber

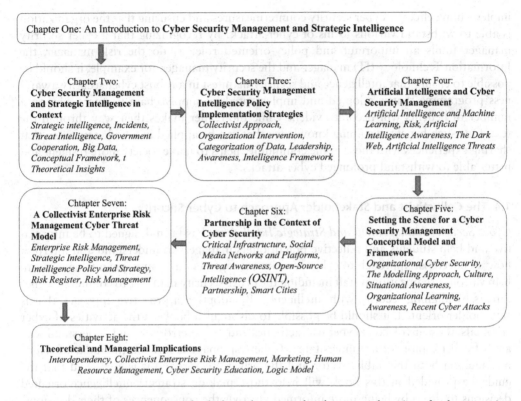

Chapter One: An Introduction to **Cyber Security Management and Strategic Intelligence**

Chapter Two:
Cyber Security Management and Strategic Intelligence in Context
Strategic intelligence, Incidents, Threat Intelligence, Government Cooperation, Big Data, Conceptual Framework, t Theoretical Insights

Chapter Three:
Cyber Security Management Intelligence Policy Implementation Strategies
Collectivist Approach, Organizational Intervention, Categorization of Data, Leadership, Awareness, Intelligence Framework

Chapter Four:
Artificial Intelligence and Cyber Security Management
Artificial Intelligence and Machine Learning, Risk, Artificial Intelligence Awareness, The Dark Web, Artificial Intelligence Threats

Chtapter Seven:
A Collectivist Enterprise Risk Management Cyber Threat Model
Enterprise Risk Management, Strategic Intelligence, Threat Intelligence Policy and Strategy, Risk Register, Risk Management

Chapter Six:
Partnership in the Context of Cyber Security
Critical Infrastructure, Social Media Networks and Platforms, Threat Awareness, Open-Source Intelligence (OSINT), Partnership, Smart Cities

Chapter Five:
Setting the Scene for a Cyber Security Management Conceptual Model and Framework
Organizational Cyber Security, The Modelling Approach, Culture, Situational Awareness, Organizational Learning, Awareness, Recent Cyber Attacks

Chapter Eight:
Theoretical and Managerial Implications
Interdependency, Collectivist Enterprise Risk Management, Marketing, Human Resource Management, Cyber Security Education, Logic Model

FIGURE 1.1 Navigational map: The linkage between the themes and topics of cyber security management and strategic intelligence.

security manager can draw on existing cyber security management knowledge and develop their strategic intelligence mindset to anticipate and prevent cyber-attacks from doing harm to the organization.

As regards non-management specialists, *Cyber Security Management and Strategic Intelligence* will be of interest to those that have a firm understanding of the technical aspects of cyber security but want to learn more about the management and human side of cyber security and intelligence that is organization specific. Indeed, the reader will as they progress through the book develop a mindset in terms of identifying how cyber security management and strategic intelligence can be applied to the issues and challenges that surface and which require intelligence-based solutions.

1.3 Adding to Management Knowledge

The more in-depth knowledge an individual possesses as regards cyber-attacks and the way in which cyber-attacks are launched, and knowing who is behind them, bodes well for being able to anticipate future attacks. Being able to identify and deal with a range of cyber threats of varying levels of risk and intensity means that a cyber security management and strategic intelligence approach needs to be adopted so that a proactive approach to intelligence gathering and analysis and policy implementation is achieved. Essentially, cyber security managers and their colleagues are concerned with devising and implementing effective cyber security countermeasures and ensuring that the organization is able to withstand various forms of cyber-attack. By recognizing that a cyber security manager fulfils an important and policy-oriented role, as do the risk manager, the Information Technology (IT) manager and the security manager, for example, it should be possible to ensure that intelligence and security manifest in a robust cyber security aware-ness programme that is adopted and implemented by supply chain partners. Hence, a number of benefits will become evident while the reader makes their way through the text. One such benefit is gaining knowledge that can be applied in a wide setting so that sharing experiences with those in the community helps to make society more resilient and better able to withstand prolonged cyber-attacks.

1.4 The Collectivist and Stakeholder Approach to Cyber Security

Cyber Security Management and Strategic Intelligence has been designed to be informa-tive and help students and reflective practitioners/managers to understand and interpret how a collectivist approach to cyber security management and strategic intelligence can help various organizational staff including the cyber security manager to counteract cyber threats by aligning security with intelligence. By adopting a proactive approach that is stakeholder oriented, it should be possible to distinguish between the activities of cyber criminals, those involved in cyber war activities and cyber terrorism, and understand why acts of cyber espionage are intensifying. Cyber espionage is now on the radar of senior managers in both the public sector and the private sector, and it is envisaged that the guidance provided in this book will help those making strategic intelligence-oriented decisions to do so by being more informed vis-à-vis the consequences of their decisions. By taking cognizance of trends and international events, it should be possible for the cyber security manager to play a much more visible role within the organization and to influence senior management. In addition, it is hoped that cyber security management is viewed as being integrated into the work of the organization's various business functions.

1.5 The Topics Covered

The reader will note that a number of main topics are covered in the book. They include an introduction to cyber security management and strategic intelligence; cyber security management and strategic intelligence in context; cyber security management intelligence policy implementation strategies; artificial intelligence (AI) and cyber security manage-ment; setting the scene for a cyber security management conceptual model and frame-work; partnership in the context of cyber security; a collectivist enterprise risk management cyber threat model and theoretical and managerial implications.

1.6 The Aims of the Book

A number of aims can be identified:

- To place cyber security management and strategic intelligence in context.
- To establish what cyber security management intelligence policy implementation strat-egies involve.

- To place AI in the context of cyber security management.
- To establish what setting the scene for a cyber security management conceptual model and framework involves.
- To establish how partnerships can be placed in the context of cyber security.
- To evaluate a collectivist enterprise risk management cyber threat model.
- To explain the theoretical and managerial implications associated with cyber security management.

Bearing in mind the aims above, the reader will: (i) increase their awareness of cyber security management and strategic intelligence; (ii) develop an understanding of why the cyber security manager needs to devise cyber security management intelligence policy implementation strategies; (iii) develop an appreciation of how AI is to be used to aid cyber security management; (iv) be able to develop a cyber security management conceptual model and framework; (v) understand why it is necessary to view partnership in terms of shared cyber security provision; (vi) produce a collectivist enterprise risk management cyber threat model and (vii) develop a theoretical and managerial implications mindset to better understand what cyber security management involves.

A number of case examples are provided that help the reader form a theoretical understanding of the subject and they should enable the reader to develop insights into specific types of problem solutions. Indeed, the cases are related to specific parts of the text and link back to the key points. By mapping the content in the case example back to the information in the chapter, it is possible to derive solutions that enrich the learning experience of individuals and result in knowledge enhancement. The case examples, which have been written to highlight specific situations, are illustrative of a range of issues and challenges confronting managers in the public sector and private sector relating to the intricacies of cyber security management and strategic intelligence. The points of interest can be discussed and placed in context. Furthermore, the questions posed can be used as a basis for developing additional questions to be answered.

It can also be suggested that *Cyber Security Management and Strategic Intelligence* has a number of strengths. The reader will be able to: (1) Develop their own appreciation of what intelligence work involves; (2) devise a cyber security management intelligence policy implementation strategy; (3) establish how AI can be used to aid cyber security management; (4) devise a cyber security management conceptual model and framework; (5) establish how a partnership arrangement can strengthen cyber security management; (6) devise an enterprise risk management cyber threat model and (7) develop knowledge in relation to theoretical and managerial implications so that cyber security management is effective.

In addition, the reader will broaden their knowledge base in terms of linking cyber security awareness, risk management and threat analysis with how to produce a risk register; deepen their knowledge of intelligence gathering; and devise a collectivist enterprise risk management cyber threat model, which identifies which member of staff undertakes specific tasks and who they report to. By accepting that cyber security is a shared responsibility, staff from various in-house business functions and staff based in external organizations (e.g. law enforcement) can work on cooperative projects and share data and information as appropriate. Both students and reflective practitioners will be guided through the process of understanding why it is necessary to adopt a proactive approach to cyber security management and strategic intelligence and they will also be made aware of the complexities involved.

1.7 The Objectives of the Book

The reader will identify with the following objectives:

- Establish how a cyber security manager undertakes strategic intelligence work.
- Evaluate how effective cyber security management intelligence policy implementation strategies are.
- Establish both the benefits and threats associated with AI in the context of cyber security management.
- Establish how to implement a cyber security management conceptual model and framework.
- Evaluate a partnership arrangement in the context of a cyber security management configuration.
- Devise a collectivist enterprise risk management cyber threat model.
- Appraise the theoretical and managerial implications embedded in cyber security management.

1.8 Learning Outcomes of the Book

As regards the main subject-specific learning outcomes, a social science approach and appreciation of cyber security management and strategic intelligence is advocated. This is achieved by linking various bodies of knowledge gained from cyber security studies, intelligence studies and management studies, with the ability to develop and test various conceptual models/frameworks. The examples referred to will provide a stimulus to learn and reflect on the issues and challenges identified. The problems highlighted and the changing nature of the central problem means that current practice has to be reflected on and evaluated so that a deeper theoretical understanding of the subject matter can be attained. The reader will both understand and challenge the assumptions upon which current cyber security management and strategic intelligence knowledge is based and will develop the confidence to apply concepts and frameworks and develop new approaches through the development and testing of their own conceptual models/frameworks.

The book has been written in such a way as to help the reader evaluate and critique current cyber security management practices and relate better to the ever-changing cyber-related environment. By applying critical reasoning and thinking, it will become apparent that there is a need to integrate more fully the different strands of cyber security knowledge and adopt a strategic intelligence perspective, if that is, the various forms of cyber-attack are to be dealt with satisfactorily.

The main learning outcomes are therefore:

i To provide the reader with sufficient knowledge of cyber security management and strategic intelligence to allow them to challenge and implement cyber security management solutions that they consider relevant.

ii To allow the reader to view cyber security management from the perspective of a strategist. The advantage being that the reader will identify cyber security issues and challenges that can be managed.

iii To provide the reader with confidence to engage in proactive cyber security management initiatives that are aimed at making the organization resilient.

iv To enable the reader to apply the cyber security management and strategic intelligence knowledge gained and to further that knowledge by discussing real-world cyber security management problems.

v To instil in the reader the belief that a proactive cyber security management and strategic intelligence approach will be sufficient to deal with various cyber threats. The key point being that future cyber threats will be anticipated and action taken that result in a more proactive approach to cyber security.

vi To help the reader find unique solutions to complex cyber security problems and implement cyber security management solutions that increase the resilience of the organization.

vii To ensure that the reader places cyber security management at the heart of security and champions a security culture within the organization that results in security and intelligence being interlinked.

1.9 Reflection

This chapter outlines the content and purpose of the book and makes the case for cyber security management and intelligence to underpin and be instrumental in the enterprise risk management approach, which is a relevant but sometimes undervalued body of knowledge. The approach adopted will help to promote the collectivist approach to cyber security and ensure that staff in partner organizations adopt an integrative approach to security with cyber security management playing a prominent role that helps to strengthen the cyber security management decision-making process. The aims, learning objectives and learning outcomes of the book are cited. A navigational map is provided that outlines the linkage between the themes and topics of cyber security management and strategic intelligence, and the holistic approach to security is made evident.

1.10 Conclusion

By adopting a cyber security management and strategic intelligence perspective, the cyber security manager and their colleagues will be able to integrate the various dimensions of cyber security into a cyber security knowledge base. This will allow a strategic intelligence framework to be developed and consolidate security operations both in-house and among partner organizations. Through the process of integrating security with strategic intelligence, the cyber security manager will be able to utilize the enterprise risk management concept and promote more fully the cyber security management concept to colleagues. By being committed to a holistic view of security and advocating that cyber security is dependent upon collectivist decision-making, support from partner organizations and various stakeholders will be forthcoming.

2

CYBER SECURITY MANAGEMENT AND STRATEGIC INTELLIGENCE IN CONTEXT

2.1 Introduction

This chapter starts with placing cyber security management and strategic intelligence in context (Section 2.2) and continues with defining cyber security and cyber security management (Section 2.3). Cyber security incidents (Section 2.4) are given attention, and this is followed by developing an appreciation of cyber security (Section 2.5). Collectivist cyber threat intelligence (Section 2.6) is followed by intra-government and inter-government cooperation (Section 2.7). Understanding big data and related consequences (Section 2.8) is followed by developing theoretical insights into cyber-attacks (Section 2.9). Reflection and questions (Section 2.10) precedes the conclusion (Section 2.11).

2.2 Placing Cyber Security Management and Strategic Intelligence in Context

In order to place cyber security management and strategic intelligence in context, it is advisable to reflect on what strategic intelligence is and how it can be interpreted. For example, Paiuc et al. (2024, p. 785) suggest that strategic intelligence is concerned with "the collection and analysis of intelligence for policy and military planning, mainly at national and international levels". However, they acknowledge that the concept of strategic intelligence can be applied to management and organizational decision-making as indeed do other authors. The objective of strategic intelligence is to build an overview of the environment in which the organization competes so that the risks identified can be mitigated.

Paiuc et al. (2024, p. 787) have defined strategic intelligence as: "the organized gathering, analysis, and interpretation of information that is needed to support decision-making and strategic planning…. It is a crucial instrument for opportunity identification, threat analysis, and effective strategy formulation". The organization known as Shaping Tomorrow (2024) suggests that strategic intelligence is used to help managers formulate future strategies, policies and plans. It covers many aspects of interest to managers and requires the utilization of data from a number of data sources. In addition, it covers time

DOI: 10.4324/9781003570905-2

horizons that are well in advance of the present. Broadly speaking, strategic intelligence is used to provide an overview of the situation, and this is achieved through applying situational analysis, which is used continuously to identify impending situations or events that are likely to have an impact on the organization. Strategic intelligence is mainly associated with geopolitical events that cause turbulence and disruption and which have ramifications for managers and the way in which the organization is managed. Strategic intelligence is applied to aid long-term decision-making and draws on evidence and expert views and interpretations from various academic and non-academic sources.

But it is more than this. Montgomery and Weinberg (1979, p. 41) are of the view that strategic intelligence systems allow managers to establish what the purpose of intelligence work is and what kinds of information need to be collected and analysed to solve specific types of problems/counter future threats. The cyber security manager and their colleagues can adhere to this view and think in terms of "defensive intelligence" as it is oriented towards "avoiding surprises"; "passive intelligence", which is concerned with benchmark data that is used for objective evaluation; and "offensive intelligence" that is associated with identifying opportunities/threats not previously known (Montgomery and Weinberg, 1979, p. 41). Such an intelligence approach advocates understanding and identifying environmental factors and their known/anticipated impacts and resulting consequences. The strategic connotation is to be interpreted from the organization's competitive standing and its ability to remain in business. This is because strategic intelligence involves (Paiuc et al., 2024, pp. 787–788): business intelligence; geopolitical intelligence; competitive intelligence and risk management.

Strategic intelligence has been linked with leadership and the need for a certain type of leadership style (Paiuc et al., 2024) and there is agreement as regards what constitutes an effective intelligence operative. To be effective, certain managerial capabilities are required. These include specific types of detailed knowledge (e.g. outward-looking) and analytical skills (e.g. inward-gazing) (Levine et al., 2017, p. 2395). Big data analytics is now being applied to *datafication* and "is the conversion of all structured, semi-structured and non-structured information pockets into quantifiable units permitting the extraction of new forms of value" (Lim, 2016, p. 622). This is according to Lim (2016, p. 622) shifting "the focus of inquiry from *causation* to *correlations*: that is the mere knowledge that something is happening, rather than why it is happening, suffices for the formulation of an adequate response". There is no doubt that various models exist and will be developed to help cyber security managers and their colleagues simulate certain threat environments, enhance decision-making through scenario analysis and planning and utilize game theory to extend their understanding of the uncontrollable factors in the cyber threat environment.

The Center for Strategic and International Studies based in Washington, DC, USA, has done much to publicize the type and significance of cyber incidents from 2006 to the present. It is appreciated that there are possibly additional cyber incidents that have not been reported by the Center for Strategic and International Studies (2024) owing to the sensitive nature of the attack and, retaliatory action may have been carried out that has not been reported also. Indeed, Grove et al. (2000, p. 90) make clear that although passive defences are in place they should be coupled with active defence measures because this should deter attacks. Some of the more recent incidents highlighted by the Center for Strategic and International Studies (2024) are included in Table 2.1 with a categorization system and rating of risks assessment. The categorization system was developed from the work of Viotti and Kauppi (2001, pp. 254–255). The selective cyber incidents reported on have been categorized according to broad logical interpretation, which involves considering psychological, ideological and environmental factors. However, for an in-depth understanding of why a threat actor undertakes such action, and risks being identified and held accountable for the damage caused, a more detailed analysis needs to be undertaken. Hence, the categorization system is an extension of the analysis and can be used by the cyber security manager and their colleagues to identify how a cyber threat incident materializes and what its antecedent conditions are. To understand this, it is necessary to reflect on what Viotti and Kauppi (2001, pp. 78–85), refer to. They refer to the interests and objectives of governments and, bearing this in mind, they state warfare (security), commerce (economy) and human rights (identity) are key themes/constructs and link them to threats and opportunities. Viotti and Kauppi (2001, p. 80) indicate that a nation's *objectives* are determined by *interests + threats + opportunities*.

To appreciate what is involved, it is necessary to consider a cyber-attack from being implemented from the stance of power and the exercising of that power. The exercising of power can be viewed from that of an individual, a group, an organization or a government agency and there may well be other types of classification that can be utilized. Viotti and Kauppi (2001, p. 86) add to our understanding of this by explaining that:

> "power is defined as the actual or potential influence or coercion a state or other actor can assert relative to other states and nonstate actors because of the political, geographic, economic, and financial, technological, military, social, cultural, or other capabilities it possesses".

In order to interpret the actions of a threat actor(s), it is useful to deploy the following cyber threat incident classification system: IIP = identity, ideological and political (which includes cultural, social and psychological factors); SG = security and geographic (which includes environmental factors); EF = economic and financial and TM = technological and military. This form of categorization, which is used in Table 2.1, reduces the level of complexity for those who are unfamiliar with the cyber security landscape and allows the cyber security manager to explain a range of incidents to their peers and receive help in further categorizing cyber threat incidents. In addition, a risk rating approach can be incorporated to place in context the actual or potential damage associated with an incident or a set of incidents. This is achieved by using a risk rating system whereby risks are placed on a scale from 1 (low risk) to 5 (high risk). The higher the number of incident characteristics, the higher the risk rating score is. However, it is appreciated that there are other forms of risk rating that can be used, and it depends upon what is considered appropriate/easy to interpret.

When formulating a risk rating system, the cyber security manager should take into account the impact that results or the potential impact that results from the incident(s) and its effect on the organization. In the case of an attack on critical infrastructure, the consequences for those who utilize the products and services related to and supported by the critical infrastructure affected need to be established and linked with the organization's business continuity plan and strategy. By adopting a proactive approach to risk management, it should be possible to identify organizational vulnerabilities and review and revise the organization's resilience capability.

TABLE 2.1 Significant cyber incidents, their categorization and risk rating from January 2024 to June 2024

Month and Year	Target Country or Target	Nature of Cyber Attack and Categorization	Industry/Target	Source of Attack/Hackers
June 2024	Japan	Attacks on networks EF and TM Risk rating 3	Satellite	From outside the country
June 2024	Indonesia	Ransomware EF Risk rating 2	Government services	Not disclosed
June 2024	Ukraine	Phishing emails, images containing malicious Microsoft Excel spreadsheet IIP, SG, EF, TM Risk rating 5	Military	Belarus
June 2024	Germany	Cyber-attack on IT services IIP Risk rating 2	Political party	Russia
June 2024	Government of Palau	Cyber attack SG, EF and TM Risk rating 4	Government documents	China
May 2024	Canada	Espionage activity SG and TM Risk rating 3	Eight Members of Parliament	China
May 2024	India	Phishing emails IIP, SG, EF and TM Risk rating 5	Government, aerospace and defence	Pakistan
May 2024	UK	Bank details and personal details SG and TM Risk rating 3	UK's special forces	China
May 2024	Poland and the Czech Republic	Microsoft Outlook vulnerability IIP, SG, EF and TM Risk rating 5	Government and infrastructure networks	Russia
May 2024	Germany	Vulnerabilities in Microsoft Outlook IIP, SG, EF and TM Risk rating 5	Political parties and defence and aerospace companies	Russia
April 2024	Russia	DDoS attacks against servers, websites and domains IIP, SG, EF and TM Risk rating 5	Political party	Ukraine
April 2024	Belarus	Website put out of service IIP and SG Risk rating 3	Security service agency	Belarus (pro-democracy hackers)

(*Continued*)

TABLE 2.1 (Continued)

Month and Year	Target Country or Target	Nature of Cyber Attack and Categorization	Industry/Target	Source of Attack/Hackers
April 2024	UK	Honey traps (e.g., compromising images) IIP, SG, EF and TM Risk rating 5	Members of Parliament	Not disclosed
April 2024	El Salvador	Personal information and Chivo's source code EF Risk rating 2	National cryptocurrency wallet Chivo	Not disclosed
March 2024	African Union	Cyber attack SG, EF and TM Risk rating 4	African Union's systems and devices	Not disclosed
March 2024	Israel	Information technology network IIP, SG, EF and TM Risk rating 5	Nuclear	Iran
March 2024	Germany	Ransomware via a Phishing attack IIP, SG and TM Risk rating 4	Political parties	Russia
March 2024	India	Cyber espionage IIP, SG, EF and TM Risk rating 5	Government and energy sectors	Not disclosed
April 2024	Belarus	Website put out of service IIP Risk rating 2	Security service agency	Belarus (pro-democracy hackers)
March 2024	Microsoft	Honey traps (e.g., compromising images) IIP, SG, EF and TM Risk rating 5	Members of Parliament	Russia
February 2024	French health insurance companies	Personal data: Birth date, social security and marital status information EF Risk rating 2	French citizens	Not disclosed
February 2024	The Netherlands	Cyber espionage IIP, SG, EF and TM Risk rating 5	Military network	China
January 2024	Canada	Cyber hack IIP, SG, EF and TM Risk rating 5	Global Affairs Canada's secure VPN	Not disclosed

The information in Table 2.1 only covers the period from January 2024 to June 2024, and not all the incidents reported by the Center for Strategic and International Studies (2024) during this period have in fact been included in the analysis. Indeed, a number of other cyber incidents were documented including an incident in March 2024 relating to the targeting of several European Union (EU) members of the Inter-Parliamentary Alliance on China and Italian MPs; an attack on Canada's financial intelligence system FINTRAC in March 2014; an attack in March 2024 on Microsoft that resulted in Russian hackers stealing source code and gaining unauthorized access to the company's internal systems in November 2023; and there were also espionage campaigns against the embassies of Georgia, Poland, Ukraine and Iran that started in 2023 and espionage attacks on several governments: the UK, India, Indonesia and Taiwan in February 2024.

The range of incidents reported by staff based at the Center for Strategic and International Studies (2024) acts as a reminder that the cyber security manager and their colleagues need to think of cyber security in a broad and multifaceted way. There are a large number of points to take cognizance of and much effort needs to be put into identifying the skills required to undertake cyber-attacks of this nature. Questions can be posed relating to how the perpetrators gain the skills required and where they obtain the skills and expertise from. In addition, the resources needed to undertake such attacks, and the benefits derived from them are also key considerations. Sophisticated technology is now in place to track and identify those that carry out cyber-attacks and also, patterns of behaviour often provide insights into who is behind such attacks and what their objectives are. There is no doubt, judging from the type of attacks listed in Table 2.1, that cyber-crime is beginning to give way to cyber war or as Valeriano and Manesss (2018) argue, "cyber conflict". Possibly, cyber war is rather a harsh connotation, but it has to be said that no nation can sit back and just defend itself against ongoing aggressive behaviour. To sit back and continually defend means that a nation is not developing cyber technology that can be used to counteract such aggression, and this is where AI will prove useful as it can both help a nation to defend its networks and computer systems and be used in a proactive manner in the form of countermeasures. To fully understand why cyber warfare/conflict is evolving requires the cyber security manager and their colleagues to look more deeply into the disciplines of international relations and international affairs and understand why nations compete in the way they do. It also requires that due care and attention be given to predict how a failing nation is likely to react to ongoing political situations and what measures need to be put in place to create world harmony. Understanding the underlying conditions associated with why nations compete and why they cooperate should provide the cyber security manager with a better understanding of the cyber security landscape. It has to be remembered also that the United Nations (UN) Charter contains a number of articles that relate to the defence of a nation and what a nation-state can do to protect its citizens from an aggressor (Grove et al., 2000).

Bearing the above in mind, the cyber security manager needs to consider how the relationships that exist (e.g., business, economic, social, political and technological) and the types of connectivity deployed involving partner organizations can be brought into the equation and monitored on a daily basis. This does require the cyber security manager to monitor the environment for technological breakthroughs that are associated with: (i) Providing the organization with a sustainable competitive advantage; (ii) identifying disruptive technology within the industry that allows an organization to gain advantage over other organizations in the industry owing to new technological applications and (iii) identifying a new resource(s) that can be used to make the organization more resilient. As regards the latter, an example could be new cyber security threat detection software that enables the organization to defend itself against certain types of cyber-attacks.

The cyber security manager can play a pivotal role in organizing an intelligence function that is concerned with (Montgomery and Weinberg, 1979, pp. 42–52): Setting intelligence priorities; identifying sources of intelligence; collecting intelligence; sorting and processing data and information; transforming data into information through evaluation; analysing the data/information; establishing patterns that highlight certain outcomes/actions; interpreting the outcomes/actions and disseminating the results. The feedback in relation to the findings, both from internal experts and external experts, can be utilized to project forward what will transpire from a certain outcome/action/impact. In other words, if an event occurs and action is taken to remedy the situation, what will be the outcome of that action? Furthermore, how will the response cause a new action/reaction? This then requires further thought and an answer to the following question: How will the secondary occurrence be managed? Such an approach to intelligence work can be viewed as proactive and strategically oriented because it goes beyond an initial impact and reaction or consequence, and it looks at a chain of actions and reactions.

Cyber-attacks are known to vary through time and because of this cyber security policy needs to ensure that the various forms of cyber-attacks that are launched on an organization are dealt with in an effective and timely manner. A commitment to and adoption of the strategic cyber security management approach (Trim and Lee, 2023) is necessary because without such an approach, it is unlikely that the organization will remain resilient and be able to sustain itself in the long term. Those that formulate cyber security management policy and implement cyber security strategy, do so with the knowledge that they have the support of the board of directors. Accepting that cyber-attacks are increasing in sophistication means that organizational resilience is a collective responsibility, and a cyber security culture needs to be put in place that is a subset of the broader security culture of the organization.

The cyber security manager will, by working with various managers including the risk manager, the information technology (IT) manager, the security manager and also functional managers such as the marketing manager, the finance manager, the technology manager and the human resource management/personnel manager, help put in place training and staff development programmes that raise the cyber security awareness and operational dexterity of staff so that in-house staff and staff in partner organizations work in unison to eradicate organizational vulnerabilities and ensure that the organization is able to counteract cyber-attacks and remain sustainable. By acknowledging that the threat environment is subject to change, a commitment to a proactive cyber security management and strategic intelligence approach will prove helpful in terms of relating vulnerability with risk; risk with impact and impact with sustainability.

2.3 Defining Cyber Security and Cyber Security Management

Morris et al. (2020, p. 3) are of the view that cyber security can be interpreted from several stances and "Cybersecurity within a business or organisation is commonly protection focused on proprietary information, maintaining the integrity of databases, ensuring timely access to systems and information by authorised users, and preventing unauthorised access and damage to systems and their components". Emphasis is placed on creating a secure trading environment that ultimately enables the organization to develop successful relationships with its stakeholders and maintain its operations in a sustainable and profitable manner that is known to be value driven. Accepting that malicious attacks can disrupt and cause lasting damage, it is important for the cyber security manager to acknowledge that they need extensive cyber security knowledge of how systems, subsystems and embedded software operate (Morris et al., 2020, p. 3). Of importance is understanding how technology is utilized to shape and integrate manufacturing processes within supply chain operations and link with customer relationship management systems (e.g., online marketing activities).

Referring to the work of Ferdinand (2015) and Jenab and Moslehpour (2016), Rajan et al. (2012, p. 1) suggest that "Cybersecurity management can be defined as an organization's strategic-level capability to protect information technology (IT) systems, information resources, and digital processes in an emerging cyber threat environment". Such a view can be interpreted from a structuration theory perspective whereby "human interaction draws on social structures and at the same time produces, reproduces or changes these structures" (Tsohou et al., 2015, p. 41). By viewing human interaction as being incorporated and influenced by social systems, it is possible to define the logic of *structures* as containing three properties (Tsohou et al., 2015, p. 41): signification, domination and legitimation. Bearing this in mind, it can be suggested that the cyber security manager needs to be able to communicate well with their colleagues and thus influence cyber security awareness; use their power of domination to allocate resources, possibly to improve threat detection, reiterate the values of the organization and establish social structures of legitimation that ensure that the systems and procedures in place support a security culture. Cyber security is at the heart of security and people are held accountable for their actions (e.g., the risk manager engages in risk management and manages the content that goes into the risk register(s).

2.4 Cyber Security Incidents

According to the International Monetary Fund (IMF, 2024, p. 74), there are a number of factors that contribute to the rapidly rising cyber incidents and these can be attributed to the increase in digital connectivity, the increasing dependency on the use of technology, financial innovation and geopolitical tensions that have resulted in various forms of open conflict. It can be reported that financial firms have been the main focus of cyber-attacks and the direct losses of institutions in this sector are put at almost US$12 million from 2004 to something like US$2.5 billion in losses since 2020 (IMF, 2024, p. 74).

Taking over an organization's computer system and network(s) and holding it to ransom has proved highly profitable as various threat actors (e.g., individuals/groups of people intent on causing harm to an organization through the use of malware) have forced senior managers into negotiating with them until a settlement is reached. Engaging with and entering into discussions with such individuals and organizations is frowned upon and, in some countries, it is illegal to pay a ransom. Counteracting such cyber threats requires continual action on behalf of senior management because not only do known vulnerabilities (e.g., faulty software, inadequate internal security systems and lax security systems in supply chain organizations) place the organization at risk but also new vulnerabilities materialize that require the swift intervention of external cyber security experts.

The theft of intellectual property is sometimes linked to an insider who is intent on stealing secrets to order. The ramifications of such an act can result in the circumvention of a patent(s) and the development of an alternative, more advanced product, which is launched onto the market and results in more intensive competition. If a data/information breach occurs, it is likely that reputational damage will occur, and existing customers will be perturbed from buying the product because they do not feel safe to buy it from the organization as their online presence appears to be less than secure. Such an event may affect a consumer's confidence and cause them to shy away from buying products online.

Top management is aware that it is no longer possible to assign a single senior manager or department to deal with cyber threats because the nature of cyber-attacks has changed through time and the level of complexity is beyond what a single department/function (e.g., IT) can deal with on its own. Bearing in mind that those carrying out cyber-attacks are relentless and persistent in their actions, it can be suggested that to effectively deal with cyber-attacks, a private–public sector dialogue is needed that results in top management putting in place a robust intelligence strategy to counteract cyber threats, across industry sectors. This is because although email phishing attacks (e.g., a general email sent to a wide group of people to trick them into downloading malware), spear phishing attacks (e.g., a more personalized and sometimes individual-specific scam aimed at entrapping a targeted person) and social engineering attacks (e.g., an individual is targeted so that they provide or release sensitive information or passwords that are beneficial to an attacker), remain predominant, new forms of cyber-attacks are emerging that are inventive and deeply harmful at the same time. The UK's National Cyber Security Centre is aware of such developments and has set up an online system whereby an organization can share cyber threat information with other organizations in the industry in which it competes. This has helped build threat awareness and has allowed senior managers whose organizations have been targeted in some way to reach out and receive help. Threat-sharing schemes prove beneficial but at the same time, any organization that admits that it has been a victim of a cyber-attack and has suffered a sizeable impact may have other known vulnerabilities that the management does not want to disclose.

Ransomware attacks on international companies have become commonplace in recent years and in 2020, CWT, a US travel management company, paid US$4.5 million in bitcoins to hackers in the way of a negotiated settlement (Stubbs, 2020). However, ransomware attacks have progressed beyond the perpetrator merely withholding data and information until a ransom is paid. Today, there is no guarantee that the victim of a ransomware attack will have access to their data and systems once they have paid the ransom demanded. This suggests that the objectives of those involved in cyber-crime are changing and because of this, their behaviour has to be considered less predictable. The cyber security manager and their colleagues need to understand this and develop a different psyche to better understand what is at stake and how they need to convey their fears to a wider audience. Indeed, reports surface from time to time alleging that certain types of cyber-attacks are motivated due to political reasons as opposed to economic gain, but sometimes, the two types of attacks are connected. In some instances, the victim of a cyber-attack is known to retaliate but this is not possible if the source of the attack is not known.

The problem in part can be attributed to the proliferation of data and data sources and the fact that the software in place does not always function in the way expected and may well contain vulnerabilities from the outset. This provides those intent on launching a cyber-attack with the opportunity to do so and, naturally, an attacker will attempt to exploit a vulnerability/weakness in order to gain an advantage. Furthermore, staff are very thinly spread within organizations due to downsizing over the years and new business models that embrace online business more intensively than previously also require staff to undertake more than one task. Because of this, it is not always possible for a member of staff to respond to an incident in real time. Delays in acknowledging that a data breach has occurred only compound the problem and, consequently, organizations that take a long time to respond to an incident than they should, suffer additionally from cascading effects. Insufficient cyber security resources mean that organizations run the risk of having more than one vulnerability exploited. It is also worrying to note, as acknowledged by Sivarajah et al. (2017, p. 264) that:

> "the growth of data in volumes in the digital world seems to out-speed the advance of the many extant computing infrastructures. Established data processing technologies, for example database and data warehouse, are becoming inadequate given the amount of data the world is current generating".

2.5 Developing an Appreciation of Cyber Security

It is important at this juncture to make clear what cyber security involves because there are a number of misconceptions about the subject. The European Commission (2013, p. 3) has indicated that cyber security can be interpreted as the "safeguards and actions that can be used to protect the cyber domain, both in the civilian and military fields, from those threats that are associated with or that may harm its interdependent networks and information infrastructure". This definition suggests that preserving the availability and integrity of networks and the infrastructure that supports the networks and maintaining the confidentiality of the information that flows through the networks is key. Such a view places emphasis on government representatives encouraging various researchers and research bodies to collect and maintain data and information relating to cyber-attacks and foster international cooperation that encourages individual nation-states to put additional resources into counteracting cyber-attacks. In addition, there appears to be a growing interest in co-developing cyber security initiatives and legislation, which result in the sharing of AI technology that can be used to analyse vast quantities of threat intelligence data and automatically implement a solution.

Looking specifically at the UK's National Health Service (NHS), it is clear that senior managers in the NHS are committed to providing digitally enabled care and can claim success with ventures such as the electronic prescription service (National Health Service, 2019). However, although there is recognition that cyber security is important, there is limited guidance in the way in which the NHS is investing to ensure that patient data and research data (derived from experiments undertaken in bioindustry laboratories) are made safe from cyber-attacks. What senior managers and policymakers need to note is that the continued reliance on biological information and increased patient–doctor connectivity as represented by the Internet-of-Medical-Things (IoMT) (Elgabry, 2023, p. 2) are likely to put additional pressure on the limited resources that have been invested in security and require Internet-connected medical devices to be given higher security protection than is the case at present.

The UK has been subject to several cyber-attacks over time and in 2021, an attacker obtained copies of the electoral register and in 2024 an attacker successfully obtained the personal details of the UK military personnel. The data obtained may not have been of strategic importance, but the question has to be asked: Why would an overseas government-funded agency undertake such an act? Speculation exists as regards whether it was in relation to the UK government's stand on issues of international affairs or whether it was intelligence-driven and disruptive in nature. As regards the latter, such acts are carried out in a cumulative manner and when aggregated can give rise to cascading effects and ultimately the failure of a system. Such attacks go beyond destabilizing a nation. They are crafted with intent and linked with a longer-term objective. For example, by causing disruption to an economy and reducing the confidence of investors, share prices fall and the shares can be acquired cheaply by the attacker or an organization that has an affinity with the attacker. Thus, a catastrophic cyber impact represents a double-win situation as an attacker not only damages or neutralizes an opponent or part of their activity or capability but also eventually becomes the owner and controller of the asset they were keen to acquire. So, the perpetrator of an attack has much to gain because they can develop a cost-effective attack base, remain hidden and extend their threat capability by sharing intelligence and linking and working with other threat agents.

It is because of the changing nature of cyber-attacks, characterized by acts of cyber-crime being transformed into acts of cyber war that senior managers need to take cognizance of. Indeed, there appears to be a renewed confidence among threat actors that those undertaking such attacks can do so without being identified and held to account. They consider that they are beyond reproach, and it has to be said that what they are doing is strategic intelligence led. Knowing this reinforces the fact that the cyber security manager needs to play a full and proactive role in helping organizational staff to counteract both internally orchestrated and externally orchestrated cyber-attacks and cyber intrusions. They can do so because the skills that the cyber security manager possesses together with the knowledge accrued over the years enables them to visualize how an event will turn out. A cyber security manager is, therefore, able to solve cyber security–related problems by drawing on past experience, analysing complex data and planning and implementing counterintelligence strategies. The outcome of this approach manifests in planning becoming reinterpreted as foresight planning, which provides the cyber security manager and their peers with environment-specific knowledge that is of use to security experts both in-house and external to the organization (e.g., law enforcement officers). Through close cooperation with internal IT staff and external computer forensics experts, knowledge can be developed that challenges how the business model is developing. Initiatives involving placing data and information in the cloud and the deployment of blockchain technology require an objective analysis. Evidence of this can be found in the fact that blockchain-based supply-chain management (BC-SCM) systems may be vulnerable to cyber-attack (Al-Farsi et al., 2021), and cloud computing vis-à-vis vulnerability analysis, which is used to evaluate current emerging threats associated with cloud technology (Singh and Pandey, 2020), can be considered ongoing. It is because the level of complexity is increasing that more advanced methods need to be found to monitor cyber-attacks. A collectivist approach (Trim and Lee, 2023) to cyber security can be used to ensure that appropriate cyber security policies, programmes and strategies are put in place that strengthen the organization's defences and at the same time raise the profile of cyber security staff. The cyber security manager can help devise a fear appeal(s) (e.g., "danger control process") that results in an individual averting a threat by changing their behaviour (Evans et al., 2016, p. 4671). Fear appeals may have ethical connotations associated with them and may not always be understood. The emphasis is to get people to think through a situation and understand what the consequence of their action is likely to be, should they decide to act in a certain way. Hopefully, the outcome will be positive as opposed to negative. A positive outcome in relation to a cyber security awareness programme would be that a member of staff protects their company-designated passwords in a way that allows the integrity of the security systems in place to be maintained.

2.6 Collectivist Cyber Threat Intelligence

The cyber security manager and their colleagues know that there are various types of threat actors in existence and that each threat actor is unique and motivated by a specific cause/objective. Some threat actors are motivated by financial gain (e.g., cyber criminals), some are motivated by the publicity they receive for the harm/damage inflicted (e.g., cyber terrorists) and some are of the view that the cause they represent or are fighting for can be furthered through some form of disruptive political process (e.g., cyber hacktivists). Although financial gain is a main motivator, some threat actors operate through a form of justification. An example of the latter is a group of hackers that carry out instructions made available via a rogue government department via the Dark Web. Possibly, their intention would be to discredit and disrupt or possibly steal technology and sensitive information that can help their country close the gap on the country that they consider has the lead and needs to be caught up. Because cyber criminals are not visible, their motivations and patterns of behaviour remain hidden, and it is difficult to predict what they will do and when they will do it. Threat actors work in a way that is logical to them and often engage a large pool of experts to carry out their illegal activities such as forwarding phishing emails or making scam telephone calls to gain access to an individual's/ the target's computer. Knowing that people use online banking facilities provides threat agents with a means to avail themselves of somebody's assets without worrying about the emotional stress that it causes.

The UK Government (2019, p. 1) has provided guidance in terms of what threat agents do and suggests that cyber threat intelligence (CTI) can be used to counteract the actions of those intent on breaking the law. CTI is mainly concerned with investigation and incident response and the processes involved. It requires those undertaking CTI to establish the tactics, techniques and procedures that threat actors use (and are possibly likely to use in the future) to disrupt the use of networks. Establishing why threat actors do what they do and what capability they have allows those undertaking CTI tasks to carry out specific actions during a data breach and also mitigate the resulting impact so that the harm caused is minimized. To achieve this, the cyber security manager and their colleagues need to think like a threat actor/agent and ensure that the reporting and risk communication processes in place are effective in terms of limiting the consequences associated with the impact. If an impact cannot be prevented, then the main objective is to limit the escalation of the damage caused and prevent the cascading effects associated with the impact so that the damage does not cause a ripple effect. It has to be remembered that supply chain members and/or organizations in the marketing channel are also at risk from the ripple effect and need to be safeguarded. A formalized CTI process can be considered beneficial in terms of making CTI available to a wider community. The results of a CTI analysis can be shared with law enforcement personnel and staff in intelligence and security agencies, as well as other stakeholders. Information sharing can be considered central to the collectivist approach to cyber security and fosters open dialogue that manifests in a proactive approach to cyber security management.

The message is clear. By acting in a proactive manner, the cyber security manager can create and implement a collectivist CTI policy and strategy framework that helps staff in the organization to eradicate cyber security vulnerabilities through a networked, partnership arrangement so that it remains in business. However, the objective is unlikely to be achieved in isolation. It requires senior management to establish how managers lower down the hierarchy appraise an organization's risk management policy and devise an adequate enterprise risk management model (Bromiley et al., 2015). This can be considered a worthwhile goal because the cyber security manager, working with the risk manager and various other managers such as the marketing manager, can pool relevant knowledge that facilitates cross-border cooperation and results in newly developed areas of expertise. By leveraging intelligence-related knowledge and utilizing strategic intelligence-oriented frameworks, it should be possible to think in terms of an organization establishing a security culture that integrates cyber security within the strategic planning process of partner organizations. This can be considered acceptable because by doing so, a more sustainable and resilient business model will be developed that has stakeholder interests at heart. Indeed, counteracting cyber-attacks can be thought of as right for society and fits with the view of DeBerry-Spence et al. (2023), who are conscious of the need to keep the general public safe. So, cyber security can be placed in the context of protecting stakeholder interests and increasing the well-being of society. However, to achieve this, it is important to look beyond the role of government and for collective action to be taken by senior managers that satisfies the demands made by shareholders.

Initiatives in cyberspace can be viewed as an opportunity to support public and private sector developments but at the same time, policymakers must ensure that the myriad of computer networks that constitute critical information infrastructure are deemed secure from cyber-attack. This is and will remain the focus of policy advisors and government representatives for some time because inter-government cooperation is essential for ensuring that computer networks are kept secure from attack (Harknett and Stever, 2009) and business can function as normal.

One way in which senior managers can help to develop the right mindset within the organization is to promote the use of scenario-based exercises that aid learning. For example, the UK's National Cyber Security Centre (2024) makes it clear that exercises, playbooks relating to cyber security incidents and establishing expertise to counteract cyber security incidents are fundamentally important with respect to dealing with unexpected consequences. It is suggested that scenarios can help managers to establish possible vulnerabilities and playbooks can be used to document what type of response should be provided in the case of specific types of cyber-attack. Furthermore, various types of risk can be highlighted, and exercises can be devised that help identify how the knowledge gaps of employees can be filled.

The National Cyber Security Centre (2024) makes a distinction between scenario-based exercises and a more forward-looking approach. The following advice is provided: "The aim of future scenario planning is **not** to forecast, but to encourage learning so that decision makers can consider alternative future possibilities" (National Cyber Security Centre, 2024). The emphasis is to establish different potential futures and how managers can plan accordingly to deal with the futures identified. This can be achieved by getting staff to focus on the "what if" type of questions and get them to challenge existing assumptions/perceptions. To achieve this, managers (National Cyber Security Centre, 2024) must place emphasis on developing future scenarios that include *scope* (stakeholders and timescales); differentiate between *trends* and *uncertainties*; outline *plausible futures* and focus on "*so what*"? By this is meant the variety of outcomes and the course of action as well as divergencies. Next, it is important to *communicate the lessons learnt*; and lastly, *understand the limitations of the approach*. The advice provided by the National Cyber Security Centre (2024) is that attention be given to the level of accuracy so that questions are asked about the potential realism of the futures identified and it also suggests that care needs to be taken vis-à-vis which futures are investigated because resources need to be committed to this.

Scenario analysis and planning can be used to get people, from different business functions, into a team building and group working routine. An experienced cyber security expert, who is known to be sensitive to the feelings of others, can be brought in to manage the scenario exercise. Remembering that cyber security staff are thin on the ground, it can be deduced that it is essential to get staff to buy into cyber security and help promote the need for it. The cyber security expert managing the cyber security exercise can use their social influence and also ensure that those involved bond with each other (Ifinedo, 2014, p. 70). This will help the individuals concerned to form work-based relationships with people that they need to work with, prior to and during a cyber-attack on the organization.

Bearing the above in mind, it is useful to reflect on what CTI is and who within the organization is responsible for it. The UK Government (2019, p. 6) provides guidance by stating that: "Cyber Threat Intelligence is the process of collecting, processing and analysing information regarding adversaries in cyberspace, in order to disseminate actionable threat intelligence, by understanding adversaries' motivations, capability, and modus operandi, to inform cyber security mitigation measures".

It is clear from this quotation that the cyber security manager, the risk manager, the IT manager and the security manager are all concerned with and have an involvement in CTI. It is likely, that in some organizations, the cyber security manager and the IT manager will report to the Chief Information Officer (CIO) and the security manager will report to the Chief Security Officer (CSO). The CSO is likely to have a wider brief than the CIO because they deal additionally with physical security. However, today, the focus is on information and communications technology (ICT) and the utilization of different types of platforms. Because of this, it is possible that an organization will combine the roles normally undertaken by a CIO and a CSO and integrate them into the role of a Chief Information Security Officer (CISO), and there may be a separate role for the Chief Digital Officer (CDO) (UK Government, 2019, p. 58). The objective is to ensure that interoperability allows employees to access a number of networks and carry on their business activities in a controlled and safe environment. Networks, whether physical or wireless, link software with hardware and this allows individuals to communicate and carryout business transactions in real time. Knowing how networks and computers are linked and managed is how the threat actor gains an upper hand and is able, through whatever means, to carry out a cyber-attack. Because there are a number of attack vectors (e.g., the use of social engineering) that can be used and defending in cyber space is beyond the capability of one person and/or one department, senior management needs to ensure that cyber security management is viewed as a collective responsibility. Consequently, working in unison, staff will update their cyber security knowledge and skill base, and pass on their knowledge to those lower down the organizational hierarchy. The logic of this is that by updating their cyber security skill and knowledge base, staff will be compliant and carry out their duties in the way expected.

The logic of this can be deduced from understanding why a network may be vulnerable or prone to attack. It can be noted that: "Threat Hunting is the proactive, iterative and human-centric identification of cyber threats that are internal to an IT network and have evaded existing security controls" (UK Government, 2019, p. 6). Threat hunting is essential because of the complexity involved. Indeed, not only do cyber security experts need to consider the threat landscape in totality but they also need to be aware of the fast-moving conditions that bring into play new threats as well as the incomplete information that is available to them and a number of hidden features that are unknown to them (Lozano et al., 2023, p. 131).

Another aspect that the cyber security manager needs to consider is the organization's digital footprint. The information in cyberspace, whether it is on a website or a social media network site, as well as other information that has been put into the public domain by various individuals and companies and associations, and which can be found on the world wide web, constitute an organization's digital footprint. The information can be used by cyber criminals to find ways to penetrate the organization's defences and the starting point maybe social engineering attacks or phishing attacks. It is for this reason that staff need to ensure that only relevant and accurate information is on the world wide web and that the data and information available is vetted and cannot be used against the organization. This is because making too much information available may mean that a criminal, intent on gaining access to an organization, can use the information to build up a profile of it and can then use the profiled information to fool the organization's staff into thinking that they are negotiating with a legitimate business representative only to find out later that this is not the case. Indeed, there have been a number of situations whereby a company has been outmanoeuvred by a criminal/criminal gang when they thought that they were dealing with a legitimate individual.

The UK Government (2019, p. 7) has this to say on the topic of the digital footprint: "Digital Risk and Intelligence (DR&I) is the process of monitoring, detecting and remediating threats within the public domain, through the control of an organisation's digital footprint". What is clear is that there is a clear link between digital risk and intelligence and threat hunting. For example, the cyber security manager and their colleagues need to know what data and information are available and what data and information are needed in order to establish a defensive strategy based on the data and information about the organization and its employees that is within the public domain. To help understand what managers in organizations need to do in terms of investing in an organization's CTI function, the UK Government (2019, pp. 15–16) has provided the following advice: "A Cyber Threat Intelligence function shall seek to collect, analyse and disseminate actionable intelligence to their organisation's defenders. A CTI function should be designed to support and improve the effectiveness of the defenders in a department". To be effective, it is recommended that the CTI function undertakes protective monitoring and risk management. It is also necessary for CTI staff to engage in change management, incident management and what is known as asset management, and to think in terms of a number of phases of their work-related activities: direction, collection, processing, analysis and dissemination (UK Government, 2019, pp. 15–16). These phases referred to are normally associated with the intelligence process and provide a sound backdrop for formalizing CTI.

In order to provide comprehensive CTI, it is important that the cyber security manager organizes and puts in place a formal threat assessment function. The parameters for formal threat assessment can be determined by senior management but rather than just rely on a top-down approach it is suggested that the cyber security manager takes responsibility for ensuring that cyber security staff are influential in determining what goes into threat assessment, and who is the beneficiary of it. The organization will be subject to cyber-attacks and because of this it is essential that incident response reports are produced and maintained that provide information about the attackers and their successes, the tools, techniques and processes they use as well as how the organization engages in risk mitigation (UK Government, 2019, p. 19). It is also useful to keep a record of penetration test report results (e.g., vulnerability assessments/red teaming activity), which has the objective of establishing if various functions or systems are vulnerable to attack (UK Government, 2019, p. 19).

In order to establish how a threat actor operates, it is important to undertake profiling. Profiling can be done according to specific criteria, but it needs to be in-depth and requires an analysis outlining the strengths and weaknesses of the threat actor, which are then mapped against their capabilities so that an analysis can be undertaken to link their strengths with the vulnerabilities to be exploited. The analysis will include an assessment of both the threat actor's weaknesses as well as the organization's weaknesses/vulnerabilities, which is important because the Dark Web is a source from which a threat actor can draw information and expertise and develop their knowledge to turn a weakness into a strength.

A threat actor can make their attack tools available for sale on the Dark Web and can also purchase such tools if necessary. A market for illicit software has been established over a number of decades and criminals can, by joining forces with other criminals that are deficient in a specific area of illegal activity or technological expertise, establish joint operations with other threat actors and develop an expertise in a certain type of disruptive behaviour. Although a rogue state actor (e.g., state agency) may well have access to direct funding sources, a threat actor that operates in the market independent of government is likely to be deficient of funds and may well identify with other criminal organizations and form partnership arrangements that are profit oriented. For example, a tripartite cyber-criminal entity may emerge that is formed of three parts: The criminal entrepreneur that possesses finance and seeks new markets and has the ambition to put a deal together that provides the necessary resources; the criminal research and development department that undertakes the development of malware and the third spoke of criminal activity, the expediter of the criminal activity. Such a tripartite arrangement has the power to bring new criminal initiatives to market and as they can operate from overseas, are unlikely to be discovered until a certain period of time has passed and have gained some success and/or moved on to a different location.

IBM (2024) suggests that threat actors (e.g., individuals or groups of people) can be categorized into different types. The way in which this can be done is to establish what motivates a threat actor and the objectives they set themselves, what level of skill or knowledge they have and where they can draw on additional knowledge and what resources they have and what resources they will need and can draw on. It is also useful to identify if a threat actor is also working for an intermediary or is carrying out their tasks alone. By segmenting threat actors according to set criteria, it is possible to rank and rate the threat they pose in a logical way; understand how they make strategic moves and if necessary, disguise their actions and establish how they are likely to invoke contingencies if their plans do not go as expected. For example, a ransomware attack is associated with a disruption in order to achieve financial gain, which is normally paid in bitcoins. Those intent on an act of cyber espionage are likely to be carrying out a commission and are likely to be working directly for a competitor (usually based overseas) or an overseas government department/agency. The objective is to steal sensitive data that can be utilized to gain a specific advantage, namely reducing the development costs and the development time in relation to producing a similar but different technology or technological application. By drawing on the most up-to-date research data, it is possible to go one step ahead and build-in a more advanced capability to the technology/technological application, while saving large amounts of money and time and reducing the risk of failure. Learning from others not only provides a unique insight into solving recurring problems but also allows the perpetrator to gain knowledge and improve their all-round capability. Hence, by stealing data/information, it is possible to produce a state-of-the-art technological application that strengthens the country's strategic advantage.

The following groups of threat actors have been defined by IBM (2024): *Cybercriminals; nation-state actors; hacktivists; thrill seekers; insider threats* and *cyberterrorists*. *Cybercriminals* (e.g., individuals/groups that are motivated by financial gain and deploy established methods such as ransomware attacks and phishing scams) focus on acquiring money transfers or data in relation to credit cards and login credentials. Also, intellectual property is targeted and so too is private/sensitive information that can be used to yield a result. *Nation-state actors* are supported and funded by nation-states and governments. Several objectives can be identified including stealing sensitive data and also gathering confidential information or carrying out actions to disrupt critical infrastructure. Various methods are deployed to obtain such objectives, and they include espionage or cyberwarfare. Such activities are well funded. *Hacktivists* use hacking techniques to promote a range of political or social agendas, which they are committed to. Such activities also involve spreading free speech and also uncovering human rights violations. The main motivation behind such an involvement can be classified as a desire to affect positive social change. Those undertaking such actions consider that the means they use are justified. Individuals, organizations or government agencies are subject to attack and one group identified as being involved in such activities is Anonymous, which is an international hacking collective that focuses on promoting freedom of speech. Anonymous has been known to use the Internet to further its cause. *Thrill seekers* are motivated by fun and are also motivated by curiosity. For example, script kiddies do not possess high-level technical skills and tend to use existing tools and techniques to carry out cyber-attacks on vulnerable computer systems and networks. Although they are motivated by amusement/ personal satisfaction, their actions can be disruptive and are known to cause damage by exploiting a situation that becomes public and leads to additional cyber-attacks. *Insider threats* are known to result from human error (e.g., an employee installs malware unintentionally or loses a company-owned device that ends up in the hands of a cybercriminal who then uses it to gain access to the organization's network). Also, it can be suggested that malicious insiders exist and are motivated to steal data that they then sell for financial gain or, if this is not the case, they may decide to inflict damage to data/applications because they feel aggrieved in some way. An example of the latter is a person who has been denied promotion, who feels resentful of the organization and decides to undertake an illegal act against it. *Cyberterrorists* can be nation-state actors, independent operatives or those acting on behalf of a nongovernment group that is politically or ideologically driven to undertake a cyber-attack or engage in a series of cyber-attacks. They are known to pose a high level of threat and may also be violent in their actions.

Knowing why a threat actor does what they do is important, but additional knowledge is needed to understand how a cyber-attacker does what they do. IBM (2024) suggests that threat actors use a number of methods to attack an individual or organization including *Malware, ransomware, phishing attacks, social engineering* and *denial of service (DoS) attacks*. *Malware* is malicious software that is aimed at damaging or disabling computer systems. It is spread via email normally in the way of attachments and can be downloaded from infected websites. Malware can also materialize in compromised software. Malware is used to steal data, take control of computer systems and also to attack other computers. Malware appears in the form of viruses, worms and Trojan horses, and can be considered highly deceptive. *Ransomware* is used to take control of a computer system, lock up a victim's data or device and only allow the situation to be remedied provided the victim pays a ransom to those orchestrating the attack. If a victim does not pay the ransom demand, it is possible that the data is locked and unavailable to the owner and will be sold online. Big game hunting (BGH) attacks are well coordinated and can inflict much damage on organizations and providers of critical infrastructure. *Phishing attacks* appear via email, text messages and voice messages but can also materialize via fake websites. The objective is to deceive the user and get them to share their sensitive data that results in them downloading malware. *Phishing attacks* can be divided into *spear phishing attacks* (e.g., messages are aimed at an individual(s) or group of individuals that appear to come from a legitimate source/sender that is known to them or has a relationship with the individual/group). A *business email compromise* is a spear phishing attack that is sent from co-workers or a colleague's impersonated or hijacked email account and the fraudulent email has a defined purpose. The *whale phishing* method is a spear phishing attack that is well crafted and aimed at high-level executives/corporate officers. The method of deception known as *social engineering* covers a number of attacks that exploit a person's feelings and emotions. The objective is to manipulate the person targeted by getting them to compromise their personal or organizational asset(s) or security so that the attacker is able to take advantage of the situation. *Social engineering* involves various approaches including leaving a malware-infected USB drive to be picked up and inserted and also social interaction is devised to trap a person into meeting and having certain expectations of the person that they have been engaging with online. *DoS attacks* are used by an attacker to flood a network or server with traffic, and consequently, it is then not available to users. A distributed denial-of-service attack (commonly referred to as DDoS attack) ensures that a distributed network of computers sends malicious traffic to a specific target computer.

Understanding why a threat actor does what they do, how they operate and where they get their expertise from is useful in terms of the cyber security manager developing an understanding of the need for strategic intelligence. For example, large technology-driven companies that operate on an international scale are likely to attract the attention of threat actors because they are resource rich. Evidence of this appears in the form of brand leadership; high levels of profitability; the deployment of up-to-date technological systems; work practices involving outsourcing; unique supply chain partners that have high levels of knowledge and/or links with government; expertise and a sustainable competitive advantage. An industry leader is likely to encounter a number of attacks over the years and some threat actors work tirelessly to penetrate a specific organization's defences.

IBM (2024) acknowledges this and has provided additional guidance in terms of what constitutes an *advanced persistent threat* (APT) and a *backdoor attack*. APTs are sophisticated cyberattacks that occur over long periods of time. They can result in a threat actor operating undetected in a computer system. The objective is to conduct espionage and reconnaissance for a future attack, and eventually steal sensitive data. Because of what is involved, it is considered that APTs stem from nation-state actors as well as threat actors that have access to large amounts of funding. With regards to *backdoor attacks*, the objective is for the attacker to enter and exit a system undetected. They focus on exploiting an opening in an operating system, application or computer system that is insufficiently protected. A *backdoor* can be created through an attacker using malware or a *backdoor* may exist to enable a software developer/hardware manufacturer to deploy upgrades or security patches. However, the opportunity exists for a hacker to gain access to a computer system and then exploit it.

Recently, a cyber-attack on Indonesia's national data centre proved highly disruptive as can be understood from the following example provided by Karmini (2024). A hacking group demanded a US$8 million ransom for unlocking disrupted services involving over 200 government agencies. The attack affected both national and regional governments and although some government services (e.g., immigration services at airports) were restored, some were not. Karmini (2024) explains that Indonesia has suffered ransomware attacks in the past and makes reference to the country's central bank which was subject to a ransomware attack in 2022 and also, the Health ministry's COVID-19 app was hacked the year before. In addition, Karmini (2024) states that in 2021 the personal data and health status of 1.3 million people were held for ransom and in 2023 "a hacker group known as the LockBit ransomware had claimed to have stolen 1.5 terabytes of data managed by Indonesia's largest Islamic bank, Bank Syariah Indonesia".

What the cyber security manager and their colleagues need to remember is that a threat actor is unlikely to reduce or stop what they are doing, even if they have achieved their goal. This is because threat actors view their actions as market specific and are financially driven to keep working in the way that they do. Success breeds success and their ventures become highly profitable. Hence, cyber criminals are able to reinvest and expand their operations and diversify into a number of illicit activities. Although a country's government agencies are involved in helping to protect critical infrastructure and strategically important industries against cyber-attacks, they have limited resources. In addition, government representatives need to operate within the law and follow due process. So, a nation's cyber defences are focused mainly on protecting against specific forms of cyber-attacks on critical national infrastructure and critical information infrastructure. They will on occasion, however, carry out attacks on hostile operators and shut down their illicit operations. What needs to be noted is that this does involve complexity because an attack on an overseas-based perpetrator may require the assistance of other government agencies based in other countries.

Understanding how senior managers can influence government policymakers is important, and this is normally done through specially arranged meetings, conferences, seminars and workshops. Senior managers also get involved with trade associations and lobby government and policymakers to change the laws or introduce interventions that curtail the actions of those carrying out illegal cyber activities.

2.7 Intra-Government and Inter-Government Cooperation

In the UK, the National Protective Security Authority (NPSA) assumes responsibility for the UK's National Technical Authority vis-à-vis physical and personnel protective security and focuses on ensuring that the UK is resilient in terms of national security threats. Staff at NPSA are associated with the UK's security service (MI5) and their staff work closely with the Government Communications Headquarters (GCHQ), which is associated with the Foreign, Commonwealth & Development Office.

The GCHQ (GCHQ, 2024) mission has been defined this way:

"Our mission is simple: we help to keep the country safe, in the real world and online. We focus on communications: how to access, analyse and – occasionally – disrupt the communications of the UK's adversaries; and on the nation's cyber security".

The GCHQ works with various stakeholders including the intelligence service (MI6), the security service (MI5), the police, the Ministry of Defence, private sector organizations, academia and overseas partners. The National Cyber Security Centre (NCSC), which is a part of GCHQ, adopts a proactive approach to safeguarding the UK's digital capability and is heavily involved in promoting cyber security awareness and various cyber security educational initiatives.

Intra-government and inter-government cooperation can be classified as incremental in nature because different government departments and agencies are responsive to different laws, and the support mechanisms in place (e.g., bureaucracy) change through time as experienced individuals move from one post to another post, and personal relationships are disrupted and rebuilt. International agreements can be "bilateral" and involve two countries only or they can be "multilateral" and involve a number of countries. The Unites Staes of America is strongly committed to such arrangements and states (US Government, 2024): "Treaties and other international agreements are written agreements between sovereign states (or between states and international organizations) governed by international law. The United States enters into more than 200 treaties and other international agreements each year". The US government is committed to international relations and peace, and upholding human rights, and in 2001 was instrumental in the formation of a treaty relating to cybercrime.

Preventing certain types of cyber-attacks, especially from overseas-based threat actors (sometimes referred to as "malicious actors") is difficult because of the different laws that are in place and the fact that some governments are lax when it comes to implementing such laws. For example, a cyber-criminal syndicate may be based in a country that is known to have strict cyber security laws in place and because of this they cross the border/operate from a safe haven and launch their attacks from an inadequately governed country. Because consumers are subject to different degrees of protection worldwide, those intent on making money from illicit acts do so by operating from an inadequately regulated country (e.g., a rogue state), which shields them and provides impunity from prosecution. This can prove problematic to the cyber security manager and their colleagues because even if a threat actor is known and action is taken to disrupt their activities and close them down, it may not be possible to do so immediately.

Accepting that the sophistication and intensity of cyber-attacks will increase, senior managers need to consider investing more time and effort into corporate governance and also appoint a CSO and a CIO to comply with legal requirements. This can be considered essential as regards the implementation of cyber security policy and strategy. It should also provide a firm base from which cyber security awareness can be established and embedded in the organization's culture via various forms of intervention stemming from and incorporating organizational learning.

Although a proactive approach to cyber security is to be applauded in the sense that cyber security awareness should improve cyber security and security generally, it has to be said that more needs to be done with respect to helping people in society to become more aware of the various types of cyber threat that are evolving, and which can yield untold harm. Indeed, by adopting a collectivist approach (e.g., collaboration involving various stakeholders that share cyber threat information/intelligence and solutions) to counteract the various cyber threats that exist, the cyber security manager and their staff will be well placed to work with staff throughout the organization and establish a clearly defined set of responsibilities and communication channels that result in cooperation between the parties involved (Li and Liao, 2018, p. 159) and which allows risk communication to function as well as expected. This requires commitment and an understanding of which cyber security factors are deemed controllable and which cyber security factors are deemed uncontrollable. Through the application of CTI, the type of cyber security factors can be separated into those requiring help from outside/international sources and those requiring assistance from inside/national sources. By mapping vulnerabilities onto expected impacts, a risk management policy can be established that allows the cyber security manager and their colleagues to equate risk with certain types of vulnerability and campaign in-house for resources to invest in specific forms of cyber security protection.

Governments around the world are also adopting a proactive approach to cyber security through partnership arrangements. The US government has been actively involved in building and promoting cyber security partnerships involving various governments and institutions for a number of years. For example, in April 2022, the United States of America and 60 countries launched the Declaration for the Future of the Internet (DFI); and also, the Quadrilateral Security Dialogue ("the Quad"), which involves the United States, India,

Japan, and Australia, has proved instrumental in bringing partner countries together to advance cyberspace shared goals through information sharing (The White House, 2023, p. 29). Information sharing between computer emergency response teams is considered important and various initiatives, such as the Indo-Pacific Economic Framework for Prosperity (IPEF) and the Americas Partnership for Economic Prosperity (APEP), should do much to support regional governments in their quest to establish a thriving digital economy (The White House, 2023, p. 30). Areas of specific need have been designated for attention and include the development of technical standards as well as mechanisms to facilitate cross-border data flows that are aimed at protecting an individual's privacy. There is also a focus on data localization requirements and resilience in the context of supply chain security. The US–EU Trade and Technology Council (TTC) has a number of objectives, one of which is to combat shared threats; the United States, Australia and the UK are engaged in a trilateral security and technology pact ("AUKUS") that is aimed at securing critical technologies, improving cyber coordination and, in addition, sharing advanced capabilities (The White House, 2023, p. 30). Sharing cyber threat information is considered a priority of the US government and so is exchanging cybersecurity practices and expertise. Partnerships such as the International Counter-Ransomware Initiative have been established to help stakeholders counteract emerging cybersecurity challenges and attention is also being given to ensuring that an adversary does not evade the rule of law. This means the United States will continue to consolidate law enforcement mechanisms such as the European Cybercrime Centre, which is focused on bringing perpetrators of crime to justice (The White House, 2023, p. 30). The US government is keen to build effective hubs, based on effective models, with partners in various parts of the world.

As regards the Trilateral Security Dialogue (TSD) involving the United States, Australia and Japan, Warren et al. (2024, p. 27) have indicated that standards need to be viewed from the perspective of the further interoperability of systems and there is a need to embrace a two-step approach: (i) "a technical inter-TSD AI-technology sharing framework" and (ii) "an international-focused governance strategy for AI". Through the process of adopting common standards, it is thought that trust in AI exchange will occur and design, implementation and legal accountability, for example, will transpire.

2.8 Understanding Big Data and Related Consequences

The need to take cognizance of the threats posed by those who undertake cyber-attacks has been given attention and placed in the context of big data. Sivarajah et al. (2017, p. 265), in their review of the work of Zicari (2014), acknowledge that big data is logically grouped into three main categories that are based on clearly identifiable but integrated topics that encompass the data life cycle. The three categories are: *Data challenges, process challenges* and *management challenges*. Sivarajah et al. (2017, p. 265) suggest that *data challenges* incorporate the characteristics of the data itself and include "data volume, variety, velocity, veracity, volatility, quality, discovery and dogmatism"; *process challenges* include the techniques involved and these are "how to capture data, how to integrate data, how to transform data, how to select the right model for analysis and how to provide the results" and *management challenges* relate to "privacy, security, governance and ethical aspects".

Categorizing data in this way has the advantage of specifying its value and also ensures that it is analysed using appropriate methods. For example, the analytical tools and models available allow large amounts of data to be collected, sorted, structured and analysed using AI. Specifically designed algorithms can go a step further and predict the interlocking associations and create and run scenario analyses. The cyber security manager, working with the risk manager and other function heads (e.g., Marketing and Finance), can establish how they are to interpret the patterns in the data and implement appropriate strategies that are logical components of the organization's overall strategy. Reflecting on the above, it is possible to develop a conceptual framework that incorporates the main topics discussed. (See Figure 2.1).

It can be noted from Figure 2.1 that the cyber security manager and their colleagues need to be aware of the laws in place that govern all aspects of cyber security. Taking cognizance of binding international treaties and their consequences is also very important. Furthermore, there are various institutions that also promote cyber security from various standpoints including increasing business operations, devising and promoting standards and regulations, advocating ethical approaches to using AI for business and the rights of workers vis-à-vis surveillance and monitoring. Building up a picture of how these different components relate and fit together is necessary because the cyber environment is not fixed or static. It is flexible and subject to change. Hence, the work of government departments needs to be viewed as aligning with the objectives of international institutions (e.g., the IMF, the Organisation for Economic Co-operation and Development (OECD), the UN and the World Bank) and how cyber security maintains the quality of life and aids new forms of business development. In some cases, lobbying occurs that gives rise to new laws and or new cooperative arrangements and agreements between nations. However, because some governments are lax in terms of implementing cyber security laws and providing support, the cyber security landscape is uneven and because of this, the cyber security manager and their colleagues need to know how to navigate through the issues and challenges that manifest as the organization they work for innovates and contributes to digitalization and the development of a digital society.

FIGURE 2.1 Conceptual framework outlining the main topics underpinning cyber security management and strategic intelligence.

It is clear from Figure 2.1 that organizational learning is considered influential. Organizational learning is according to Morgan et al. (1998) a process and needs to be viewed from two perspectives (Lee, 2009, p. 186): adaptive learning and generative (double-loop) learning. Indeed, adaptive learning can be viewed as improving the quality and the efficiency of existing operations through the utilization of knowledge and, generative learning, which is a step beyond adaptive learning, relates to staff formulating new "practices, perspectives and frameworks" that when applied, helps the organization to develop its capability (Lee, 2009, p. 186).

Taking into account the international dimension of cyber-crime and the fact that cyber criminals operate across borders and may be based in one country and undertake attacks on organizations and individuals in other countries suggests that cooperation involving organizational staff and law enforcement personnel is essential and needs to be viewed as ongoing. However, police forces and indeed intelligence and security agencies around the world operate in different ways and are accountable to different government departments. This adds to the complexity of cyber security and, in addition, means that there may well be delays in undertaking investigations into specific acts of criminal activity if that is the investigation is of an international orientation and law enforcement officers are subject to different laws.

It is useful to reflect on a cyber-attack on a bank and the consequences of it. Bank staff may need to close down banking activities for a while in order to investigate the problem and ensure that the bank's operations are secure. An impact on a bank will cause customers to suffer psychologically as they are denied access to their bank account and also some transactions may not be fulfilled due to technical delays. Delays can cause secondary problems and also rumours throughout the industry may convince some customers to ask for the removal or transfer of their deposits to other banks and this may result in the closure of their accounts. Should a bank suffer a major impact, it is likely that there will be a response from industry members and corporate clients, and it is likely that staff based in the nation's central bank will also become involved and work closely with staff at the affected bank. Industry representatives brought in to assess the impact and its consequences and the impact on other banks will write reports and report to various authorities. This may raise issues of governance and compliance, and this may result in new legislation arising. This is because some banks borrow funds from the interbank market on a daily basis and failure to do so could have severe ramifications for the bank because it may be denied access to funds and also their clients.

An investigation into a cyber-attack on a bank is also likely to warrant the involvement of special cyber security advisors and forensic experts, and this can prove costly and add to the delay in getting the bank operational again. Those providing critical national infrastructure and critical information infrastructure services may also participate in the discussions because of the fact that there may well be knock-on effects relating to the functioning of the industry itself and also broader-based issues relating to the vulnerability of the technology that governs connectivity may warrant attention. Furthermore, various independent banking sector institutions and trade associations may also participate in the discussions and so will staff from the country's central bank. It also has to be remembered that as well as individuals, a bank has business clients including retail companies, local small business concerns and local councils. So, the level of disruption can be enormous, and this is the reason why the security and intelligence agencies will monitor the situation and ensure that the cascading effects are limited, and a major economic disruption is avoided.

As regards an organization's strategic intelligence approach, the cyber security manager and their colleagues will need to work with experts in relation to undertaking situational awareness. This involves the collection, analysis and dissemination of key intelligence that is judged to be important in terms of identifying, assessing and solving cyber security–related threats and linking individual threats to known or potential vulnerabilities so that appropriate action can be taken to rectify the situation. Working closely with experts involved in country risk analysis, industry sector analysis and those possessing cyber threat expertise, the cyber security manager will develop trust-based relationships with staff in partner organizations who ensure that an event occurring in real time is dealt with in real time.

In order to develop working relationships with their peers, cyber security managers can avail themselves of the social cognitive theory, which requires an individual to learn by observing others and also develop the ability to interpret thought processes that are key to understanding personality (Pfleeger and Caputo, 2012, p. 605). During meetings with their peers, the cyber security manager can watch for and anticipate positive and negative signals and devise a strategy to deal with them. For example, during discussions with the finance director regarding the funding of cyber security awareness workshops, it may be made clear that the cost is too high. By suggesting that security is an investment, arguments can be made that outline the cost savings associated with the prevention of a cyber-attack getting through the organization's defences. So, prevention is better and less costly than a cure. Furthermore, by indicating how risk mitigation is to be planned and implemented, the investment aspect is reiterated, and this should result in support from senior management.

Through connectivity and the process of interaction, the intelligence systems of partner organizations will become integrated, and this will speed up the flow of information so that if one company in the partnership arrangement is targeted and an impact manifests, then the other partner members can react quickly to dilute the impact and its effect and ensure that the partnership remains operational. This suggests that a business continuity plan and planning process is in being and the partnership arrangement is resilient. But this needs to be planned for and appropriate staff need to be in place such as a business continuity manager or risk manager, for example, who have a clear mandate and report to senior management.

It can be noted from Figure 2.1 that in order for organizational cyber security to be comprehensive, staff need to be cyber security aware and need to have the ability to identify and deal with various forms of cyber threats that materialize from time to time. An organization's ability to counteract cyber threats will be enhanced through a formalized counteracting cyber threats policy that outlines who in the organization is responsible for the different components of the CTI policy. Such a policy will also make clear who specific individuals report to. As well as indicating what needs to be done and by whom, senior management needs to be specific about important issues such as the operating budget and how the budget is funded. Without clear guidance as regards the resources to be drawn on and utilized, the appropriate controls are unlikely to be in place for the continuity of the resourcing of the cyber security budget. By specifying the appropriate mechanisms and outlining the structures in place, it should be possible to adopt the enterprise risk management approach as a means of holistic risk management because to do so means that every department within the organization has a member of staff that feeds their intelligence (trends, results and data) into the enterprise risk management model that is in being. In addition, a holistic approach to risk management should ensure that staff based in partner organizations contribute fully to cyber security policy because they are committed to a collectivist cyber security framework that is viewed as being co-owned by the partner organizations.

It is now apparent that in order to have a collectivist cyber security framework in place, a commitment to organizational learning is required that gives rise to staff being cyber security aware and able to undertake various strategic intelligence work. One of the outputs of organizational learning is, therefore, a strategic cyber security management strategy. This is symbolic of a proactive approach to cyber security. A proactive approach requires that the cyber security manager and their staff utilize cyber security knowledge, expertise and various models, tools and techniques and deploy appropriate forms of AI. AI can be viewed as transformational in nature and can help staff to undertake risk assessment. By having a risk assessment policy in place, the cyber security manager and their colleagues can utilize organizational intelligence, and this can manifest in an organizational intelligence system that draws on data and information from staff in partner organizations.

2.9 Developing Theoretical Insights into Cyber-Attacks

Reflecting on the above, it is possible to highlight a number of theoretical insights that managers can give some thought to. For example, Agrafiotis et al. (2018) are of the view that the harm caused by cyber-attacks needs to be looked at in terms of the impact they have on an organization and also the level of risk that management is prepared to accept. In addition, modelling can play a useful role as regards senior management making an overall assessment of the different forms of harm that can be caused, which range from financial to psychological. The following example provided by Agrafiotis et al. (2018, p. 10) provides an insight into the harm caused to an organization and the resulting knock-on effects. Agrafiotis et al. (2018, p. 10) refer to what happened to JP Morgan Chase, a large US bank: "..... hackers obtained administrator access to several of their servers. Information regarding names, phone numbers, email and physical addresses of account holders was exfiltrated, affecting 76 million households and seven million small businesses......" The customers whose information had been leaked needed to monitor their finances to establish if they had been the subject of fraud and indeed some were. For example, those behind the attack sent fake emails directing customers to impostor websites and this resulted in a number of customers falling victim to financial fraud. Consequently, the bank was required to reappraise its IT infrastructure and employ extra staff to help implement change.

As regards modelling cyber security attacks, modelling is viewed as a way of reinforcing what needs to be done in terms of monitoring the external threat environment and at the same time establishing how cyber security personnel implement the necessary systems and controls that thwart the actions of those that engage and implement cyber-attacks. Various studies exist outlining the attacks on specific systems (Ahmadian et al., 2019), and most of these studies are highly complex involving mathematical interpretations.

The Cyber Attack Modeling and Impact Assessment Component (CAMIAC) approach involves using a number of techniques (Kotenko and Chechulin, 2013, p. 5): "attack graph generation, real-time event analysis, prognosis of future malefactor's steps, attack impact assessment, and anytime approach". It can be suggested that these techniques are useful because they draw on "a comprehensive security repository, efficient attack graph (tree) generation techniques, taking into account known and new attacks based on zero-day vulnerabilities, stochastic analytical modelling and interactive decision support" (Kotenko and Chechulin, 2013, p. 5). Hence, they are considered useful because they can help the cyber security manager and their colleagues to establish cyber security countermeasures.

The Kill Chain Attack modelling technique is well known and is used to plan intrusions. It is a structured form of attack that encompasses a number of steps detailed in the form of a chain of action. According to Al-Mohannadi et al. (2016, p. 70), the Kill Chain Attack modelling technique is composed of seven key steps: *Reconnaissance; Weaponization; Delivery; Exploitation; Installation; Command and control* and *Action on objectives*. Step 1 *Reconnaissance* is characterized by the attacker collecting information that provides a basis for the attack. The source of the information may well be the Internet. In Step 2, *Weaponization*, the attacker prepares the method of attack such as getting a virus ready and planning the attack on the victim/target. Step 3 *Delivery*, here the attacker implements the attack (e.g., possibly via an email attachment or in the form of a link to be downloaded). Step 4 *Exploitation*, the victim downloads the payload sent and the exploitation starts. Step 5 Installation, the malware is installed on the victim's computer. Step 6 *Command and control*, this is where the attacker authorizes access to the internal assets guarded by the victim. Finally, Step 7, *Action on objectives*; it is here that the attacker is able to realize their objective and achieve their goal.

The cyber-attack modelling approach can be thought of as conceptual in nature and composed of a number of steps that require cyber security staff to test for vulnerabilities through simulating attacks on the organization. The objective is to identify possible vulnerabilities; review the risk management process and allocate funds to ensure that the potential vulnerabilities are made secure. Various scenarios can be used to mimic the way in which an attacker carries out an attack or set of attacks and the solution identified may involve cooperation with staff in partner organizations as security is deemed a shared responsibility.

What can be learned from the above is that cyber security managers need to be confident in exploring situations of complexity and must be prepared to take risks so that they develop an understanding of how cyber security management and strategic intelligence are shaped and shape the world of cyber security threat prevention. By partaking in theory building, the cyber security manager can develop insights into the world of cyber security and explain how cyber security specialists, through making deductions, arrive at informed guesses that help to change the perception of the cyber security specialist. For example, by being apathetic and reactive in their approach, the cyber security manager will be defensive and react continually to those carrying out cyber-attacks. By being proactive and anticipating the actions of those carrying out cyber-attacks, the cyber security manager will be well placed to understand what motivates the perpetrator of such attacks and how such individuals plan and execute cyber-attacks. Such knowledge is beneficial because it allows the cyber security manager to logically define possible solutions to evolving situations. The solutions have relevance because they are based on and incorporate reality. One approach that can be drawn on to help the cyber security manager interpret events and build theoretical knowledge is understanding how social scientists build theory and how theory is used to interpret complex situations.

It can be suggested that social science is different from natural sciences because at the heart of social sciences are people and their interactions. Natural sciences incorporate and are based on laws, whereas social science works in a different way and requires in-depth studies that provide evidence in terms of cause and effect in relation to people and their behaviour. The cyber security manager is well aware of the problem associated with turning data from a small sample into a predictive reality because people do not always act in the way expected and are motivated by different stimuli. Hence, generalizability is not always possible and because of this, it is difficult for the cyber security manager to establish a theory because there are a large number of uncontrollable factors that can be held responsible for changing an individual's reality. Considering how people are influenced and what motivates them to change their behaviour requires an understanding of how people are influenced in terms of negative and positive outcomes, fear appeals and how strong their personality is. Fear is a motivator and can be viewed from several perspectives: an individual's personal loss and what the consequences may be to them financially or from the perspective of how an error in judgment (e.g., the giving away of a sensitive password to an outsider) may result in a data breach and the consequences it has for the organization.

It is pertinent at this juncture to consider how the cyber security manager should go about developing their mindset as regards developing cyber security management theory in the context of strategic intelligence. The grounded theory approach can be considered useful and highly prized with respect to building theory. Indeed, the work of Strauss and Corbin (1990) has been used by various researchers and people in business to provide a holistic understanding of a situation. An alternative and less-complex approach would be to think and follow through the advice of Lange and Pfarrer (2017) and consider using the five building blocks of knowledge creation. The five building blocks are: Common ground, complication, course of action, concern and contribution (Lange and Pfarrer, 2017, pp. 408–410). *Common ground* can be associated with the increasing capability of the threat actors to cause harm by increasing their resource base, which provides them with unlimited funds to invest in their illicit actions. Cyber criminals are known to successfully carry out ransomware attacks and get paid in bitcoins. We can interpret this as a *common ground* in the sense that what cyber attackers do is exploit a vulnerability and then, through the process of enrichment, go on to do more damage by diversifying their attack pattern of behaviour. Cyber security specialists are aware of the harm done and need to develop countermeasures that prevent a cyber-attack from being successful. As regards *complication*, there is no doubt that those who undertake cyber-attacks are skilled and determined to take advantage of the situation. It is with this in mind that attention can focus on the details, and it can be suggested that something positive needs to be done to prevent such attacks from getting through the organization's defences. In other words, an alternative solution needs to be found because it is not appropriate to consider maintaining the current situation. With regards to *concern*, this requires the cyber security manager to consider that the "complication is of concern" (Lange and Pfarrer, 2017, p. 409). Because a common ground has been established with the risk manager, the IT manager and the security manager, for example, it is easier to devise a collectivist approach to cyber security and work together to create a cyber security awareness programme as well as think of how to develop/deploy threat detection software for example. It follows that the *course of action* requires the cyber security manager to think of how the construct/themes are related and how cyber security policy can be devised and implemented that embraces partner organizations and supply chain members. It follows that a convincing solution is applied to a compelling complication and this is evidence of theory building. Lastly, *contribution* is viewed in terms of how the idea or argument or context is used to reinforce people's understanding of a problem and how others view the possible solution. Can the cyber security policy or framework or strategy be used to galvanize the attention of senior management and get them to invest in cyber security provision? Obviously, those in powerful positions within the organization need to be convinced that the investment in cyber security is worthwhile but they also need to understand that establishing a governance framework is their responsibility.

Haveman et al. (2019) suggest that there are different ways to construct a theory and possibly the cyber security manager, taking note of this, should think less about theory building as a way to solve problems and more about developing knowledge that can be integrated into the different aspects of cyber security management. This can be done through utilizing the enterprise risk management concept and developing frameworks that draw on a range of experts to share information and who willingly engage in cyber security decision-making.

2.10 Reflection and Questions

The Cyber Security Management and Strategic Intelligence Process is outlined in Figure 2.2. It is clear that senior management is required to ensure that staff are aware that a proactive and anticipatory leadership style, characterized by cooperation and teamwork, is in being as it provides a platform upon which the strategic intelligence approach can be carried out. By cooperating with in-house staff and staff from the stakeholder community, it should be possible for the cyber security manager and their colleagues to work with government representatives, when necessary, on a number of cyber security–related initiatives. These may include implementing new standards and regulatory measures and ensuring the laws are in place to protect the customer's privacy.

Cyber-crime threat detection is beneficial in terms of helping the cyber security manager to focus the attention of senior managers on ensuring that cyber security and intelligence

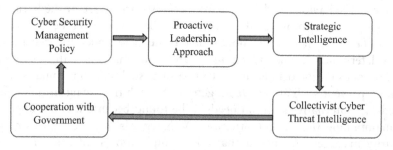

FIGURE 2.2 The cyber security management and strategic intelligence process.

work are coupled and the work of cyber security intelligence staff is necessary for monitoring the environment so that current and future cyber-attacks can be identified and categorized. Categorizing cyber threats and cyber-attacks is important because it allows senior managers to establish when a specific type of cyber-attack will occur and how the impact/potential impact and the knock-on effects are likely to undermine the functioning of the organization. By monitoring the environment, it is possible to establish who is responsible for an attack and what their motive is. For example, an insider may want to take revenge on the organization by sabotaging data files and/or making confidential and sensitive information available to an outside organization. Furthermore, an external threat actor may decide to defraud the organization and/or disrupt the functioning of the organization by spreading false rumours (disinformation) about it, which results in reputational damage. Establishing who is responsible for an attack and what their motives are provides other organizations in the community with insight that they can act upon to lobby the government for tougher regulatory controls to protect organizations in the industry. It also proves beneficial as it provides valuable data and information to law enforcement agencies so that they can target their efforts and utilize their limited resources more effectively.

Question 1: Why is it important to categorize cyber threats?
Question 2: How can those orchestrating cyber-attacks be monitored?
Question 3: What regulatory controls are needed to provide more comprehensive cyber security?

2.11 Conclusion

By placing cyber security management and strategic intelligence in context, it is possible to have a broad-based view of the subject and appreciate what managers need to do in order to play their role in making the organization more resilient in terms of counteracting cyber-attacks. Because cyber-attacks are wide ranging and beyond the control of a single department, it is advised that a collectivist approach to cyber security is adhered to. However, in order to embrace such an approach, it is important to have the necessary people in place within the organizational structure and ensure that cyber security staff are motivated to contribute to various cyber security initiatives in the way expected. There are a range of interventions that can be used to protect against cyber threats, but it is important to acknowledge that cyber security managers and their colleagues need to be in a position to be one step ahead of the threat actor. This can be achieved through a commitment to cyber threat detection and the use of scenarios, which can be deployed to answer the "what if" type question. It is hoped that such an approach will focus senior management's attention on implementing a proactive cyber security management approach as opposed to a reactive cyber security management approach. The objective is to be one step ahead as opposed to one step behind and, additionally, to ensure that the organization's digital assets are protected.

Case 1: Digital services: issues and reflections

Mr. Thompson took up his new appointment as Marketing Director at a company that was known to operate its sales through traditional sales outlets located in shopping centres and retail park locations. When agreeing to join the company, Mr. Thompson had suggested that he would help marketing staff to devise and implement an e-service strategy that would complement the company's existing marketing and sales operations. However, there was limited knowledge within the company as regards what an e-service involved and how it could be managed. Most of the staff had worked their way up from sales and were extensively focused on setting targets and achieving the targets set. They were keen to market the company's products but did not show an interest in security.

Mr. Thompson considered that the best way forward was to commission an external software company to produce a chatbot that once installed could operate and be managed via the company's website. Chatbots have been in use for some time and were considered highly successful in terms of entertaining customers and potential customers and providing instant and accurate information about the company's products. When commissioning the company to provide a chatbot, Mr. Thompson placed emphasis on customization that enabled the chatbot, through specific algorithms, to seek direct answers to questions relating to customer choice and delivery. Furthermore, the chatbot could collect non-personal information and store the information for future use.

The logic was to provide and build a trustworthy online marketing service that would be promoted through electronic word-of-mouth and positive customer reviews. It was envisaged that this would help widen the customer base and at the same time help marketing staff to match the products available with customer needs. This was considered appropriate because although there had been an increasing trend showing consumers were buying products online, it was thought that a certain percentage of consumers would return to buying face to face from physical outlets because online operations had difficulties from time to time and there had been numerous reports in the media about customers being scammed.

The chatbot e-service was launched six months after the idea was first put forward and appeared to work well for the first three weeks. After that period, it was noted that customer feedback started to be less positive than was the case to start with and also some highly critical product reviews had been noted. Mr. Thompson decided to look into the situation and get staff to undertake a strengths, weaknesses, opportunities and threat analysis. He was surprised at what he discovered.

It was clear from the analysis that the staff could not distinguish between the company's internal situation, which involved listing the strengths and weaknesses of the company and making a match with the external situation, which involved assessing the threats that the company faced and highlighting the opportunities available. Furthermore, the staff were unable to focus the findings of their analysis in terms of setting priorities and objectives and were confused about how to carry out further analysis involving a positioning strategy within the industry. The perceptual map that the staff devised was unrealistic in terms of the company's actual position and the corporate objectives set. It seemed that there was no real appreciation of a digital strategy and how it could be devised and placed within the company's overall marketing strategy. There was further confusion as regards the communications strategy, how it incorporated promotion and the payment system and how the end customer could choose to customize the product. The information the customers were given seemed to confuse them and their interaction with the chatbot was incomplete and in some instances, drew incorrect information from it. Feedback received from the customers suggested that they considered that the chatbot was hallucinating and the product received was either late or did not meet the requirements provided and overall, they were disillusioned and rather angry with their experience and the service level provided.

Mr. Thompson decided to organize an in-house training session to promote the use of e-service and decided to incorporate cyber security awareness as this was considered important vis-à-vis linking the product display material on the website with the payment system. Attention was given to these aspects because it seemed that some customers had purchased products from a similar website that was owned and managed by a different company and, in addition, there was a high level of returned products. Although instructions were provided on the company's website and the terms and conditions were made known, it was thought that a high percentage of customers only skimmed through the details and were not prepared to put much time and effort into reading through all the information.

What emerged from the training session surprised Mr. Thompson. It was clear that marketing staff were unable to place themselves in the position of the customer and to think of how the chatbot could and should relate to customer needs. Staff considered that the process was automatic, and they were not able to think of how problems arose and what they needed to pay attention to. Some staff said that all inquiries should be followed up by staff in the IT department as staff in that department were better able to handle the technical issues that arose. However, a representative from the IT department made it clear that marketing staff did not engage with staff in IT and marketing staff were known to secure orders but did not follow through and resolve the recurring problems.

A representative from the finance department was also on the training course and suggested that it was worrying to note that over the past two weeks, a high percentage of returns had been received. Customers appeared to be ordering more items than they needed, and this was causing problems because of the cost associated with receiving returned items and the fact that they could not be resold as new. The company could not sustain such a situation for long because it impacted profitability and distracted people away from their day-to-day activities, which meant that they were not completing their normal daily tasks on time.

When attention focused on extending the company's e-service provision, more confusion occurred. The staff were not aware of how a social media influencer could be perceived differently from a virtual influencer. There was also confusion about the concept of augmented reality and how companies were deploying it. Also, some staff suggested that they had heard that a virtual influencer had been cloned and that a fake website was using a very similar virtual influencer to obtain orders for its products. The staff seemed reluctant to embrace technology and seemed to want to return to traditional marketing methods. This resulted in an in-depth discussion regarding cooperation between the company's separate business departments and what information should be placed in the company's risk register. Again, staff were unclear about this and did not seem to know who should do what. It was suggested that the company's suppliers should also participate in future discussions regarding digitalization because staff in partner organizations were struggling to introduce the blockchain concept that the senior management had proposed.

It was clear that staff throughout the partnership arrangement did not know how to devise and implement a digital strategy and did not possess the skill or the knowledge to integrate the digital strategy into the company's marketing strategy. What shocked those attending was that the person assigned to talk about the digital strategy in greater depth had unfortunately left the presentation material on the bus and had to go to the bus depot to retrieve the material. This was extremely worrying because the information pack was known to contain details of customers and contracts with suppliers. The details in the package could be used to launch a cyber-attack on the company and its partners and, in addition, there was information in the presentation pack outlining who in the organization undertook specific tasks and who they reported to. There was also a sub-report within the package outlining the different types of customer databases in existence (e.g., business-to-customer and business-to-business) and who had access to such data and where the data was stored. Senior management had in fact just signed an agreement with a cloud provider for the company to store data in the cloud they operated, and a second contract was about to be signed with another cloud provider. Also of worry was the fact that an in-depth analysis had been undertaken of customer complaints and the complaints had been tabulated and the findings interpreted. The results were linked to specific retail stores and the chatbot service managed by the company.

Mr. Thompson reflected on the situation and considered that the company needed to devise and implement a strategic intelligence policy that could focus the minds of managers on both the external environment and the internal environment and create a culture that enabled staff to better understand the issues and challenges confronting the company. He set about designing a workshop for senior management that would provide answers to three main questions.

Question 1: How could a digital services strategy be incorporated within a digital strategy that was integrated into the marketing strategy?

Question 2: What cyber security problems were likely to emerge that need to be addressed?

Question 3: How can staff in partner organizations be involved in cyber security management?

Case 2: Strategic intelligence and cyber security management

Jennifer Hall was the cyber security manager of a rapidly growing organization in the UK that had ambitious plans to expand overseas. Jennifer was aware of the fact that cyber security management and strategic intelligence was a new and emerging body of knowledge and was prepared to put time and effort into helping staff to understand what it involved and ensure that staff throughout the organization harnessed such knowledge on a daily basis. Indeed, she had recently presented a talk to industry representatives highlighting the fact that the uncontrollable factors in the cyber threat environment were becoming more prominent and that managers were struggling to adequately understand the economic, social, political and technological factors that were combining to provide increased uncertainty on a day-to-day basis.

Jennifer was aware that she needed to provide leadership and identify new resources that would enable the organization to become more resilient by implementing cyber security threat detection concepts. She was also aware that she needed to establish an intelligence function that was able to set intelligence priorities and establish patterns of cyber-attacks that would help staff to focus on and find solutions to new forms of cyber-attacks. Staff were, however, thinly spread and it seemed that she needed to draw on external advice and devise a proactive cyber security strategy as the organization only had an informal cyber security policy in place.

One of the tasks she set herself was to set up a weekly meeting with the risk manager, the IT manager, a newly appointed security manager, as well as managers from the other business functions to discuss cyber security issues. At their first meeting, they defined cyber security and put in place a cyber security strategy. The objective was to monitor and formalize cyber security management policy and to make sure the organizational vulnerabilities were made known and addressed before a cyber-attack caused an impact that proved harmful to the organization. This was not an easy task because nobody within the organization had defined who the threat actors were and had not established what they might do and how this might impact the organization. It was known that ransomware attacks were commonplace, and some companies were prepared to settle or negotiate settlements with the perpetrator of the attack.

Jennifer wanted to adopt a proactive approach to cyber security and considered it important to set up a CTI unit to monitor the actions of those carrying out cyber-attacks. She realized that a collectivist CTI policy and strategy needed to be devised and implemented but all the other managers were too busy to provide her with help and she was left alone to do this. She also realized that anything to do with critical information infrastructure and critical national infrastructure needed government cooperation in some form. To be effective, she had to ensure that the organization's CTI policy was clearly defined and took into account organizational networks, which conveyed the organization's data and information. Indeed, for a network to be sustainable, it had to be managed and as well as understanding the technical issues involved, attention had to be given to understanding that networks also involve people and, therefore, trust building is essential. The digital footprint of the organization is also another consideration to be kept in mind and one that needed increased attention.

Understanding how threat actors undertake their activities is essential as regards developing a cyber security management and strategic intelligence perspective. Jennifer was aware of this and decided that a knowledge bank would be developed that made reference to the various types of perpetrators of cyber-attacks. This was considered necessary because threat actors are experts at drawing on resources and cooperating with other perpetrators when necessary.

An interesting point that emerged was when Jennifer talked with Sheila Lee, head of risk management within the organization, and discovered that for staff to engage in cyber security problem-solving more effectively, they need to think more deeply about the strategic issues confronting the organization and understand how the networks in place helped organizational staff to be more effective in their day-to-day operations. It was known that to achieve this, staff needed to develop new knowledge that could be exploited and, in some instances, staff in partner organizations had been approached to help but at times this had proved problematic. It seemed that staff were not always prepared to share information or offer help. External business partners tended to guard information closely and at times refuse to engage in discussions. Generally, organizational staff were not prepared to talk about cyber-attacks on their organization. The value of computer emergency response teams (CERTs) was well known, and Jenefer was aware of how important it was to provide and receive cyber threat information from government representatives and to exchange information with them. It was hoped that providing information about cyber-attacks to those who were influential and prepared to do something to stop them from occurring would be beneficial to the industry.

Having appraised the organization's cyber security policy and framework, Jennifer was aware that the situational awareness undertaken was done in a logical and sustainable manner; however, the intelligence and insights produced were not always stored within the organization's memory. This was considered a weakness because organizational staff need to know what to do and where to receive instructions from during a cyber-attack upon the organization. Guidance was available but not always utilized in the way expected. Although staff talked about the enterprise risk management approach, in reality, the approach adopted was disjointed and the risk management process involved a number of ad hoc approaches, which sometimes caused confusion and irritation with staff in partner organizations. Overall, the way in which vulnerabilities were identified was less than satisfactory and ways had to be found to get staff to cooperate more.

Jennifer Hall decided to think through some of the issues raised over the past weeks and decided that she needed to find answers to specific questions:

Question 1: How can various cyber-attacks be categorized in terms of (i) Cyber-crime; (ii) cyber war; (iii) cyber terrorism and (iv) cyber espionage?

Question 2: Why is it important to place the organization's digital footprint in the context of an organization's cyber security strategy?

Question 3: Why is it important to include organizational learning in the organization's cyber security management and strategic intelligence framework?

References, websites and further reading

Agrafiotis, I., Nurse, J.R.C., Goldsmith, M., Creese, S., and Upton, D. (2018). A taxonomy of cyber-harms: Defining the impacts of cyber-attacks and understanding how they propagate. *Journal of Cybersecurity*, pp. 1–15. DOI: 10.1093/cybsec/tyy006

Ahmadian, S., Tang, X., Malki, H.A., and Han, Z. (2019). Modelling cyber attacks on electricity market using mathematical programming with equilibrium constraints. *IEEE Access*, 7, pp. 27376–27388. DOI: 10.1109/ACCESS.2019.2899293 (Accessed 8th May, 2024)

Al-Farsi, S., Rathore, M.M., and Bakiras, H.B. (2021). Security of blockchain-based supply chain management systems: Challenges and opportunities. *Applied Sciences*, 11 (12), pp. 1–29. https://doi.org/10.3390/app11125585

Al-Mohannadi, H., Mirza, Q., Namanya, A., Awan, I., Cullen, A., and Disso, J. (2016). Cyber-attack modeling analysis techniques: An Overview. In: *Proceedings of the IEEE 4th International Conference on Future Internet of Things and Cloud Workshops*, pp. 69–76. 22–24 August. Vienna, Austria. DOI: 10.1109/W-FiCloud.2016.29

Bromiley, P., McShane, M., Nair, A., and Rustambekov, E. (2015). Enterprise risk management: Review, critique, and research directions. *Long Range Planning*, 48, pp. 265–276. https://dx.doi/10.1016/j.lrp.2014.07.005

DeBerry-Spence, B., Trujillo-Torres, L.E., Sengupta, R., Matsumoto, K., and Jia, C. (2023). Marketing's role in promoting the common good: A systematic examination and an agenda for future inquiry. *Journal of Public Policy & Marketing*, 42 (2), pp. 95–114. DOI: 10.1177/07439156221145330

Elgabry, M. (2023). Towards cyber-biosecurity by design: An experimental approach to Internet-of-Medical-Things design and development. *Crime Science*, 12 (3), pp. 1–5. https://doi.org/10.1186/s40163-023-00181-8

European Commission. (2013). *Cyber Security Strategy of the European Union: An Open, Safe and Secure Cyberspace*. High Representative of the European Union for Foreign Affairs and Security Policy. Report JOIN (2013) 1 final (7th February). Brussels: European Commission.

Evans, M., Maglaras, L.A., He, Y., and Janicke, H. (2016). Human behaviour as an aspect of cybersecurity assurance. *Security and Communication Networks*, 9, pp. 4667–4679. DOI: 10.1002/sec.1657

Ferdinand, J. (2015). Building organisational cyber resilience: a strategic knowledge based view of cyber security management. *Journal of Business Continuity and Emergency Planning*, 9 (2), pp. 185–195. http://www.ingentaconnect.com/content/hsp/jbcep/2015/00000009/00000002/art00011

Grove, G.D., Goodman, S.E., and Lukasik, S.J. (2000). Cyber-attacks and international law. *Survival: The International Institute for Strategic Studies Quarterly*, 42 (3), pp. 89–193.

Harknett, R.J., and Stever, J.A. (2009). The cybersecurity triad: Government, private sector partners, and the engaged cybersecurity citizen. *Journal of Homeland Security and Emergency Management*, 6 (1), pp. 1–14. DOI: 10.2202/1547-7355.1649

Haveman, H.A., Mahoney, J.T., and Mannix, E. (2019). Editors' comments: The role of theory in management research. *Academy of Management Review*, 44 (2), pp. 241–243. https://doi.org/10.5465/amr.2019.0034

Ifinedo, P. (2014). Information systems security policy compliance: An empirical study of the effects of socialisation, influence, and cognition. *Information & Management*, 51, pp. 69–78. https://dx.doi.org/10.1016/j.im.2013.10.001

IMF. (2024). *Global Financial Stability Report. The Last Mile: Financial Vulnerabilities and Risks.* Washington DC: International Monetary Fund (April).

Jenab, K., and Moslehpour, S. (2016). Cyber security management: A review. *Business Management Dynamics*, 5 (11), pp. 16–39.

Kotenko, I., and Chechulin, A. (2013). Cyber attack modeling and impact assessment framework. In: Podins, K., Stinissen, J., and Maybaum, M. (eds.). *Proceedings of the 5th International Conference on Cyber Conflict*, pp. 1–24. Tallinn, Estonia: NATO CCD COE Publications.

Lange, D., and Pfarrer, M.D. (2017). Editor's comments: Sense and structure – The core building blocks of an AMR article. *Academy of Management Review*, 42 (3), pp. 407–416. https://doi.org/10.5465/amr.2016.0225

Lee, Y-I. (2009). Strategic transformational management in the context of inter-organizational and intra-organizational partnership development. In: Trim, P.R.J., and Caravelli, J. (eds.). *Strategizing Resilience and Reducing Vulnerability*, pp. 181–196. New York: Nova Science Publishers, Inc.

Levine, S.S., Bernard, M., and Nagel, R. (2017). Strategic intelligence: The cognitive capability to anticipate competitor behavior. *Strategic Management Journal*, 38, pp. 2390–2423. DOI: 10.1002/smj.2660

Li, Z., and Liao, Q. (2018). Economic solutions to improve cybersecurity of governments and smart cities via vulnerability markets. *Government Information Quarterly*, 35, pp. 151–160. http://dx.doi.org/10.1016/j.giq.2017.10.006

Lim, K. (2016). Big data and strategic intelligence. *Intelligence and National Security*, 31 (4), pp. 619–635. DOI: 10.1080/02684527.2015.1062321

Lozano, M.A., Llopis, I.P., and Domingo, M.E. (2023). Threat hunting architecture using a machine learning approach for critical infrastructures protection. In: Trim, P.R.J., and Lee, Y-I. (eds.). *Managing Cybersecurity Threats and Increasing Organizational Resilience*, pp. 129–154. Basel, Switzerland: MDPI.

Montgomery, D.B., and Weinberg, C.B. (1979). Toward strategic intelligence systems. *Journal of Marketing*, 43, pp. 41–52.

Morgan, R.E., Katsikeas, C.S., and Adu, K.A. (1998). Market orientation and organizational learning capabilities. *Journal of Marketing Management*, 14, pp. 353–381.

Morris, D., Madzudzob, G., and Garcia-Pereza, A. (2020). Cybersecurity threats in the auto industry: Tensions in the knowledge environment. *Technological Forecasting & Social Change*, 157, pp. 1–8. https://doi.org/10.1016/j.techfore.2020.120102 (Accessed 20th April, 2024)

Paiuc, D., Săniuță, A., and Parincu, A.M.T. (2024). Strategic intelligence: A semantic leadership perspective. *Encyclopaedia*, 4, pp. 785–798. https://doi.org/10.3390/encyclopaedia4020050

Pfleeger, S.L., and Caputo, D.D. (2012). Leveraging behavioral science to mitigate cyber security risk. *Computers & Security*, 31, pp. 597–611. DOI: 10.1016/j.cose.2011.12.010

Rajan, R., Rana, N.P., Parameswar, N., Dhir, S., Sushil, and Dwivedi, Y.K. (2012). Developing a modified total interpretive structural model (M-TISM) for organizational strategic cybersecurity management. *Technological Forecasting & Social Change*, 170, pp. 1–18. https://doi.org/10.1016/j.techfore.2021.120872

Singh, V., and Pandey, S.K. (2020). Cloud computing: Vulnerability and threat indications. In: Pant, M., Sharma, T., Basterrech, S., and Banerjee, C. (eds.). *Performance Management of Integrated Systems and its Applications in Software Engineering*, pp. 11–20. Singapore: Springer. https://doi.org/10.1007/978-981-13-8253-6_2

Sivarajah, U., Kamal, M.M., Irani, Z., and Weerakkody, V. (2017). Critical analysis of Big Data challenges and analytical methods. *Journal of Business Research*, 70, pp. 263–286. http://dx.doi.org/10.1016/j.jbusres.2016.08.001

Strauss, A., and Corbin, J. (1990). *Basics of Qualitative Research*. Newbury Park, CA: Sage.

The White House. (2023). *National Cybersecurity Strategy*. Washington: The White House (1st March).

Trim, P.R.J., and Lee, Y-I. (2023). *Strategic Cyber Security Management*. Oxford: Routledge.

Tsohou, A., Karyda, M., Kokolakis, S., and Kiountouzis, E. (2015). Managing the introduction of information security awareness programmes in organisations. *European Journal of Information Systems*, 24, pp. 38–58. DOI: 10.1057/ejis2013.27

UK Government. (2019). *Cyber Threat Intelligence in Government: A Guide for Decision Makers & Analysts*. Kew, London: Information Policy Team (March). file:///C:/Users/HP%20User/Desktop/Cyber-Threat-Intelligence-A-Guide-For-Decision-Makers-and-Analysts-v2.0.pdf (Accessed 6th June, 2024).

Valeriano, B., and Maness, R.C. (2018). Chapter 20 International relations theory and cyber security: Threats, conflicts, and ethics in an emergent domain. In: Brown, C., and Eckersley, R. (eds.). *The Oxford Handbook of International Political Theory*, pp. 259–272. Oxford: Oxford University Press.

Viotti, P.R., and Kauppi, M.V. (2001). *International Relations and World Politics: Security, Economy, Identity*. Upper Saddle River, New Jersey: Prentice-Hall, Inc.

Warren, A., Hunt, C.T., Warren, M., Bartley, A., and Manantan, M.B. (2024). *Developing an AI Capacity Framework for the Trilateral Security Dialogue (TSD): US, Australia, and Japan*. Pacific Forum, RMIT University and Australian Government. https://pacforum.org/publications/developing-an-ai-capability-framework-for-the-trilateral-security-dialogue-tsd-us-australia-and-japan/ (Accessed 31st July, 2024).

Zicari, R.V. (2014). Big Data: Challenges and opportunities. In: Akerkar, R. (ed.). *Big Data Computing*, pp. 103–128. Baton Rouge, Florida: CRC Press, Taylor & Francis Group.

Websites

Center for Strategic and International Studies. (2024). Significant Cyber Incidents. https://www.csis.org/programs/strategic-technologies-program/significant-cyber-incidents (Accessed 20th July, 2024).

GCHQ. (2024). *Our mission to help keep the UK safe*. Government Communications Headquarters. https://www.gchq.gov.uk/information/welcome-to-gchq (Accessed 13th June, 2024).

IBM. (2024). What is a Threat Actor? https://www.ibm.com/topics/threat-actor#:~:text=IBM-,What%20is%20a%20threat%20actor%3F,to%20digital%20devices%20or%20systems. (Accessed 7th June, 2024).

Karmini, N. (2024). *Indonesia won't pay an $8 million ransom after a cyberattack compromised its national data center*. Associated Press. https://apnews.com/article/indonesia-ransomware-attack-national-data-center-213c14c6cc69d7b66815e58478f64cee (Accessed 25th June, 2024).

National Health Service. (2019). *The NHS Long Term Plan*. www.longtermplan.nhs.uk (Accessed 12th July, 2023).

National Cyber Security Centre. (2024). Using cyber security scenarios. https://www.ncsc.gov.uk/collection/risk-management/using-cyber-security-scenarios (Accessed 9th May, 2024).

Shaping Tomorrow. (2024). Strategic Intelligence. https://www.shapingtomorrow.com/services/strategic-intelligence (Accessed 18th July, 2024).

Stubbs, J. (2020). 'Payment sent' - travel giant CWT pays $4.5 million ransom to cyber criminal. https://www.reuters.com/article/world/us/payment-sent-travel-giant-cwt-pays-45-million-ransom-to-cyber-criminals-idUSKCN24W26O/ (Accessed 4th August, 2023).

US Government. (2024). *Treaties and International Agreements*. US Department of State. https://www.state.gov/policy-issues/treaties-and-international-agreements/ (Accessed 25th June, 2024).

Further reading

Inkpen, A.C. (1996). Creating knowledge through collaboration. *California Management Review*, 39 (1), pp. 123–140.

Trim, P.R.J. (2002). Counteracting industrial espionage through counterintelligence: The case for a corporate intelligence function and collaboration with government. *Security Journal*, 15 (4), pp. 7–24.

Trim, P.R.J., and Youm, H.Y. (eds.). (2014). *Korea-UK Collaboration in Cyber Security: From Issues and Challenges to Sustainable Partnership*. British Embassy Seoul: Republic of Korea (18th March). https://eprints.bbk.ac.uk/id/eprint/9561/1/9561.pdf

Trim, P.R.J., and Youm, H.Y. (eds.). (2015). *Korea-UK Initiatives in Cyber Security Research: Government, University and Industry Collaboration*. British Embassy Seoul: Republic of Korea (16th March). https://eprints.bbk.ac.uk/id/eprint/15897/1/15897.pdf

3

CYBER SECURITY MANAGEMENT AND STRATEGIC INTELLIGENCE POLICY IMPLEMENTATION STRATEGIES

3.1 Introduction

The logic underpinning the collectivist approach to cyber security (Section 3.2) is followed by organizational intervention (Section 3.3) and then the categorization of data (Section 3.4). Next, appropriate leadership and the stakeholder approach (Section 3.5) are discussed and followed by widening the attack front (Section 3.6). International considerations (Section 3.7) precede establishing a cyber security awareness mindset (Section 3.8) and placing the cyber security management and strategic intelligence framework in context (Section 3.9). Lastly, reflection and questions (Section 3.10) is followed by a conclusion (Section 3.11).

3.2 The Logic Underpinning the Collectivist Approach to Cyber Security

A collectivist enterprise risk management cyber threat model can be developed to help senior managers provide adequate organizational intervention and thus make sure staff are compliant with government policy. Such an approach will strengthen the organization's defences and ensure that a cyber-attack intelligence knowledge base is developed that can be accessed by staff from partner organizations.

Bearing in mind that digitalization has focused the minds of senior managers on the need to move away from traditionally defined ways in which intelligence is organized, collected, analysed and then disseminated allows a mental appreciation of a wider set of tools and techniques that are adapted for specific types of intelligence work. To fully appreciate how managers from different business functions can couple their interest in intelligence work with those of their colleagues, it is important to understand that the concept of cyber security management and the role it plays provide unique insights into how cyber security, intelligence and security are related in order that senior managers devise and implement a conceptual collectivist enterprise risk management cyber threat model that incorporates cyber security threat detection.

DOI: 10.4324/9781003570905-3

Cyber security management and strategic intelligence requires, therefore, that the cyber security manager and their staff, consider that it is necessary to: (i) establish how a strategic intelligence approach can be used to develop an integrated cyber security mechanism to counteract cyber-attacks and (ii) provide guidance to staff as to how staff in the wider stakeholder community can develop a strategic CTI mentality that can help staff in partner organizations to find unique solutions to recurring problems. To prove successful, it is necessary for the cyber security manager to embrace the concept of mutuality and ensure that intra-organizational and inter-organizational decision-making are focused on creating a security culture that has at the heart of it, a commitment to maintaining cyber security awareness. Cyber security awareness is ongoing and very much associated with organizational learning and the learning organization approach, which is deemed useful in terms of the development and transfer of knowledge.

3.3 Organizational Intervention

Given the fact that cyber-attacks are becoming more sophisticated, it can be argued that organizational intervention is necessary because staff have to be continually reminded of the need for security and also people leave and enter an organization at various periods of its history. Furthermore, working from home has to some extent isolated remote workers and they are not always able to get support and assistance when needed (e.g., from their peers and staff in their security and IT departments). Hence, intelligence work can be viewed as engagement led and a necessary activity with regard to ensuring that the outcome of uncontrollable factors does not lead to or give rise to vulnerabilities. The key point to note, therefore, is that cyber security management and strategic intelligence involve reducing complexity by building trust-based relationships with in-house staff and staff in partner organizations that strengthen organizational resilience by ensuring that organizational intervention is aligned with organizational security policy (e.g., staff are compliant in their actions) that is aimed at achieving clearly defined corporate security objectives.

Organizational interventions that ensure cyber security awareness is maintained through cyber security skill enhancement training programmes and staff development programmes can be considered necessary and should be viewed as a positive outcome of internal marketing (Trim and Lee, 2019). Hence, to explain how a collectivist enterprise risk management cyber threat model can be developed, it is necessary to consider the four pillars upon which it is based. The four pillars can be defined as organizational cyber security; government and institutional commitment to societal well-being; strategic intelligence and organizational learning. Organizational cyber security is key because of the need for staff to be compliant in their actions. In order to be compliant, employees need to understand why data and information are to be kept secure and how data and information are to be safeguarded when placed with partner organizations.

3.4 The Categorization of Data

Reflecting on the fact that various types of data in various forms can be stolen or manipulated in some way, it is essential that data is categorized in a logical way. Risk Management Solutions, Inc. (2016) have categorized data into one of five groups and this form of segmentation proves helpful in terms of a cyber security manager knowing which type of data may be at a higher risk than other types of data. The categories identified by Risk Management Solutions, Inc. (2016, p. 25) include: (i) Personal Identity Information (PII) such as an individual's full name and social security number; (ii) Payment Card and Credit Card Information (PCI), which includes credit card numbers and bank account numbers; (iii) Protected Health Information (PHI) such as healthcare records and medical device identifiers; (iv) Commercially Confidential Information (CCI), such as proprietary business information and trade secrets, for example; and (v) Intellectual Property (IP) such as copyright, patents and blueprints. Bearing in mind the range of data and the linkage between the data sets, it is clear that the cyber security manager needs to know how the network of data is linked because an individual working for a bank may be at risk of extortion because the criminal intent on stealing digital funds from a bank will want to target and make vulnerable the individual in order that they can be manipulated and then exploited. Furthermore, by knowing the weaknesses of an individual and how they can be made vulnerable (e.g., an individual may suffer from an illness and need a certain type of medicine), a criminal can hack into a set of medical records and suspend the authorization of medical provision, therefore disrupting the healthcare provision. Consequently, the individual in need of healthcare may be cajoled into doing something illegal (downloading and transferring sensitive data to individuals outside the company) in return for the reactivation of a supply of medicine. Understanding how the perpetrator thinks and how they are likely to carry out their attack(s) allows the cyber security manager to couple data availability with risk and put in place a number of contingencies. However, this may bring to the surface ethical issues and considerations and how an individual should be helped/advised to protect their private data.

As well as the threat from a data breach, cyber security managers are aware that a disruption in connectivity may result due to the actions of those involved in cyberprotests, cyberactivism, and hacktivism (Martin and Kracher, 2008, p. 292). Those intent on causing damage or disruption may not be motivated by the same set of conditions or objectives. Martin and Kracher (2008, pp. 293–294) state:

> "Conducting protest activities over the Internet allows groups to garner public support and exposure, and therefore wield the power that accompanies such support and exposure. Business protests using online tactics communicate to managers and firm decision makers that their constituents are aware of certain practices and oppose them".

Martin and Kracher (2008) are right to suggest that deceiving through various means such as stealing somebody's identity, utilizing stolen credit card numbers and selling counterfeit goods is not the same as online business protests that are not associated with criminal intent but what are classified under sociopolitical intent (Martin and Kracher, 2008, p. 295). This is because in order to identify and assign priority to eradicating actual and potential risks, the allocation of limited resources must be to good effect. It is at this juncture that the cyber security manager needs to think of what if any cyber insurance is needed. If resources are limited and it is not possible to employ staff to manage risk-based assets (e.g., provide database support), then one way in which to deal with the problem is to insure against a data breach and/or compromised computer system. Referring to the concept of hacking, Martin and Kracher (2008, p. 298) define the streams of online business protests and suggest that hacking is a subset of online business protests and name informational protest websites, blogs, e-mail campaigns, online petitions, spoofs and parasites. Hacking, they suggest, can be subdivided into hacktivism (e.g., hijacking, e-mail bombs, defacement graffiti and virtual sit-ins) and cyber terrorism. As regards e-mail bombs, defacement graffiti and a virtual sit-in, these both feed into the client side and the server side. Recognizing that cyber terrorism is a subcategory of hacking, raises the stakes and forces senior management into putting in place strong leadership, the aim of which is to ensure that all possible eventualities associated with a cyber-attack are known and the appropriate contingencies are in place to counter the moves of those intent on causing damage.

3.5 Appropriate Leadership and the Stakeholder Approach

Radoynovska (2024) indicates that leadership, which underpins strategic decision-making, is a strong component of stakeholder theory. Writing on stakeholder theory, Freeman et al. (2020, p. 220) are of the view that leadership is about solving specific kinds of performance-related problems and a key consideration is the relationships involved. This means managers need to adopt a more strategic view of stakeholder engagement and consider what the higher purpose is. This shared purpose as it can be referred to is about

> "aligning all the stakeholders of the business around that purpose. In the absence of an articulated shared purpose, businesses revert to the default purpose, which has long been defined as profit maximization. A system with that as its implicit or explicit purpose will soon find stakeholders operating at cross-purposes"
>
> *(Freeman et al., 2020, p. 220).*

Barney and Harrison (2020) endorse the fact that stakeholder theory is complicated and needs to be viewed as holistic and incorporate various relationship-building processes. These relationship-building processes are in fact intra-organizational and inter-organizational in orientation and are subject to a range of influences as people and technology interact and change and reconfigure organizational structures. Stakeholder engagement can be interpreted as two-way formal and informal communication that gives rise to mutuality (Kujala et al., 2022, p. 1158). Kujala et al. (2022, p. 1160) define stakeholder engagement as "the aims, activities, and impacts of stakeholder relations in a moral, strategic, and/or pragmatic manner". The moral component of stakeholder engagement is a crucial aspect and covers legitimacy, trust and fairness. It is important to understand this because these aspects give rise to

> "stakeholder empowerment and/or the democratization of the relations between the organization and the stakeholders. Furthermore, the moral component relates to morally desirable impacts for the stakeholders and the organization, such as enhanced social and ecological well-being, giving voice to stakeholders..."
>
> *(Kujala et al., 2022, p. 1160).*

Such an approach takes into account the ethical considerations that managers need to be aware of in terms of investing in adequate cyber security protection (Fleischman et al., 2023).

3.6 Widening the Attack Front

According to Cavelty and Wenger (2022, p. 1), as regards politically relevant problems,

> "cyber security evolves at the intersection between fast-paced technological development, the political and strategic use of these tools by state and non-state actors, and the various attempts by the state and its bureaucracies, society, and the private sector to define appropriate responsibilities, legal boundaries, and acceptable rules of behavior..."

This view can be described as informative and relevant because human beings are behind the development of technology (e.g., AI) that can protect against cyber-attacks and also are responsible for the cyber-attacks that have plagued society for some considerable time. In addition, the development of AI-operated systems and a growing reliance on innovation and technology to counteract new forms of cyber-attack is placing increased emphasis on technology-led cyber security solutions. There are a number of cyber security threat detection models and applications in being to select from, but it could be that an organization needs more than one type of defence system.

At this stage, it is relevant to suggest that our focus on cyber security would not be complete unless we referred to government intervention. Government intervention can be viewed as positive (e.g., the domestic government introduces laws to protect against all sorts of cyber intrusion) or negative (e.g., a rogue government supports organized criminal groups in their illicit undertakings). Although cyber security is viewed as defensive, it has to be said that cyber war has raged from time to time and is likely to escalate from an attack-defence response to a defensive-attack response to an attack-attack response. Such an escalation would ultimately result in cyber war and cyber terrorism on an increased scale. It can also be suggested that if harmful cyber activity is viewed as productive by a rogue nation, then cyber espionage will become more accepted as a tool for data harvesting as technological developments leave some nation-states behind and ruling governments decide to close the gap on competitor nations by deploying alternative methods of restoring the balance between countries. As well as overtly stealing data and information, some governments, possibly those of failing states, will increasingly seek to bolster their standing by engaging and authorizing disinformation activities that are aimed at destabilizing nations that are achieving high growth targets and have a stable political environment. Schünemann (2022, p. 32) is of the view that disinformation is the process of spreading false information, the objective of which is to cause disruption and harm. Disinformation is achieved through rumours that result in a benefit to the instigator of disinformation and a loss/disadvantage to the individual or entity targeted.

Haunschild et al. (2022, p. 55) indicate that bots are used "to intervene in online discourse through confusion or misinformation, e.g. by associating a hashtag with non-related content for distraction ("misdirection") or to hide relevant content amidst unrelated content ("smoke screening")". In addition, astroturfing is used to manipulate public opinion and political decisions through the process of strengthening own views and distorting or discrediting opposing arguments via a so-called legitimate grassroots organization (Haunschild et al., 2022, p. 55). What this highlights is that the cyber domain is expanding, and aspects of psychological warfare are now entering the arena, which means that governments need to be aware of how innovative cyber-attacks will disrupt the business environment. Furthermore, attention has to be given to government priorities as regards solving or utilizing resources to solve such problems and this focuses attention on where and how the government will acquire the resources needed (e.g., higher taxation or increased borrowing or both).

3.7 International Considerations

Although nation-states view security mainly from their own perspective, it can be argued that cyber-attacks are to be viewed as having an international reach and because of this, senior managers need to think in terms of formalizing cooperation with a range of overseas law enforcement, security and intelligence bodies. The 2009 cyber-attack on South Korea and the United States was noted for the extent to which online networks and hard drives in personal computers were disabled by being hijacked and controlled by remote means (Andreasson, 2012, pp. 61–63). Consequently, document files and computer programs were erased. The disruption witnessed the authorities undertake a wide search for the source of the problem. Indeed, eight servers in Japan were found to have been used to carry out the attack (Andreasson, 2012, pp. 61–63), which was orchestrated from another country.

Realizing that sophisticated and intense cyber-attacks can be waged across industrial sectors, the UK government declared that the UK would work closely "with key allies and like-minded partner countries on the development of cyber security policy, co-ordinating domestic action where we can bring mutual enhancements to national security" (Cabinet Office, 2012, p. 5). The magnitude of the problem confronting senior managers is much clearer once we include other illegal business activities into the equation such as counterfeiting, which is also known to provide criminal gangs with exceptionally high returns on their investment and affect reputable brands through reputational damage when the purchased item does not perform in the way expected and electronic word-of-mouth gives rise to an outpouring of discontent via online reviews. Counterfeit software is known to cause harm and can be viewed as constituting an organizational vulnerability if it is installed. Indeed, research undertaken by Cuntz and Qian (2021) suggests that counterfeiting needs to be considered highly problematic because it does have detrimental effects on R&D and net sales. Counterfeiting can be classified as ongoing and disruptive. It is known to be an international problem because it is widespread and evident in a range of industries (e.g., products and components). Much of the faulty software on the market has been illegally copied and lacks the updates to make it function in the way expected. Faulty software is normally installed without senior managers in the organization knowing that this is the case; subcontractors are mostly responsible for cutting costs and installing faulty software. Such business practice increases the level of vulnerability and manifests in specific types of cyber-attacks getting through the organization's defence and causing damage to networked services.

The 1st Conference on Cyberspace, which was held in London in November 2011, did much to promote the problems associated with cyber-crime and the UK government's National Cyber Security Strategy 2016–2021 (HM Government, 2016) has put several measures in place that strengthen the capability of UK law enforcement. The European Commission, through publishing a report entitled: "Cyber security strategy of the European Union: An open, safe and secure cyberspace", has done much to focus the minds of policymakers, their advisers and industry leaders and make sure that organizations take responsibility for their all-round security (European Commission, 2013). Indeed, the European Commission (2013, pp. 4–5) has outlined five areas of attention vis-à-vis cyber security: Cyber resilience, reducing cybercrime, cyber defence policy and capabilities, industrial and technological resources and a coherent international cyberspace policy and has boosted research and cooperation across industry sectors. An additional dimension is for the government to engage with the university sector and invest funds into cyber security research and education. Such an approach is mirrored by the US government which has over the years provided leadership and funding for a range of cyber security initiatives. Indeed, US government officials have revitalized the country's cyber security strategy (The White House, 2023, p. i) through various steps that acknowledge that cyber security is essential as regards supporting critical infrastructure and privacy in terms of data and communications. Cyber security is central to and supports the democratic functioning of society and it also underpins the defence of the nation. It is clear that policymakers in the United States are aware of which threat actors carry out the various forms of cyber-attack as is evidenced in the following quotation (The White House, 2023, p. 3): "Malicious cyber activity has evolved from nuisance defacement, to espionage and intellectual property theft, to damaging attacks against critical infrastructure, to ransomware attacks and cyber-enabled influence campaigns designed to undermine public trust in the foundation of our democracy". It is now clear that malicious cyber activity is possible on a much wider scale than previously because there are a range of offensive hacking tools and services available including commercial spyware, which can be utilized by organized criminal syndicates (The White House, 2023, p. 3).

The US government is committed to funding research, training and education in cyber security. This is important because by engaging with the higher education sector, governments can spearhead the development of cyber security master's degrees and community educational programmes that strengthen the country's cyber security research base. Policy initiatives such as these can be viewed as stakeholder reinforcing and can aid community building when social conflict occurs (Barrios et al., 2016) and the community needs to be brought together.

The South Korean government is well aware of the need for a community spirit and has shown much commitment to championing cyber security by outlining, in the Informatization White Paper (Korea Internet and Security Agency, 2010), the growth and opportunities associated with ICT. South Korea hosted the 3rd Conference on Cyberspace in October 2013 and has since the date encouraged university researchers to work closely with researchers abroad to devise and implement international security standards, policies and workable cyber security frameworks. It is useful to reflect on the fact that South Korean politicians are concerned about geopolitical developments, as indeed are US government representatives, and as a consequence, those involved in the preparation of international standards relating to cyber security do not "ignore what is happening in other countries" (Pearce, 1976, p. 120) because company information flows are integrated and can be penetrated should a vulnerability be identified and exploited by a cyber-criminal or rogue state agency. It is because of the vulnerabilities involved and the fact that if trading is disrupted, resulting knock-on effects cause a dislocation of day-to-day business operations. It is because of this that governments around the world share cyber-attack information, introduce news laws and regulatory conditions and expand their security and intelligence agencies.

3.8 Establishing a Cyber Security Awareness Mindset

It is clear from the above that the cyber security manager and their staff need to work with the marketing manager and the human resource manager to establish a cyber security culture that is underpinned by cyber security awareness. There are several ways that this can be achieved, through organizational learning–inspired security training and staff development seminars and programmes, for example. One way in which to proceed is to ask staff to watch the cyber security videos that are available on various websites as some of them contain a great deal of information. Table 3.1 includes a list of selected cyber security training videos that can be accessed. Their usefulness and accompanying learning outcomes are listed. The videos cited cover various aspects of cyber security and complement each other well. They can be considered informative from both a cyber security technical standpoint and a cyber security management perspective.

With regards to staff development programmes in particular, Table 3.2 contains information relating to the usefulness and learning outcomes of selected cyber security academic articles and conference papers that can be used by training managers and experts in cyber security educational provision to provide background reading material and/or module outlines for cyber security staff development programmes. Some of the material is of a technical/specific nature, and the content moves beyond cyber security awareness and attempts to provide a deeper understanding of the subject matter and the link with a high-level educational provision.

TABLE 3.1 The usefulness and learning outcomes of selected cyber security training videos

Cyber Security Video	Usefulness	Key Learning Outcome
NCyTE Center: An introduction to small unmanned aerial systems (sUAS) cyber security. Dr. Craiger. NCyTE Center website (National Cybersecurity Training & Education Center). https://www. ncyte.net/home (Accessed July and August, 2023).	Outlines specific types of attack: GPS spoofing and jamming; man-in-the-middle and hijacking. Outlines how and why a device is targeted.	Identify the vulnerabilities. Identify more than one attack surface. Man-in-the-middle attacks delete, modify or inject communications to take control from the user and this is relatively easy if the device is not fully protected/has a low level of built-in security.
NCyTE Center: Penetration testing a small unmanned aerial system (sUAS): Dr. Craiger. NCyTE Center website (National Cybersecurity Training & Education Center). https://www. ncyte.net/home (Accessed July and August, 2023).	Having a good knowledge of computer coding will help a person understand how malware is introduced into a computer system and network. Outlines how cyber security can prove effective. Need to understand what a network is and how vulnerable to attack it is. Hackers know what they are doing (e.g., to steal data).	Identify the source of the code and how it is used. Indicates which aspect of cyber security has priority. Understand how network feeds are used. Undertake vulnerability tests. Establish how encryption can thwart a hacker.

(Continued)

Table 3.1 (Continued)

Cyber Security Video	Usefulness	Key Learning Outcome
NCyTE Center: Cyber supply chain attacks and risk management: Dr. Craiger. NCyTE Center website (National Cybersecurity Training & Education Center). https://www.ncyte.net/home (Accessed July and August, 2023).	Supply chains are interconnected. There are vulnerabilities in a supply chain and ransomware is a problem. Ransomware attacks are known to be high in cost. Physical components and software may not be secure. Risk must be quantified.	The weakest link will allow a cyber attacker to have access to a system. A ransomware attack has an effect beyond its initial victim. Establishing the cascading effects of a ransomware attack is important. Do the products and software conform to confidentiality, integrity and availability? A risk mitigation policy and strategy must be in place.
NCyTE Center: Maritime transportation system cybersecurity: An overview: Dr. Craiger. NCyTE Center website (National Cybersecurity Training & Education Center). https://www.ncyte.net/home (Accessed July and August, 2023).	Cyber-crime affects the global business environment. Not everybody has perfect information. Critical national/information infrastructure are interconnected. Cyber security is a process. Information communication technology links networks to networks and is formed of systems of systems. Information communications technology connects different organizations within and across industries. Cyber threat detection is ongoing.	Cyber security staff need to liaise with various cyber security specialists. To deal with a cyber-attack in real time requires a team effort. Need to have a good knowledge of the dependencies and interdependencies between industries and companies. The cyber security process needs to be managed. Management models need to take into account and deal with systems of systems. Cyber security management is to prevent attacks on systems of systems succeeding. Risk management requires foresight.
NCyTE Center: Maritime transportation system cyber-attacks and mitigation strategies: Dr. Craiger. NCyTE Center website (National Cybersecurity Training & Education Center). https://www.ncyte.net/home (Accessed July and August, 2023).	Sophisticated attacks on logistics/logistical systems may be difficult to detect. Mitigation and risk mitigation strategies need to be well defined. Intelligence threat data needs to be shared across industry sectors. Criminals and threat actors have a high level of skill and knowledge.	Expertise is needed to deal with and predict cyber-attacks on digital systems. The risk manager and various other senior managers need to take responsibility for risk mitigation. Senior managers need to respond to cyber-attacks in real time. Cyber security staff need to constantly develop their skill and knowledge base.

(Continued)

Table 3.1 (Continued)

Cyber Security Video	Usefulness	Key Learning Outcome
Birkbeck, University of London: A collectivist approach to cyber security involving government, industry, academia and society: Dr. Trim. Available on YouTube at: https://www.youtube.com/watch?v=3MiZ_Kp8_oI (Accessed July and August, 2023)	Place cyber security within the context of cyber security management. View cyber security management as involving resilience and business continuity planning. Integrate risk management throughout the organization. Prioritize the risks and place them in a risk register. Cyber security countermeasures need to be developed. Ensure that staff are committed to cyber security. Ensure there is stakeholder commitment to security. Organizational learning can help managers to maintain a cyber security culture within a security culture.	Identify the role of the cyber security manager. Develop an organizational resilience model that includes business continuity planning. Identify the role of a risk manager. Assign a risk manager and various assistant risk managers. Cyber security countermeasures need to be based on appropriate threat assessments. Establish a cyber security culture. Link security with resilience planning. Commitment to organizational learning needs to be continuous.
OWASP Suffolk Chapter: Cyber security - Thinking like the enemy: Dr. Cochrane. OWASP Suffolk Chapter. Available on YouTube at: https://www.youtube.com/watch?v=ZWvD3BLvPSM (Accessed on 29th March, 2024).	Understand that people are vulnerable because of their behaviour, hence technology alone will not solve the problem. Being aware that a DDoS attack is used as a diversion for a tunnel set-up or infiltration of the organization. Those carrying out cyber-attacks will not stop. Those involved in the Dark Net are becoming really powerful.	Cyber security specialists need to think like an attacker and anticipate future threats. Fake information could trigger a major conflict. Organizations need to share attack information and cooperate more fully. Artificial intelligence is better at pattern recognition than humans.

TABLE 3.2 The usefulness and learning outcomes of selected cyber security academic articles and conference papers

Academic article/Conference paper	Usefulness	Key Learning Outcome
Kavak, H., Padilla, J.J., Vernon-Bido, D., Diallo, S.Y., Gore, R., and Shetty, S. (2021). Simulation for cybersecurity: State of the art and future directions. *Journal of Cybersecurity*, pp. 1–13. DOI: 10.1093/cybsec/tyab005.	The Internet is increasing dependency on information communications technology. Cyber-attacks appear in patterns.	Highlight the growing influence and dependence on information communications technology. Identify the pattern of attack and assign threat-detection priorities.
Veksler, V.D., Buchler, N., Hoffman, B.E., Cassenti, D.N., Sample, C., and Sugrim, S. (2018). Simulations in cyber-security: A review of cognitive modeling of network attackers, defenders, and users. *Frontiers in Psychology*, pp. 1–12. Doi: 10.3389/fpsyg.2018.00691.	Attackers and defender models need to include domain-specific knowledge. The more the simulation focuses on policy, the wider the set of skills and knowledge required.	Domain-specific knowledge needs to be brought into the organization's simulation exercises. Policy-related simulations need to include public sector and private sector considerations.
Jalali, M.S., Siegel, M., and Madnick, S. (2019). Decision-making and biases in cybersecurity capability development: Evidence from a simulation game experiment. *Journal of Strategic Information Systems*, 28, pp. 66–82. https://doi. org/10.1016/j. jsis.2018.09.003	Cyber security simulations can cover a range of activities simultaneously. Simulations can be used to identify a range of risks and link them to organizational vulnerabilities. The organization's cybersecurity capability can be established. Cyber incident patterns can be established. Simulations can help individual staff identify their own weaknesses in terms of cyber security knowledge gaps.	Simulations can be used to analyse the learning effect. Appropriate risk mitigation strategies can be identified. Investments in cybersecurity capability building can be identified. Policy can be developed to deal with cyber incident patterns across the industry. Simulations can help an individual to identify what additional cyber security knowledge they need and where to obtain it from.

(Continued)

Table 3.2 (Continued)

Academic article/Conference paper	Usefulness	Key Learning Outcome
Mäses, S., Randmann, L., Maennel, O., and Lorenz, B. (2018). Stenmap: Framework for evaluating cybersecurity-related skills based on computer simulations. *Proceedings Learning and Collaboration Technologies. Learning and Teaching: 5th International Conference, LCT 2018.* Held as Part of HCI International 2018. Las Vegas, NV., USA. July 15–20, Proceedings, Part II. Zaphiris, P., and Ioannou, A. (Eds.): LCT 2018, LNCS 10925, pp. 492–504. https://doi.org/10.1007/978-3-319-91152-6_38	Cyber security simulations need to be logical and conform to a certain structure. Those who undertake a simulation exercise need to provide feedback related to its effectiveness. Cybersecurity exercises can have a number of formats.	Cyber security simulations need to be evaluated – they need to be realistic and ensure the trainee/learner gains the skills/knowledge required. Those who have participated in a simulation can help design future simulations. Cybersecurity exercises can be undertaken on an individualistic basis or in a team.
Gedris, K., Bowman, K., Neupane, A., Hughes, A.L., Bonsignore, E., West, R.W., Balzotti, J., and Hansen, D.L. (2012). Simulating municipal cybersecurity incidents: Recommendations from expert Interviews. *Proceedings of the 54th Hawaii International Conference on System Sciences,* pp. 2036–2045. https://hdl.handle.net/10125/70862	Educational simulations and related experiential learning exercises can help prepare staff to deal with cyber-attacks. Cyber security scenarios need to involve a number of stakeholders. Various learning approaches can be used to teach cyber security. The scenarios used can focus on current forms of cyber-attacks and how and why they are carried out. To make clear why organizations and critical national/information infrastructure are attacked.	Educational simulations and related experiential learning exercises need to be as realistic as possible. Cyber security scenarios need to be team oriented and involve law enforcement officers. The approaches to teaching cyber security include competitions, simulations, games, tabletop exercises and playable case studies. The scenarios developed can focus on ransomware and the mindset of the attacker. To establish how vulnerable the separate components of a supply chain are.

(Continued)

TABLE 3.2 (Continued)

Academic article/Conference paper	Usefulness	Key Learning Outcome
Nguyen, T.T., and Reddi, V.J. (2021). Deep Reinforcement Learning for Cyber Security. *IEEE Transactions on Neural Networks and Learning Systems*, 1, pp. 1–17. Doi: 10.1109/ TNNLS.2021.3121870	Deep reinforcement learning (DRL) can help solve various types of cyber security threat–related problems. Evolving threats are difficult to identify and defend against. The types of cyber-attack need to be placed in context. A vulnerability analysis needs to be ongoing. Training data for AI algorithms is expensive to collect.	Deep reinforcement learning (DRL) is complex. Need to engage in foresight planning and anticipate future cyber threats. Cyber threats need to be listed in order of priority. A vulnerability needs to be linked to a specific type of cyber-attack. Simulations can help produce training data for AI algorithms.
Tioh, J-N., Mina, M., and Jacobson, D.W. (2017). Cyber Security Training: A Survey of Serious Games in Cyber Security. *2017 IEEE Frontiers in Education Conference (FIE)*, pp. 1–5. DOI:10.1109/ FIE.2017.8190712	Interlinkage of topics and subtopics. Ongoing need for safe cyber security practices. Need for cyber security awareness. Educational games need to enhance learning through engagement and motivation.	Topics and subtopics need to be current. Defined cyber security practices need to be in place. Cyber security awareness is ongoing. Learning needs to be viewed as motivational and game players need to be fully engaged.

3.9 Placing the Cyber Security Management and Strategic Intelligence Framework in Context

A commitment to harnessing cyber security technology is evident. In May 2024, the UK government's Viscount Camrose, who was the Parliamentary Under Secretary of State at the Department for Science, Innovation and Technology, put out a "Call for views on the Cyber Security of AI" in relation to evidence that would help formulate policy in terms of harnessing AI and at the same time ensure that the end-user would be protected from AI risks. The importance of and the increased role played by AI was recognized and emphasis was placed on cyber security provision bearing in mind that the AI industry in the UK was known to employ in excess of 50,000 people and contributed to £3.7 billion to the UK economy (UK Government, 2024).

Reflecting on what AI involves, del Rincon et al. (2024, p. 4) state:

"Artificial intelligence (AI) refers to machines that exhibit the ability to comprehend and learn tasks. Within AI, machine learning (ML) is the field of study concerned with the development and study of statistical algorithms that can effectively learn tasks from data rather than execute explicit instructions".

Advances in AI, and especially Deep Learning (DL) involving artificial neural networks (ANN), are in part due to the training process and the utilization of data, the thoroughness of the model architecture, and also, the optimization of the parameters that have resulted in improved validation (del Rincon et al., 2024, p. 4). During the final testing process, which is known as inference, new data is used to evaluate the model's ability to generalize (del Rincon et al., 2024, p. 4). Bearing this in mind, it can be ascertained that developments in AI are progressing at speed and new cyber security applications will be available in the near future. It has to be remembered, however, that threat actors will continue to try and disrupt such progress and will find ways to poison the training data used and will also develop malware to counteract the defensive capability of AI cyber security applications. In addition, they will also develop their own AI cyber security attack tools and possibly widen their attack approach by creating additional harm through fake news campaigns. Fake news campaigns are aimed at spreading fear and discontent and will possibly be combined with other impact-oriented events such as natural disasters to maximize the damage caused.

The cyber security manager and their peers need to be aware of the developments in AI and how it will transform organizational and business operations. As can be noted from Figure 3.1, AI is viewed as transformational and because of this, attention needs to be given to how AI will be used to replace mundane repetitive labour-intensive roles that are prone to error and mistake. In addition, cyber security staff need to know how AI will be harnessed to help with cyber threat detection and consequently reinforce

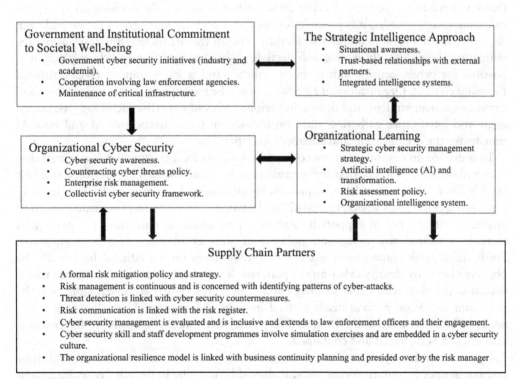

FIGURE 3.1 Extended conceptual framework outlining the main topics underpinning cyber security management and strategic intelligence.

organizational security. However, AI is only one component of cyber security management, and it is important to reflect on the main dimensions and how they link. It is clear from Figure 3.1 that the dimension *Government and Institutional Commitment to Societal Well-being* involves an acceptance of the need for organizational staff to liaise with policymakers and law enforcement staff and be committed to ensuring that staff are aware of the benefits of cyber security both in terms of the organization and the community. Staff in organizations are aware that government can only do so much to protect against cyber-attacks on critical infrastructure because they do not possess the resources to do everything and organizations and individuals in society need to be proactive in terms of ensuring that they are compliant with regulations and act in a responsible manner. This is so society in general is protected against cyber-attacks and those responsible for national security can counteract the actions of cyber attackers.

With regards to the *Strategic Intelligence Approach*, it is important that internal staff are able to carry out situational analysis and feed their analysis into an integrated intelligence system(s) that can be accessed by staff in partner organizations. For it to be accepted, it needs to be viewed as having value. Only staff with a high level of security clearance and level of responsibility will be allowed to access the information as it is made available on a "need-to-know" basis.

Organizational Cyber Security is the priority of the cyber security manager and various other managers (IT manager and risk manager) and takes as its starting point the need for cyber security awareness and places this in the context of a cyber threats policy that counteracts the actions of cyber attackers/threat actors. By devising an enterprise risk management model, it is possible for the cyber security manager to define and rank the cyber threats identified and also identify who in the organization is responsible for mitigating the risk(s). By having a collectivist cyber security framework in place, it is possible for cyber security staff to both embrace and work within an *Organizational Learning* context. *Organizational Learning* forms the backbone of a strategic cyber security management strategy and draws on various forms of expertise including risk assessment and intelligence gathering and also focuses on the utilization of AI and how AI transforms the organization and enhances its capability.

In order for an organization not to be vulnerable to a cyber-attack, it is essential that senior management accept that the organization is vulnerable to a cyber-attack via their *Supply Chain Partners* and, consequently, specific individuals need to be appointed to carry out specific tasks so that responsibility is assigned to them. Such individuals need to provide various types of support to staff in supply chain organizations to ensure that there is a formal risk mitigation policy and strategy in place that is operational. Furthermore, risk management needs to be undertaken on a continual basis with the objective being to identify cyber-attack patterns. It is important to make sure that threat detection is linked with cyber security countermeasures, which are sustainable, and the risk communication process needs to feed into the risk register. This is because a risk needs to be categorized and allocated a responder who takes responsibility for ensuring that the risk is managed and contained.

By ensuring that cyber security management is evaluated continuously through time and not at specific points in time only, it should be possible to include law enforcement officers in the process and exchange information with them on a regular basis. This is necessary because brand leaders too are only aware that fraudsters are intent on both selling counterfeit products that stem from fake pop-up websites and are also keen to acquire mailing lists that give them access to customers that they can try and scam in various ways. Cyber security skill and staff development programmes do much to highlight the actions of cyber attackers and simulation exercises can be used to deepen the organization's knowledge base and thus help the organization to establish and maintain a cyber security culture. For example, the cyber security manager can use simulation exercises and scenario analysis to make clear how those involved in carrying out cyber-attacks make their strategic moves. This should help cyber security staff to develop an organizational resilience model that incorporates business continuity planning. It should also help to signpost the role of the risk manager and make clear the lines of responsibility associated with cyber security management policy.

Looking objectively into what strategic intelligence involves, it is clear that deep insights into the subject matter can be obtained provided the cyber security manager thinks like an intelligence operative. To achieve this, it is important to distinguish between direct and indirect effects and their consequences. For example, a cyber-attack on a company that is successful and results in a data breach provides the attacker with several options. The data can be held for ransom and if a ransom demand is paid, the attacker can allow the targeted company to have access to the data. If a ransom is not paid, the attacker may sell the data on the Dark Web. Once it is sold on the Dark Web, it is available in several forms and can be sold on to specialist attackers that have several objectives in mind.

Stolen data can be traded in blocks and can be subdivided into segments or specific market offerings. For example, stolen credit card details can be sold to those who want to undertake financial fraud; sensitive personal data can be sold to those who want to engage in identity theft and personal data of a different nature that relates to the behaviour of a person and their lifestyle can be sold on to those who want to benefit from implementing phishing attacks and social engineering attacks. This kind of demarcation does not, however, fully explain matters. What the cyber security manager needs to know is that indirect associations in relation to a data breach will manifest in reputational damage that witnesses the targeted company lose clients because they feel the company is not compliant as regards safeguarding client data and may inform their suppliers and other industry contacts to avoid doing business with the company. In addition, a regulatory body may impose a fine on the organization and this may convince investors that senior management is defective in terms of governance policy. If the company has suffered a financial loss, it could be that if a cyber insurance policy is in place, it is not valid. Or, if the company needs to borrow funds to continue in business, the banks/investors may be reluctant to lend money to the company because they are of the view that it is no longer a sound investment because the company is losing market share and its profitability has declined.

Although it may be suggested that a data breach is confined and limited to a small amount of data, it has to be remembered that other criminal gangs may well decide to focus on the targeted company because they can see there is an opportunity for them to exploit a vulnerability also. Other criminals/criminal syndicates will see how they can exploit the company's vulnerabilities and will set out to do this over a period of time. The objective is to probe the company's defences until a vulnerability is found and exploited. Figure 3.1, represents an extended conceptual framework that can be used as a basis for integrating supply chain partners into the organization's enterprise risk management cyber threat model.

It is clear from Figure 3.1 that a collectivist enterprise risk management cyber threat model is developed from an appreciation of the inputs from the external environment (e.g., government and providers of critical infrastructure) and from internally derived knowledge-related inputs (e.g., risk assessment knowledge and intelligence derived knowledge), which combine to form enhanced cyber security inputs. The role played by supply chain partners is to be viewed as further enhancing the cyber security inputs. The specific inputs from supply chain partners and the inputs into supply chain partner organizations are in relation to structures and mechanisms. More specially, risk is managed through a formal risk mitigation policy and strategy. This is a joint undertaking involving the cyber security manager and the risk manager. By establishing a formal risk management process, risk management can be viewed as continuous and is concerned with identifying patterns of cyber-attacks. Threat detection is linked with cyber security countermeasures and the need to ensure that contingency plans are in place that can be implemented in real time. Because cyber-attacks are growing in intensity and sophistication, it is important for senior management to be as transparent as possible about the threats posed and how vulnerabilities are to be rectified. This means that risk communication occupies a central position, and all the risks are listed in the risk register.

To ensure that new threats and recurring threats are monitored and evaluated, it is necessary to assign cyber security management responsibility to a number of managers as opposed to just the cyber security manager. This is to make sure that the evaluation of cyber security policy is undertaken continuously, and the cyber security policy and the cyber security strategy are audited at specific times in the year. The auditing process can be overseen by an external manager and possibly staff drawn from the business continuity function can be involved in the auditing process. However, it is advisable to draw on the expertise of specific organizations that are well versed in how cyber-attacks are launched and also the strategies that those carrying out cyber-attacks implement. The involvement of law enforcement personnel is to be encouraged, and joint training programmes can be arranged with law enforcement personnel to maintain relations and foster continual engagement. Partly, such initiatives are to increase cyber security skill levels and to make sure that staff that want to pursue a career in cyber security can avail themselves of cyber security development programmes. Cyber security development programmes can be enriched through the use of simulation exercises and scenario analysis, and this can help to establish and reinforce cyber security awareness. The objective is to establish a cyber security culture that gets staff to link security with intelligence work. Should this be the case, then it is likely that the organizational resilience model in place will be linked with business continuity planning and presided over by the risk manager/business continuity manager. What is important to note is that the structures and mechanisms in place, need to be well defined and, on occasion, jointly managed. This is because the level of complexity is high and as much cover as possible is given to each aspect of cyber security.

Another point of interest that surfaces is whether the business model adopted has designed in security. The forgoing makes the case for a security culture that incorporates cyber security. However, security provision needs to be viewed from the context of the organization's security capability. Indeed, Jones and Trim (2009) are firm about the questions that should be posed to establish if an organization has a security culture, and they advocate a collectivist approach to security. Jones and Trim (2009) consider that leadership is the most important factor and make reference to the transformational approach. The transformational approach can be considered appropriate because it is based on the premise that relationships between organizational staff and departmental members are important and need to be nurtured through time. The relationship-building process fits well in terms of linking intelligence with security and requires that senior management is aware of what intervention is required from within the organization and who in the external environment is also responsible for providing intervention. Governments provide intervention by devising and implementing laws, and regulatory bodies provide the support and guidance to ensure that organizations adhere to the laws in being.

Knowing that threat actors are determined to disrupt and cause damage to those competing in the market requires that the cyber security manager develops the mindset of a political analyst. A political analyst is known to collect as much intelligence on a specific theme as possible and utilizing the skills of the trade undertakes an analysis of the data/information so as to provide a certain outcome. The key point to note is that having undertaken an analysis, the analyst is in a position to seek further information and/or engage in forward thinking. The use of scenario and simulation exercises proves useful with respect to this but sometimes, and in cases where there is much uncertainty within the environment, there may be insufficient time to undertake a more protracted analysis of the situation. However, if the time available is limited, then a decision has to be made and an action has to be implemented. What the analysts have to do prior to implementing the decision is think through the consequences of the decision. For example, in the case of predicting cyber-attacks, it is important to understand how a certain action will be interpreted and responded to. Once an action has been carried out and a response attained, the analyst has to recalibrate matters to establish if the retaliatory action will lead to a different outcome than that predicted by the analyst. For example, before an action is implemented, it is better to work out what the cyber attacker's second move will be and how further possible actions and reactions will manifest in a given outcome. So, the idea is not just to make a decision and implement it and anticipate what an isolated response will be or look like; it is necessary for the cyber security manager to look further ahead and to think of two or three forward moves and the associated retaliations. Thinking ahead is necessary and requires foresight, which can be developed in a number of ways including game play or computer simulations. An interesting aspect to consider is that the threat environment is still evolving and each time a solution is found, whether it is human in origin or as a result of AI, the criminal or bad state actor will try and counteract and respond in some way to get one step ahead. This will in turn shape environmental change and mean that environmental conditions will at some point in the future need to be responded to.

3.10 Reflection and Questions

Figure 3.2 outlines the process through which cyber security management and strategic intelligence achieve continuity and it is viewed as a continuous process. It can be noted that cyber security awareness is a fundamental requirement and staff within the organization must be prepared to update their cyber security skill and knowledge base through time. However, senior management takes responsibility for this and must ensure that

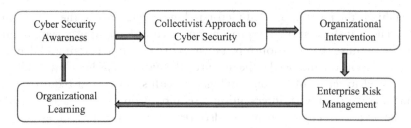

FIGURE 3.2 Cyber security management and strategic intelligence continuity.

appropriate cyber security training and staff development programmes are in being and that intelligence work is collectivist in orientation. By adopting the enterprise risk management approach, staff will view risk management from a holistic perspective and adhering to the organizational learning approach should ensure that staff view cyber security management from a proactive stance.

Cyber security intelligence initiatives can help an organization remain in business. Initiatives include new ways of viewing cyber-related problems and exploring ways to solve recurring problems, which relate to but are not cyber security–focused alone. The cyber security manager, working with various colleagues, can utilize various intelligence and knowledge-oriented approaches to devise cyber security management intelligence policy implementation strategies. Drawing also on research studies of interdisciplinary and multidisciplinary nature, the cyber security manager can think of devising a collectivist enterprise risk management cyber threat model that can help senior managers implement cyber threat detection. In order that the approach adopted is fit for purpose and the model developed has credibility, it is essential for the intelligence approach to be strategic in nature and associated with the organizational learning approach. This is because cyber security knowledge needs to be transferred between organizational partners and new knowledge developed through various forms of intervention. Hence, establishing a cyber security knowledge base is important because cyber security knowledge can be transferred between internal staff and then shared with external stakeholders.

Question 1: What is a cyber security management intelligence policy implementation strategy?

Question 2: How can a collectivist enterprise risk management cyber threat model be constructed?

Question 3: Why is it important for the cyber security manager to embrace the organizational learning approach?

3.11 Conclusion

In order that the cyber security manager and their colleagues utilize intelligence to devise cyber security management and strategic intelligence policy implementation strategies, it is essential that a full understanding of the subject of cyber security management is aspired to. By working closely with informed and proactive stakeholders, CTI can become formalized and the collectivist approach to cyber security management can be endorsed that helps to maintain a security culture with cyber security being a key component of it. What is clear is that the government cannot do everything in isolation and will need to work closely with public sector and private sector representatives and will need to make clear that acts of cyber-crime are giving way to and being reinforced by acts of cyber war. In order for the cyber security management training and staff development programmes to be effective, a deeper insight into the subject matter is required. This means the cyber security manager and the training manager need to draw on relevant videos, academic articles and conference papers so that they embrace a wider understanding of the topic and develop appropriate insights into the varied but interlinked cyber security subject matter.

Case 3: Establishing a collectivist approach to cyber security

Roger Barnes, who had been employed as the organization's cyber security manager for the past 14 months, was stern faced as he talked through the idea of integrating the organization's risk management strategy into a collectivist enterprise risk management cyber threat model that he was proposing. The objective was as he explained, to provide adequate organizational intervention throughout the year so that staff in other business functions were able to provide a high level of support and ensure that the various cyber-attacks on the organization were dealt with effectively in real time. Underpinning this view was the link between security work and intelligence work and the need to provide guidance to staff so that they could communicate with stakeholders more effectively. The point being that during times of crisis, decisions had to be made and implemented quickly and there was no room for error. He considered that it was essential that all those concerned with client relationships, in particular, and the management and servicing of the organization's IT were informed about what to do during periods of crisis. He was also aware that a cyber-attack on a supplier or channel member would also have ramifications for all partner organizations.

To date, internal staff had been extremely helpful in supporting the organization's cyber security policy, but more had to be done because some staff in partner organizations were not aware of what cyber security management involved. There had been problems from time to time because of a lack of communication or people had been away on holiday and had not been given adequate cover. Connectivity was known to be problematic at times and recently, the organization had been targeted by individuals unknown who had tried to gain access to the client databases by posing as supplier representatives. Various forms of social engineering have been deployed. Although unsuccessful, Mr. Barnes considered it only a question of time before a data breach occurred.

Staff in partner organizations used a different approach to risk management and did not place much emphasis on ensuring that the personal data of customers was safeguarded in the way that they were supposed to. One of the organizations Mr. Barnes and his colleagues dealt with on a regular basis was known to keep all customer data and information in hard copy form, in files that were stored in an unlockable filing cabinet. Often, the files were left unattended on a senior manager's desk, and on one occasion, a file had gone missing for three days. It was believed that somebody had borrowed the file over a weekend to do some work at home. Indeed, staff within that organization were often heard discussing client details in public and were known to take lunch breaks at odd times. During lunch, which was taken in the organization's onsite restaurant, the computers of staff were left on, and data and information were visible via the monitors.

A couple of staff had been told repeatedly to adhere to the organization's security policy, but their attitude was that "we do not have anything worth stealing" and the status quo was maintained.

Roger Barnes informed his colleagues that it would be appropriate to adopt the stakeholder theory approach as this would allow management to have a holistic view of business operations and help integrate risk management into all aspects of the business including partner organizations. The idea was to provide uniformity and result in intra-organizational and inter-organizational associations that resulted in trust-based relationships that allowed information to be shared both on a formal and an informal basis. Mr. Barnes was asked several questions about sharing information as opposed to exchanging information and provided insights into how individuals relate to other individuals and cited social engagement, trust building and power relationships as being the key determinants of effective information sharing. Attention focused on how supply chain partners engaged in business operations and one of the points that surfaced was that the IT systems used by some suppliers were known to be incompatible with those of the organization and because of this, problems in communication occurred. But it extended beyond this. There were also issues as regards how staff in supplier organizations undertook threat detection and risk mitigation. It was suggested that staff in one supplier used the "back of an envelope" approach and had no formal process in operation. All the calculations were informally arrived at and there was no way of knowing how realistic they were. This had caused both confusion and irritation at times. It was realized that all partner organizations needed to adopt a formal and systematic approach to risk analysis and leadership had to be provided vis-à-vis best practice.

After lunch, Mr. Barnes talked through his view as to what a collectivist enterprise risk management cyber threat model was composed of and explained it was important to include both an internal and an external dimension into the model. He also suggested that the model did not have to be mathematically determined. He advocated a conceptual approach because there were too many unknowns within the environment and the model had to be flexible enough to accommodate all the uncertainties. One of the key considerations was to monitor and predict patterns of cyber-attacks because this helped formalize the threat detection process and allowed staff to put cyber security countermeasures in place. The overarching view was that security had to be designed and the relationships between organizational staff needed to be viewed in the context of linking intelligence with security and extending outward to engage with law enforcement representatives.

In the last session of the day, Mr. Barnes and his colleagues discussed the following questions:

Question 1: It has been suggested that there is no need to share information informally within and between organizations if there is a formal information-sharing process in place. Critically appraise this view and provide reasons as to why this may not be correct.

Question 2: In relation to supply chain partners, which factors should be given attention to in order for the cyber security policy and strategy of each supplier to be integrated into the cyber security policy and strategy of the main organization?

Question 3: What should a collectivist enterprise risk management cyber threat model be composed of? Make a distinction between an intra-organizational model and an inter-organizational model.

References, websites and further reading

Andreasson, K. (ed.). (2012). *Cybersecurity: Public Sector Threats and Responses*. London: CRC Press.

Barney, J.B., and Harrison, J.S. (2020). Stakeholder Theory at the Crossroads. *Business & Society*, 59 (2), pp. 203–212. DOI: 10.1177/0007650318796792

Barrios, A., de Valck, K., Shultz, C.J., Sibai, O., Husemann, K.C., Maxwell-Smith, M., and Luedicke, M.K. (2016). Marketing as a means to transformative social conflict resolution: Lessons from transitioning war economies and the Columbian coffee marketing system. *Journal of Public Policy & Marketing*, 35 (2), pp. 185–197. DOI: 1509/jppm.15.151

Cabinet Office. (2012). *The UK Cyber Security Strategy Report on Progress – December 2012. Forward Plans*. London: Cabinet Office (December).

Cavelty, M.D., and Wenger, A. (2022). Cyber security between socio-technological uncertainty and political fragmentation. In: Cavelty, M.D., and Wenger, A. (eds.). *Cyber Security Politics: Socio-Political Transformations and Political Fragmentation*, pp. 1–13. London: Taylor and Francis.

Cuntz, A., and Qian, Y. (2021). The impacts of counterfeiting on corporate investment. *Journal of Economic Development*, 46 (2), pp. 1–40. DOI: 10.35866/caujed.2021.46.2.001

del Rincon, J.M., Nowroozi, E., Kamenou, E., Alouani, I., Gupta, S., and Miller, P. (2024). *Study of Research and Guidance on the Cyber Security of AI*. United Kingdom: Centre for Secure Information Technologies (CSIT), Queen's University Belfast (QUB), pp. 1–24. https://assets.publishing.service.gov.uk/media/663cf1b2bd01f5ed3279388e/Study_of_research_and_guidance_on_the_cyber_security_of_AI_-_Queens_University_Belfast_literature_review.pdf (Accessed 3rd June, 2024).

European Commission. (2013). *Cyber Security Strategy of the European Union: An Open, Safe and Secure Cyberspace*. High Representative of the European Union for Foreign Affairs and Security Policy. Report JOIN (2013) 1 final (7th February). Brussels: European Commission.

Fleischman, G.M., Valentine, S.R., Curtis, M.B., and Mohapatra, P.S. (2023). *Business & Society*, 62 (3), pp. 488–529. DOI: 10.1177/00076503221110156

Freeman, R.E., Phillips, R., and Sisodia, R. (2020). *Business & Society*, 59 (2), pp. 213–231. DOI: 10.1177/0007650318773750

Gedris, K., Bowman, K., Neupane, A., Hughes, A.L., Bonsignore, E., West, R.W., Balzotti, J., and Hansen, D.L. (2012). Simulating municipal cybersecurity incidents: Recommendations from expert Interviews. *Proceedings of the 54th Hawaii International Conference on System Sciences*, pp. 2036–2045. https://hdl.handle.net/10125/70862

Haunschild, J., Kaufhold, M-C., and Reuter, C. (2022). Cultural Violence and Fragmentation on Social Media: Interventions and Countermeasures by Humans and Social Bots. In: Cavelty, M.D., and Wenger, A. (eds.). *Cyber Security Politics: Socio-Political Transformations and Political Fragmentation*, pp. 48–63. London: Taylor and Francis.

HM Government (2016). *National Cyber Security Strategy 2016–2021*. London: HM Government.

Jalali, M.S., Siegel, M., and Madnick, S. (2019). Decision-making and biases in cybersecurity capability development: Evidence from a simulation game experiment. *Journal of Strategic Information Systems*, 28, pp. 66–82. https://doi.org/10.1016/j.jsis.2018.09.003

Jones, N.A., and Trim, P.R.J. (2009). Establishing a security culture: Pointers for senior management. In: Trim, P.R.J., and Caravelli, J. (eds.). *Strategizing Resilience and Reducing Vulnerability*, pp. 165–179. New York: NOVA Science Publishers, Inc.

Kavak, H., Padilla, J.J., Vernon-Bido, D., Diallo, S.Y., Gore, R., and Shetty, S. (2021). Simulation for cybersecurity: State of the art and future directions. *Journal of Cybersecurity*, pp. 1–13. DOI: 10.1093/cybsec/tyab005

Korea Internet and Security Agency. (2010). *Informatization White Paper*. Seoul: KISA.

Kujala, J., Sachs, S., Leinonen, H., Heikkinen, A., and Laude, D. (2022). Stakeholder engagement: Past, present, and future. *Business & Society*, 61 (5) pp. 1136–1196. DOI: 10.1177/0007650321166595

Martin, K.D., and Kracher, B. (2008). A conceptual framework for online business protest tactics and criteria for their effectiveness. *Business & Society*, 47 (3), pp. 291–311. https://doi.org/10.1177/0007650307299218

Mäses, S., Randmann, L., Maennel, O., and Lorenz, B. (2018). Stenmap: Framework for evaluating cybersecurity-related skills based on computer simulations. In: Zaphiris, P., and Ioannou, A. (eds.). *Proceedings Learning and Collaboration Technologies. Learning and Teaching: 5th*

International Conference, LCT 2018, pp. 492–504. Held as Part of HCI International 2018. Las Vegas, NV, USA. July 15–20, Proceedings, Part II. LNCS 10925. https://doi. org/10.1007/978-3-319-91152-6_38

Nguyen, T.T., and Reddi, V.J. (2021). Deep reinforcement learning for cyber security. *IEEE Transactions on Neural Networks and Learning Systems* 1, pp. 1–17. DOI: 10.1109/ TNNLS.2021.3121870

Pearce, F.T. (1976). Business intelligence systems: The need, development, and integration. *Industrial Marketing Management*, 5 (2/3), pp. 115–138. https://doi.org/10.1016/0019-8501(76)90035-3

Radoynovska, N. (2024). Expectations meet reality: Leader sensemaking and enactment of stake-holder engagement in multistakeholder social enterprise. *Business & Society*, pp. 1–44. DOI: 10.1177/00076503231221537 (Accessed online 22nd April, 2024).

Risk Management Solutions, Inc. (2016). *Managing Cyber Insurance Accumulation Risk.* Cambridge: Centre for Risk Studies. University of Cambridge. (February).

Schünemann, W.J. (2022). A threat to Democracies? An overview of theoretical approaches and empirical measurements for studying the effects of disinformation. In: Cavelty, M.D., and Wenger, A. (eds.). *Cyber Security Politics: Socio-Political Transformations and Political Fragmentation*, pp. 32–47. London and New York: Taylor and Francis.

The White House. (2023). *National Cybersecurity Strategy.* Washington: The White House (1st March).

Tioh, J-N., Mina, M., and Jacobson, D.W. (2017). *Cyber Security Training: A Survey of Serious Games in Cyber Security. 2017 IEEE Frontiers in Education Conference (FIE).* Indianapolis, IN: IEEE. pp. 1–5. DOI:10.1109/FIE.2017.8190712. 18th to 21st October.

Trim, P.R.J., and Lee, Y-I. (2019). The role of B2B marketers in increasing cyber security awareness and influencing behavioural change. *Industrial Marketing Management*, 83, pp. 224–238. https://doi.org/10.1016/j.indmarman.2019.04.003

UK Government. (2024). *Open call for evidence: Call for Views on the Cyber Security of AI.* https://www.gov.uk/government/calls-for-evidence/call-for-views-on-the-cyber-security-of-ai/ call-for-views-on-the-cyber-security-of-ai (Accessed 3rd June, 2024).

Veksler, V.D., Buchler, N., Hoffman, B.E., Cassenti, D.N., Sample, C., and Sugrim, S. (2018). Simulations in cyber-security: A review of cognitive modeling of network attackers, defenders, and users. *Frontiers in Psychology*, pp. 1–12. DOI: 10.3389/fpsyg.2018.00691

Websites

Cochrane, P. Cyber security - Thinking like the enemy. OWASP Suffolk Chapter. https://www. youtube.com/watch?v=ZWvD3BLvPSM (Accessed 29th March, 2024).

Craiger, J.P. An introduction to small unmanned aerial systems (sUAS) cyber security.

Craiger, J.P. Penetration testing a small unmanned aerial systems (sUAS).

Craiger, J.P. Maritime transportation system cybersecurity: An overview.

Craiger, J.P. Cyber supply chain attacks and risk management.

Craiger, J.P. Maritime transportation system cyber attacks and mitigation strategies. Available from: NCyTE Center website (National Cybersecurity Training & Education Center). https:// www.ncyte.net/home (Accessed July and August, 2023).

Trim, P. A collectivist approach to cyber security including government, industry, academia and society. https://www.youtube.com/watch?v=3MiZ_Kp8_oI (Accessed July and August, 2023).

Further reading

Kranton, R.E. (1996). The formation of cooperative relationships. *The Journal of Law, Economics & Organization*, 12 (1), pp. 214–233. https://doi.org/10.1093/oxfordjournals.jleo.a023358

Leonidou, L.C., Aykol, B., Spyropoulou, S., and Christodoulides, P. (2019). The power roots and drivers of infidelity in international business relationships. *Industrial Marketing Management*, 78, pp. 198–212. http://dx.doi.org/10.1016/j.indmarman.2017.03.003

Trim, P.R.J. (2003). Public and private sector cooperation in counteracting cyberterrorism. *International Journal of Intelligence and Counter Intelligence*, 16 (4), pp. 594–608.

4

ARTIFICIAL INTELLIGENCE AND CYBER SECURITY MANAGEMENT

4.1 Introduction

The chapter starts with insights into AI and ML (Section 4.2) and continues with balancing AI opportunities with risk (Section 4.3). Developing AI awareness (Section 4.4) precedes information about the Dark Web (Section 4.5), and this is followed by taking cognizance of AI-oriented threats (Section 4.6). Looking to the future and anticipating AI threats (Section 4.7) is followed by reflection and questions (Section 4.8) and next, there is a conclusion (Section 4.9).

4.2 Artificial Intelligence (AI) and Machine Learning (ML)

Colleagues in the marketing department who deal with customer details and manage customer relationship management systems and customer databases are aware of what levels of customer service need to be provided and how security needs to be linked into marketing department operations so that the confidential data stored in customer databases are protected and in-house marketing reports are available to only those with a high level/appropriate level of security clearance. Marketing staff are aware of what IT security systems are in place and how they are managed but AI is likely to be a game changer and will require due care and attention. Because the business operations reporting channels are known, any unusual or suspicious behaviour, whether internally or externally orchestrated, will be picked up by staff and/or the computer system log facility when an employee or unauthorized person tries to access sensitive and confidential data and information that is kept within a secure system. This is managed by sensors in the network(s) that detect activity and then send a message to the appropriate manager (e.g., IT manager). This is only part of the picture, however. AI is increasingly being used to identify and target customer groups, and it is also being used to predict and influence potential customers as it is making information available to them regarding their purchase behaviour. Hence, the use of AI needs to be placed in context, and this means that

DOI: 10.4324/9781003570905-4

both the positive and negative aspects of AI must be addressed. If privacy issues and data protection are to be addressed, staff need to be compliant and focused on avoiding reputational damage.

With reference to the financial sector, Boukherouaa and Shabsig (2021, p. 5) have a clear appreciation of how technology, through enhanced AI/ML capabilities, will continue to transform the sector for the benefit of all concerned. Boukherouaa and Shabsig (2021, p. 5) indicate that AI/ML systems are having a profound effect on client experience and make reference to enhanced communication through the use of chatbots. They also highlight investing and refer to what is known as a robo-advisor and make reference also to borrowing vis-à-vis automated mortgage underwriting. Boukherouaa and Shabsig (2021, p. 5) also refer to identity verification (e.g., image recognition) and suggest that the use of technology will provide cost savings as a result of a number of processes being automated. In addition, it is suggested that predictive analytics will be harnessed, which will allow banks to devise better product offerings, and improve business operations through more effective risk and fraud management processes. Furthermore, it is expected that regulatory compliance will be more adhered to, and AI/ML systems will "provide central banks and prudential oversight authorities with new tools to improve systemic risk surveillance and strengthen prudential oversight" (Boukherouaa and Shabsig, 2021, p. 5).

Bearing this in mind, it is worth reflecting on the fact that AI and ML systems will create new market opportunities and will help organizations reach higher levels of efficiency; however, it has to be remembered that cyber-crime is international in orientation and an organization's cost savings and return on investment have to be weighed up against the possible threats encountered, which may materialize due to an exaggerated risk appetite. Boukherouaa and Shabsig (2021, p. 20) are right to suggest that ethical questions relating to the deployment of AI will emerge that need answering and monitoring will become key. For example, customer privacy, the safe deployment of AI/ML systems and the willingness to share experiences and create new knowledge are now key considerations for managers but they have wider ramifications and go beyond day-to-day business operations.

Shabsigh and Boukherouaa (2023, p. 3) make known that the Chat Generative Pre-Trained Transformer (ChatGPT) is rapidly becoming utilized because: "Competitive pressures have fueled rapid adoption of AI/ML in the financial sector in recent years by facilitating gains in efficiency and cost savings, reshaping client interfaces, enhancing forecasting accuracy, and improving risk management and compliance". Shabsigh and Boukherouaa (2023, p. 3) make reference to the fact that GenAI (e.g., Generative AI – used to create content) is expected to deliver a number of cyber security benefits that include implementing predictive models that allow for the rapid detection of threats and improved incident response. Because GenAIs have the ability to process large and diverse data sets, it is possible to generate content that is in an accessible format and this will help improve business operations from the perspective of risk mitigation and compliance reporting (Shabsigh and Boukherouaa, 2023, p. 3).

It is useful to focus on AI in relation to the financial sector because of the fact that banks have been subjected to a large proportion of cyber-attacks on organizations and are known to invest extensively in cyber security. Furthermore, bank representatives are well aware that some consumers have allowed an attacker to take control of their bank account, and this has resulted in them losing money and contacting the bank for help. Also, business clients have been subject to cyber-attacks and consequently have paid erroneous invoices to fictitious companies, which they have later tried to reclaim. It is not surprising to learn, therefore, that financial institutions are investing in AI for a number of business-related reasons. Besides the day-to-day operations that are fundamental to a bank's existence, it has to be recognized that banks play an important and pivotal role in a nation's business and trading activities and because of this, the government is mindful of the fact that the nation's banking industry needs to be protected and safeguarded for all concerned.

Reflecting on the future development of the banking industry, Shabsigh and Boukherouaa (2023, p. 4) provide the following update relating to real-world examples that either harness generative AI applications or are considering doing so to improve their competitiveness in the financial sector: Capital One and JPMorgan Chase are using GenAI to augment their AI-powered fraud and suspicious activity detection systems. The objectives include better detection, reducing costs and improving customer satisfaction. Morgan Stanley Wealth Management is deploying OpenAI's technology as a means to utilize data sources in order to assist financial advisors by providing them with insights into companies, sectors, capital markets and regions of the world, for example. Wells Fargo is known to be building capabilities vis-à-vis automating document processing. It is achieving this by providing summary reports and increasing its use of virtual assistant chatbots. Goldman Sachs and Citadel are also considering GenAI applications for the internal development of software and information analysis.

As can be noted from the above, banks and possibly other financial institutions are intent on harnessing AI for a number of reasons. The development of AI is and will continue to be dependent on large amounts of investment. It is possible, therefore, that those developing internal AI systems will also invest in an external source and duplicate their AI project activities. This duplication will continue until it is found that one AI project is a better investment and likely to fulfil the requirement better than the other projects that are being invested in. At this point in time, the more robust AI project will continue and the less effective AI project will be discontinued.

Issues have been raised regarding the use of GenAI and discussions have occurred at the government level and company level. Shabsigh and Boukherouaa (2023, pp. 10–11) have raised a number of issues that need the immediate attention of managers vis-à-vis GenAI usage:

- The exploitation of sophisticated phishing messages and email attacks.
- Malicious actors can use the technology to impersonate individuals or organizations, and this can increase the risk of identity theft/fraud.
- Deepfakes will proliferate (e.g., more realistic videos, audio or images), and as a consequence, serious damage will be inflicted on individuals and organizations.
- GenAI models may be vulnerable to data poisoning and input attacks and this results in AI models being influenced at the training stage.
- Malicious actions will be hidden and not easily identified when the AI models are in operation.
- GenAI tools such as SEO or GenAI-generated content will be subject to manipulation and the GenAI data environment will be distorted due to and for malicious purposes.

- Because pre-2021 Internet scraped data is used to train and operate current GenAI models, and also data sets may be targeted by purpose-built cyberhacking tools, additional risks may evolve, which are unknown.
- Current GenAI models are prone to "jailbreaking" attacks and due to the words/sentences used, malicious data or instructions can be inserted via "prompt injection attack" and as a result sensitive data could be extracted.
- GenAI technology may have other vulnerabilities that remain unknown.
- Hallucinations may occur and the information provided may be inaccurate.

4.3 Balancing AI Opportunities with Risk

Although it can be argued that there are a number of advantages in harnessing the power of online marketing technology and especially AI, it can be argued that managers do need to be more aware of the consequences of using AI because of the possible impact it has on the way customers think and exercise their judgements. As regards the move towards embracing humanoid virtual influencer technology, and the human-like qualities the technology is associated with, it can be suggested that managers need a reasonable knowledge of psychology as well as an understanding of how the algorithms (behind the images that are displayed online) function. The cyber security manager is aware that AI represents a complex technology that is driven by technically gifted people and is used for harvesting huge data sets; however, the objective is to understand and relate to end users and their needs better.

The emphasis is, therefore, on marketing strategy implementation and ensuring that the organization is able to compete in the industry and maintain its sustainable competitive advantage. Managers are aware that innovations in marketing help to shape markets and bring about market transformation; consequently, they need to be aware of the wider security issues associated with dealing with customers online and pay attention to assisting their colleagues in IT to identify organizational vulnerabilities. In other words, expanding the envelope of marketing activities is likely to result in a number of uncertainties that could be transformed into business vulnerabilities.

A better understanding of the minds of consumers and how consumers behave means that additional data is needed regarding their lifestyle, and in due course, marketing plans are formed that attempt to provide more value to the customer via additional products and services. This can mean supplying products online and operating a product return policy, also online. Criminals monitor the actions of companies that operate online and devise ways in which to emulate leading brand providers and this sometimes manifests in similar websites being designed and made available to the public. The idea is to trap unsuspecting consumers into believing that they are buying a product from a legitimate brand leader's website, when in fact this is not the case. Some criminals, often those with access to large amounts of capital, also hijack legitimate websites and hold the organization to ransom and normally ask to be paid in bitcoins. Hacktivists have also been known to hijack a website and replace it with a different version. Sometimes activists take down a leading piece of text and replace it with their own text. Normally, this is done to discredit the company and, in some cases, reference is made to senior management's wrongdoing and an "apology" is provided for wrongdoing. By monitoring the organization's website, the cyber security manager can prevent a website from being hijacked or can close down an existing website and replace it with a legitimate alternative website. In the future, online marketing systems are likely to receive more prominence as Generation Z fully exploits their use and knowledge of technology and customizes their purchase behaviour around their lifestyle. Thinking ahead means that the cyber security manager and their colleagues can build security into marketing activities and embed cyber security within the marketing plan. What the cyber security manager needs to be aware of is that criminals are well aware of what organizations are doing and will always try and be one step ahead of them. The objective of the cyber security manager and their colleagues remains to ensure that the organization is able to withstand and, if possible, eradicate data/information breaches and cyber disruptions and to remain functioning.

As AI becomes more embedded in and associated with marketing activities (e.g., placing customers into defined segments, devising promotional campaigns and analyzing data to identify unforeseen threats), managers and marketing managers in particular will turn increasingly to using AI technology because the algorithms in use assume responsibility for the routine decisions that were once the prerogative of experienced marketers. What is clear is that the new world that is emerging and which may see social media influencers being partly replaced by virtual influencers means that business-to-consumer, business-to-business, consumer-to-business and consumer-to-consumer relations are changing in both degree and emphasis. This means that both intra-government and inter-government cooperation is likely to occur as consumers buy products and services online, sourced from different parts of the world, and regulatory powers are enforced to protect groups of consumers.

The increasing emphasis on the utilization of AI should result in senior managers providing guidance and ensuring, because they are held accountable, that their staff and staff in partner organizations adhere to strict AI codes of practice. In addition, senior management will need to ensure that there is an appropriate governance mechanism in place and that the role of governance is understood by employees, who are responsible in terms of conducting themselves responsibly. This means that the cyber security manager, the risk manager and the marketing manager follow the same ethical guidelines, protect the personal data of customers and ensure that staff are compliant in their behaviour. In other words, marketing and security are integrated and viewed as the same business function.

4.4 Developing AI Awareness

It is useful at this point to consider how the cyber security manager can work with the marketing manager and their staff and ensure that they possess the skills necessary to deal with the different types of cyber-attacks. All too often, access is gained to an organization's database(s) by inexperienced staff making available to people unknown passwords that allow them to access computer systems and networks when they should not. Staff can also be manipulated through targeted relationships into providing a password that results in a system being exploited and a data breach occurring. Errors of judgement such as a confidential document being left in a public place and which falls into the wrong hands can also manifest in a hack that allows data to be extracted or manipulated and deformed or erased.

There is no doubt that AI has a number of advantages associated with it and managers need to be aware of them. For example, AI can automate specific tasks, some of which are monotonous and prone to human error as people get bored undertaking them and make mistakes. By automating mailing lists and promotional campaigns (e.g., via email), it is possible to free up labour and to deploy people on more analytical tasks such as market and company/competitor analysis. However, it is not always possible to assume that staff will have the basic skills necessary to be transferred to more demanding work and specific types of training need to be provided. The human–AI interface requires thought, and senior management needs to anticipate the pace of change and how AI can be fully utilized. Eventually, managers will become reliant on AI and so will their staff. Hence, understanding that AI can be used to undertake contextualized searches, which is supportive of report writing, editing and structuring information for company presentation purposes and reports to internal and external stakeholders, is an important step forward.

AI is able to monitor continuously computer systems and networks and detect and deal with security-related vulnerabilities (e.g., detection of malware and illegal/attempted entry by persons unknown of databases containing customer and financial information) and because of this, AI is likely to be deployed to intensify and deepen security provision. It is for this reason that cyber security needs to be placed in the context of an organization's security policy and strategy (Trim and Lee, 2023).

Threats can materialize because staff do not pay attention to basic requirements. For example, an individual may, without giving the matter sufficient thought, place personal and company information in a chatbot in order to get more precise answers/information and this could lead to the organization's systems being compromised because there is no way of knowing what a chatbot does with the information provided or where such information is stored and how secure it is. Bearing in mind how resource-rich cyber threat actors can be, it has to be remembered that any organization is subject to an APT/APA that can go on over a long period of time until a vulnerability has been found and exploited. Once the information retained by a chatbot is breached, it could be sold on the Dark Web. Furthermore, those relying on the services of a chatbot may not be aware that a chatbot may provide inaccurate or misleading information through what is known as hallucination. The incorrect or misleading information is likely to be viewed as valid by the user and used in a decision-making capacity with disastrous consequences (e.g., data/information is used to make a financial forecast).

4.5 The Dark Web

Chertoff (2017, p. 27) has provided much insight into the Dark Web and suggests that it makes up a small percentage of the sites on the Internet. The Dark Web is accessible only through the use of a special browser such as The Onion Router – Tor – and, in addition, often requires a password for access to be gained. The Hidden Wiki and availability of bitcoins enable users to utilize the services available on the Dark Web. As well as services provided by cyber criminals on the Dark Web, there are also political dissidents that use the Dark Web to make information available to the outside world because it is unregulated by the government (Chertoff, 2017, p. 28) and allows them to circulate messages to a wide audience. As well as hacktivists, whistle-blowers are known to use the Dark Web because it offers anonymity.

At this juncture, it is logical to reflect on how AI and the Dark Web may combine to heighten the risk of cyber-attacks against an organization. Walters (2015) has provided insights into a whole range of cyber-attacks on US companies and is clear that attacks are escalating. Cyber-attacks are known to seek private, personal data, which is then sold to other criminals via the Dark Web. In some instances, a data/information breach is not detected until some weeks/months after a breach has occurred and because of this, it is not always possible to establish the immediate value and the cost of the data/information that has been leaked. What needs to be borne in mind is that a single attack on an organization, although disruptive, may not be so severe as a concerted grouping of attacks on an organization over a period of time. Persistent attacks and an APT are associated with probing to ensure an organizational vulnerability is uncovered that will allow the attacker to penetrate the organization's defences and gain access to its computer system and networks. Once a perpetrator has gained access to the computer system, organizational staff are hard pressed to stop the attacker from taking out data and information. If such an attack occurs at the same time as an online business protest against the organization (Martin and Kracher, 2008, p. 293), it could be that the problem intensifies and cascading effects give rise to a catastrophic failure of some kind. Reflecting on the fact that technology now is highly advanced, it could be that the firewall(s) and defences in place are unable to prevent an intrusion. In this case, the objective would be to ensure that the intruder is unable to extract the data and exit the system.

Chertoff (2017, p. 31) suggests that:

"policy to address the Dark Web requires an understanding of the benefits and risks of anonymity and of an open internet. Rash and sweeping legislation has the potential to encroach on civil liberties and to be a nightmare to enforce".

Chertoff (2017, p. 31) realizes that if the concerns relating to the Dark Web are not addressed, then illicit activities will continue, and this will present additional problems to society. The point to note is that regulating the Dark Web will require a concerted effort from governments around the world. This is because as Chertoff (2017, p. 31) indicates, the regulations applicable to the Internet will need to affect those using the Surface Web, the Deep Web and the Dark Web.

Legislation has been introduced to make the Internet safer for the user. For example, the UK implemented the Online Safety Act 2023 that is aimed at protecting society against illegal content and activity and is especially focused on protecting children against content and activity that is considered harmful to them. The act does much to address online behaviour in relation to protecting young people, especially from being targeted in relation to abusive material via social media platforms. Ofcom (the Office of Communications) is the regulator that is appointed by the UK government to ensure that the telecommunications industry, for example, adheres to the Online Safety Act 2023.

Kumar and Rosenbach (2019) make known that some activities on the Dark Web are not illegal and the actions of some of the Dark Web users are not related to criminal activity or organized crime. It is suggested that some individuals living in countries that are deemed to have oppressive regimes in place use the Dark Web to promote their cause. This implies that interaction and engagement on the Dark Web are sometimes attributed to political dissents and their fight for freedom. By voicing their concerns on the Dark Web, it is possible that they can influence policy in the country they reside without putting themselves in danger by ensuring that they can continue their lobbying activities knowing that they are free from persecution. The Dark Web may also be a facility for those that consider whistle-blowing to be essential and legitimate because they can make their views/information known without suffering any consequences. Kumar and Rosenbach (2019) also argue that the Dark Web offers those concerned with privacy and anonymity issues an opportunity to make their views felt about the way in which corporations and governments utilize data and this may be viewed as raising legitimate concerns. The main point to note is that consumer activists and the activist movement generally are likely to gain more momentum in the years ahead as technology and the dissemination of ideas and comments are considered both useful and necessary by those promoting a certain cause. Monitoring such developments can be considered necessary and will involve close cooperation between IT, marketing and security staff.

4.6 Taking Cognizance of AI-Oriented Threats

Possibly what senior management needs to be aware of is that AI can be used to create and deliver malware and that AI can be used to mimic an individual, normally someone of authority. The purpose of mimicking a person of authority can be to spread fake news and/or obtain funds through fraudulent means. One of the growing areas of threat is in fact the creation of phishing emails, generated by AI, which are deployed in conjunction with social engineering attacks. So, what senior managers need to be aware of and make known to staff is that a single AI-driven cyber-attack is unlikely to be independent of other cyber-attacks. Those orchestrating cyber-attacks are in fact aware of how to combine attacks in order to exploit an organizational weakness. Such attacks are likely to be sustained through time until a vulnerability is exploited. The cyber security manager and their colleagues need to know how to counteract various types of attacks because an aggressor has formulated an attack strategy that is logical and intent on breaching the organization's defences. In the process, the attacker learns what works and what does not work and is prepared to invest time and effort into a continuous set of attacks until some success is achieved.

It is important at this point to understand that the cyber security manager needs to extend their understanding of cyber security management and strategic intelligence by undertaking an analysis of all known forms of cyber-attack, categorize them and then rank them in order of severity/impact. The question has to be posed: How will AI be used to facilitate different forms of cyber-attack? To answer this question, it is necessary to establish a complete list of cyber-attacks and establish which form of attack is likely to be enhanced by AI. Hossain et al. (2024, pp. 13–14) have listed various types and techniques of cyber-attack; they include ransomware, spyware, adware, keyloggers, trojans, viruses, worms, rootkits, bots/botnet, SQL injection, malvertizing, XSS, Internet Protocol (IP) spoofing, Address Resolution Protocol (ARP) spoofing, Domain Name System (DNS) spoofing, DoS, DDoS, phishing, spear phishing, whaling, man-in-the-middle, brute force attacks, social engineering, malicious insider, negligent insider, zero-day target attacks, repudiation, tampering, spamming and Advanced Persistent Attack.

The knowledge of those intent on stealing data and information has to be judged and placed in the context of how fast they can obtain data/information and exit a system. A really knowledgeable attacker can enter a network and computer system in a very short period of time and may only be detected if sensors pick up their activities. A key concern is that an intruder will enter a system undetected and extract data as and when necessary. However, once the data has been accessed and distributed and made available on the Dark Web, such activities may be detected but by then it is too late.

Sophisticated threat detection software is available on the market that can be used to counteract the actions of hackers, but it has to be said that organizational staff are not always aware of such software and sometimes consider that their organization is invincible, which it is not. What is most worrying is that staff are not always aware that the organization's database has been breached. Detecting a breach can take weeks and months, and in some instances, it is not possible to quantify the damage because there are too many unknowns. Also, the technique of mirroring computer systems allows an attacker to gain access to a computer system without being detected, observe what data is being put into a computer system and understand how it is being used.

Those involved in cyber espionage activities are familiar with decoding complex data and information and have knowledge and skills that allow them to find and interpret data and information and then identify the most appropriate market for it. The attacker could be a rouge government department or it could be an independent group that is commissioned to steal specific types of sensitive data and information. Or it could be an opportunist who is aware of market forces and is out to make a profit from their illegal activities. Organizations that are market leaders and known to innovate continuously are prone to attack and so too are those organizations that have patents protecting their inventions. Organizations that are known to be underperforming may also be the target of an attack, especially from an overseas predator that is intent on gaining market entry through any means, including social engineering to obtain data/information that can be used against the organization and help cause reputational damage and thus devalue its share base. Some of the hacks that have been carried out in recent years have in fact been undertaken to steal personal data so that specific individuals can be identified, targeted and blackmailed or scared into providing data/information that is of benefit to the attacker.

The advantages associated with utilizing AI technology can be seen more in the deployment of advanced robotics and the integration of manufacturing systems. Flexible manufacturing systems have been around for many years and the lessons learned from such complex technology have filtered through into sensitive industries, such as biotechnology and bioinformatics, which will in the years ahead see an increased use of AI. Why should policymakers be concerned about the further use of AI in sensitive industries? Ney et al. (2017, pp. 765–766) have provided insights into this by referring to research that was aimed at establishing what would happen in the case of a DNA-based exploit. Ney et al. (2017) were able to identify, through a simulated attack on an identified vulnerability (e.g., downstream modified sequencing utility), what the consequences would be vis-à-vis exploiting a computer program in relation to synthesized DNA. The researchers were able to establish how an "attacker could use sample bleeding to inject specific DNA sequence reads into concurrently sequenced samples. The reads contain malicious code or be used to confuse subsequent downstream analysis (e.g., variant calling)" (Ney et al., 2017, p. 773). Such research can be deemed valuable because it can help cyber security staff to identify how a specific type of vulnerability is likely to offer an attacker the opportunity to steal data/information by deploying a ransomware attack or merely steal data, without staff realizing it has been stolen, which is then sold to a competitor, possibly based overseas.

The bioindustry is drawing attention from several audiences but especially potential investors because they are aware of the high returns on biotechnology and bioindustry investment. However, potential investors are also aware of the high costs of biosecurity, which is necessary because threat actors may be intent on deliberately contaminating bioindustry data or hacking medical research data to gain financial advantage from selling it or disrupting the supply of data to slow down further development and delay commercialization. Such eventualities need to be placed in the context of patients of specific types of medical intervention being deprived of various forms of medicine/assistance to help them recover/live a life as comfortably as possible. Cyber intrusions aimed at falsifying medical records are a problem that constantly needs to be guarded against because it not only delays a patient from receiving medical intervention on time but may also result in incorrect medicine being prescribed to a patient, which results in side effects or possibly the loss of life. In such cases, a lawsuit for compensation may materialize that manifests in reputational damage and a huge fine and compensation.

At this juncture, it is worthwhile to reflect on what cyberbiosecurity is and what it involves because having a sound appreciation of the bioindustry in mind will allow us to consider the public–private cyber security interlinkage and the government–company–customer security relationships that are in place. This is important for (i) allowing managers in the private sector (e.g., pharmaceutical industry) to market profitable products and services to staff in the public sector (e.g., health authorities, medical doctors and hospitals) and (ii) to put in place cyber security countermeasures that protect all the parties involved. What needs to be remembered is that cyber security countermeasures require that managers adopt a specific attitude and mindset to understand why threat actors act as they do and why they are intent on causing damage to an industry through acts of sabotage, theft and ransom. Those that instigate a cyber-attack for a specific purpose may launch a number of cyber-attacks through time and, in some cases, operate an APA until eventually they find a way to penetrate the organization's defences. Hence, senior managers in some industries are now familiarizing themselves with what is known as an APT and focusing their attention on how they can stop hackers from extracting data from the organization's databases because they accept that an attacker will penetrate the organization's defences at some point in time. Whether this is logical or not has to be considered from the perspective of what goes into the risk register and how those who see the information in the risk register will react to it.

Murch et al. (2018, p. 1) are clear that cyberbiosecurity requires detailed thought about the vulnerabilities covering unwanted surveillance as well as intrusions, malicious and harmful activities that

"occur within or at the interfaces of comingled life and medical sciences, cyber, cyber-physical, supply chain and infrastructure systems, and developing and instituting measures to prevent, protect against, mitigate, investigate and attribute such threats as it pertains to security, competitiveness and resilience."

In the United States alone, the value of the annual bioeconomy is considered to be US$4 trillion and accounts for almost 25% of the GDP (Murch et al., 2018, p. 2). Hence, it is clear that the bioeconomy is highly important and has a wide attack surface because it includes industries such as the chemical industry and the pharmaceutical industry and also producers of medical equipment and various renewable biological resources for example.

4.7 Looking to the Future and Anticipating AI Threats

From the above, it is clear that those intent on carrying out a cyber-attack will in the years ahead utilize AI and ML to become even more entrepreneurial, sophisticated and organized in the way in which they undertake a cyber-attack because senior managers in both the public sector and the private sector are insufficiently aware of what they need to do in order to prevent a range of cyber-attacks from succeeding. Bearing in mind the predatory nature of those carrying out such attacks, it is imperative that senior managers develop their awareness of the different types of attack (e.g., DoS, man-in-the-middle, phishing/spear phishing, ransomware, trojan horse and SQL injection) and also, make assumption/realistic assumption(s) as to whether the attack(s) is related to an act of cyber-crime, cyber warfare or cyber terrorism. Although AI can be used to detect and eliminate cyber-attacks, it has to be recognized that threat actors are contaminating training data that is used in the development of AI algorithms and also, in the years ahead, it will become more difficult to distinguish between acts of cyber-crime, cyber warfare and cyber terrorism. Cyber espionage will become more prominent and naturally, this is causing concern among policymakers and will require various initiatives in the form of public–private sector cooperation to counteract it because of the consequences.

Increasingly damaging forms of cyber-attack will require industry–government–consumer cooperation, and result in a collectivist approach to cyber threat detection intelligence policy and strategy. At the forefront will be the intelligence, security and law enforcement agencies that operate on behalf of the government. However, these agencies have limited funds, and more help is needed. It is because of the move from cybercrime to cyber warfare that senior managers need to invoke governance and put in place structures and mechanisms that ensure organizational staff are both compliant and supportive of government cyber security policy. They will also need to monitor and participate in university research vis-à-vis cyber security projects because the specialization needed is clear to see. Corporate social responsibility in the form of community-centred cyber security projects will do much to raise people's interest in cyber security and organizations can engage with schools and host cyber security competitions that stimulate awareness and at the same time make known cyber security management career paths.

With reference to the need to harness AI, the European Union Agency for Cybersecurity (ENISA, 2021, p. 12 and p. 4) has provided advice as regards how managers can utilize AI better by having a fuller appreciation of what ML represents; hence, ML can be defined as: "the ability for machines to learn from data to solve a task without being explicitly programmed to do so". ENISA (2021, p. 3) suggests that there is a need to understand how ML algorithms operate and what they can do and managers need to view this from the perspective of core functionalities and critical stages. It is suggested that:

> "The aim of the ML algorithm taxonomy is to focus not only on the functionalities of the algorithms but also on the ML models' workflow represented by the lifecycle. This lifecycle summarises the principle steps to produce an ML model".

ENISA (2021, p. 3) suggests several steps can be added to the lifecycle process and makes reference to data creation and data analysis. However, in order to simplify matters, it is useful to condense the number of steps involved. Although data cleaning needs to be included, data creation is viewed as external to the ML lifecycle (ENISA, 2021, p. 21) and may be excluded. Advice such as this is important because Huang and Rust (2021, p. 42) point out that AI is being used in a range of business contexts in various industries and managers can use ML to effectively segment a market and target customers more effectively. Hence, the advantages associated with AI are known but the problems presented by AI are not so obvious.

Bresniker et al. (2019, p. 46) have indicated that AI can help cyber security specialists detect thousands of threats and can aid the cyber security knowledge process by automating tasks and training new cyber security analysts. Bresniker et al. (2019, p. 46) suggest that AI/ML will, in the future, be used to (i) produce pattern-matching tools for highlighting security issues in networks; (ii) allow cyber security staff to use their time more effectively to respond to events in real time and (iii) ensure that action is formulated to deal with the threats identified. Whatever risk management approach is used, it is important to realize that the risk management process needs to be shared by managers in various business functions. This highlights the importance of a collectivist enterprise risk management cyber threat model that is incorporated into the structure of the partnership arrangement.

The use of AI chatbots is also receiving increased attention as managers use software-generated images to interact and converse with customers online. Research has shown that consumers have emotions towards a chatbot and express their closeness towards AI chatbots (Gkinko and Elbanna, 2023, p. 5), however, it is known that avatars have been used to spread disinformation and products like ChatGPT are being used to produce fake documents. This requires managers to take cognizance of the fact that as well as the training data used to construct the algorithms used in AI analysis is susceptible to outside manipulation, it is important to recognize that fake news can be difficult to detect, and manufactured rumours and fake stories together can prove destructive. Various researchers have looked into how and why disinformation is produced and the consequences associated with it (Albright, 2017; Klein and Wueller, 2017; Carrapico and Farrand, 2021), and this is an area of immediate and future attention as recognized by governments around the world.

The complexity associated with AI has been made clear by Bonfanti (2022, p. 65) who states:

> "Simply put, artificial intelligence will integrate and support cyber defensive and offensive activities, which may involve both the logical and the semantic layers of the cyberspace. Most of the features and functionalities which make artificial intelligence appropriate to cyber defence also make it suitable to offense".

Bonfanti (2022, p. 65) is right to suggest that AI can produce targeted cyber intelligence and can be used for both aggressive and protective purposes. It is thought that those carrying out cyber-attacks will use AI to enhance vulnerability discovery and carry out exploitive attacks and use AI to prompt sophistication in malware design and functioning that will enable AI-powered malware to evade detection and possibly "creatively respond to changes in the target's behavior" (Bonfanti, 2022, p. 74). There are other issues to consider as well. Wenger and Cavelty (2022, p. 256) state:

> "The socio-technical expansion of cyberspace is led by private technology firms, yet state actors shape the tighter coupling of technical systems with sociopolitical

institutions. This in turn means that governments share the responsibility to secure cyberspace with actors from the economy and society".

Wenger and Cavelty (2022, p. 256) place much emphasis on socio-technical and sociopolitical transformation, and this can be considered justifiable bearing in mind that the cyber security manager will need to be more actively involved in cyber governance discussions. This is because, as Wenger and Cavelty (2022, p. 256) proclaim, the use of wireless and satellite-based Internet facilities will mean that people are at a greater risk than before because cyber security is being stretched across different policy fields. Reflecting on these points, it can be suggested that to maintain some sort of order in the new interconnected world, governments around the world need to ensure that AI is used responsibly and if a company or a government abuses AI use, then they need to be held to account. This assumes that it can be argued that people in society know how AI should be used and can distinguish between harmful use and good use. Whatever view is adopted, however, will necessitate the cyber security manager to engage in debate regarding the ethical use of AI and how AI is to transform business practice and business operations for the good of society.

An area of growing concern to security specialists is how technology is utilized to produce deepfakes. Deepfakes are created to deceive and cause disruption because at issue is trust and how people relate to the images or voice messages and the context within which the imagery is used. A deepfake is a DL technique that enables fake videos to be created by swapping the face of an individual with that of another person (Tolosana et al., 2020, p. 131). Individuals will either directly or indirectly be affected by deepfakes because the objective of the perpetrator is to cause psychological shock and harm by creating a scenario whereby the viewer is not sure of what is being said and how to interpret it. So deepfakes can be viewed in terms of cause and effect. Kietzmann et al. (2020, p. 136) suggest that in order to create deepfakes, those concerned need to have expertise, access to various types of expensive hardware and software and training in various aspects of the process. ML and, in particular, DL are used to produce deepfake content of a most convincing nature and it can be assumed that the level of sophistication will increase through time as those deploying these forms of deception are out to gain an advantage of some kind. "Digitally manipulated synthetic media content" is supposed to look as lifelike as possible (Mustak et al., 2023, p. 1) in order to convince/fool the viewer/audience and achieve the desired deceptive results.

Cyber criminals and those involved in acts of cyber war, cyber terrorism and the growing area of cyber espionage are known to utilize technology in whatever way they can to achieve their objectives(s), which they consider are justified. Financial terrorism is known to be on the agenda of policymakers worldwide, and reporting on the financial sector, Khan et al. (2023, p. 80182) state:

> "…. cyberattacks are getting more and more serious. Artificial intelligence is being used by the banking sector to build cyber defence systems to reduce unwanted access and cyberattacks. Banks in Qatar are aware of the danger posed by cybercrime and the importance of cybersecurity for long-term development. The banking sector is now going through a significant technological change".

Obviously, ways are being found to counteract the threats posed and these include biometric authentication (e.g., identification verification) (Khan et al., 2023, p. 80185).

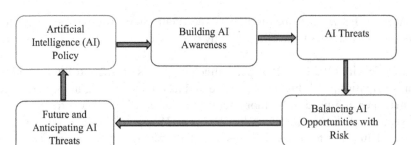

FIGURE 4.1 Artificial intelligence (AI) policy and threat detection.

However, it has to be acknowledged that although proof of identification is logical, people may be at risk due to identity theft (Khan et al., 2023, p. 80185) as a result of the continued sophistication of the criminal fraternity.

4.8 Reflection and Questions

Figure 4.1 outlines an organization's AI policy and links it to threat detection. Of key interest is the need for senior management to build AI awareness on a continual basis because AI capabilities are increasing rapidly. AI is being used for threat detection, but it can and will be weaponized and used in different ways from those expected. It is because of this that staff need to balance AI opportunities with risk and develop a mindset that requires those in management positions to think in terms of future AI threats.

There are several areas of concern regarding the way in which AI is developing and being used to support, improve and indeed transform business operations. However, the cyber security manager is well placed to understand the benefits associated with the use of AI and ML and has knowledge of how the deployment of AI tools can contribute to a sustainable business and its further development. Monitoring threats and dealing with various kinds of cyber-attacks, especially intrusions, place emphasis on establishing an in-depth cyber security intelligence system and framework that is managed and, to some extent, controlled by AI. Increased digitalization will, it can be assumed, place more emphasis on the need to undertake a thorough risk management assessment and the need to adhere to governance and compliance more so than is the case at present.

Question 1: How will AI enhance an organization's cyber security?
Question 2: What is an in-depth cyber security intelligence system and framework composed of?
Question 3: Who in the organization is responsible for undertaking risk management?

4.9 Conclusion

The use of AI can be expected to accelerate as new applications are developed and cost savings demand that labour is replaced by technology. Having said this, AI is expected to create job opportunities as people are redeployed on decision-making-related work and new industries emerge that rely more on the interpretative abilities of humans. Government policymakers will be charged with putting into practice laws that protect consumers and force organizations to strengthen their cyber security defences. What is clear is that government–industry–consumer interaction is essential in determining how AI is to be used and who has responsibility for it.

Case 4: Artificial Intelligence (AI) and cyber security

It has been suggested that AI and ML in particular will transform cyber security as it will allow mundane and repetitive tasks, normally associated with humans, to be carried out at speed by the technological systems in place. A good example of this is the interpretation of data from sensors in networks that highlight intruder activities and implement follow-up action that involves informing the appropriate responder (via the computer log) of the situation and implementing specific action to ensure that a data breach does not result. But AI is more than this. Much has been written about AI and managers in organizations appear positive about adopting and utilizing AI, but there are many unknowns that need to be addressed.

Managers are considering the investment needed in AI and how to justify such investment and there are also risks that need to be quantified. Bearing this in mind, it is unlikely that any one individual within an organization will have full knowledge of how AI is to be used to enhance the business decision-making process. The contamination of training data is an issue to be addressed and is likely to be given attention because it will impact AI effectiveness. There are also issues of customer privacy and over-reliance on AI, which can cause confusion and gaps as regards day-to-day activities. It is unlikely that staff will want to share bad experiences of AI usage with external staff, and what is placed in a risk register may vary.

AI is associated with analytical and predictive qualities, and it is these managers need to focus on. Models for fostering threat detection to improve incident response vary in degrees of complexity and often external advice and support are needed to perfect the system in use. So, the consequences of using AI need to be understood and AI usage needs to be placed in the context of human–computer interaction, if an all-around view is to be established. AI can also be used to protect against the hijacking of the organization's website, but it is not clear how this can be done. Possibly, by understanding through profiling the behaviour of Generation Y and Generation Z, it is easier to predict how AI can be used to reinforce cyber security policy. But again, managers need to be sure of what they are doing and what they want to achieve.

AI is not just to be associated with security enhancement, it will be used in a wide number of business activities and because of this, an organization-specific AI policy is needed vis-à-vis business-to-consumer, business-to-business, consumer-to-business and consumer-to-consumer relationship building. This places emphasis on governance, and the need for staff to be conversant with compliance policy. Developing AI awareness is an issue; however, managers need to embrace the idea that AI will transform business operations for the better.

Cyber threat actors are known to be investing in their AI capability and because of this, they will be able to implement APAs on the organization and its partner members. The Dark Web is a source of intelligence, but it is not recommended that staff access the Dark Web. Those who do access the Dark Web are thought to gain much in terms of cyber security management and strategic intelligence but there are risks involved.

Managers are aware that cyber intrusions vary in intent and an issue that is currently of concern is falsifying of data and malware that can delete computer files. Managers are aware that cyber security countermeasures require action to counteract acts of sabotage, theft and ransom but this is only part of the picture. The growing intensity of cyber-attacks means that industry–government–consumer cooperation is needed and society must play a more active role in cyber security provision than is the case currently. This is because acts of cybercrime are now being superseded by acts associated with cyber war and the level of complexity is causing increased concern to managers. This is because the technology in use enables a perpetrator to produce fake documents and deepfakes, and this is worrying managers because in the case of false documents, staff are not always able to distinguish between legitimate and illegitimate business transactions. As a result, much psychological discomfort is evident and increased uncertainty is likely to cause additional stress. The way to counteract the various methods of digital-enhanced manipulation is now high up on the agenda of senior managers. Such attacks are relentless and carried out with no concern for the victim or the consequences of such actions.

Question 1: What should the cyber security manager consider when planning to use AI to monitor continuously the organization's computer systems and networks?

Question 2: Is it possible for AI to monitor all the threats that an organization is confronted with?

Question 3: How will threat actors use AI to facilitate different forms of future cyber-attack? Such attacks may not be known at present.

References, websites and further reading

Albright, J. (2017). Welcome to the era of fake news. *Media and Communication*, 5 (2), pp. 87–89. https://doi.org/10.17645/mac.v5i2.977

Bonfanti, M.E. (2022). AI and the offense – defense balance. In: Cavelty, M.D., and Wenger, A. (eds.). *Cyber Security Politics: Socio-Political Transformations and Political Fragmentation*, pp. 64–79. London and New York: Taylor and Francis.

Boukherouaa, E.B., and Shabsig, G., with AlAjmi, K., Deodoro, J., Farias, A., Iskender, E.S., Mirestean, A.T., and Ravikumar, R. (2021). *Powering the Digital Economy Opportunities and Risks of Artificial Intelligence in Finance*. Washington, D.C.: International Monetary Fund. DP/2021/024 (August).

Bresniker, K., Gavrilovska, A., Holt, J., Milojicic, D., and Tran, T. (2019). Grand challenge: Applying artificial intelligence and machine learning to cybersecurity. *Computer*, 52, pp. 45–52. DOI: 10.1109/mc.2019.2942584

Carrapico, H., and Farrand, B. (2021). When trust fades, Facebook is no longer a friend: Shifting privatisation dynamics in the context of cybersecurity as a result of disinformation, populism and political uncertainty. *Journal of Common Market Studies*, 59 (5), pp. 1160–1176. https://doi.org/10.1111/jcms.13175

Chertoff, M. (2017) A public policy perspective of the Dark Web. *Journal of Cyber Policy*, 2 (1), pp. 26–38. DOI: 10.1080/23738871.2017.1298643

ENISA (2021). *Securing Machine Learning Algorithms*. Athens, Greece. DOI: 10.2824/874249

Gkinko, L., and Elbanna, A. (2023). Designing trust: The formation of employees' trust in conversational AI in the digital workplace. *Journal of Business Research*, 158, pp. 1–10. https://doi.org/10.1016/j.jbusres.2023.113707. (Accessed online 15th March, 2023).

Hossain, S.K.T., Yigitcanlar, T., Nguyen, K., and Xu, Y. (2024). Local government cybersecurity landscape: A systematic review and conceptual framework. *Applied Sciences*, 14, 5501, pp. 1–33. https://doi.org/10.3390/app14135501

Huang, M-H., and Rust, R.T. (2021). A strategic framework for artificial intelligence in marketing. *Journal of the Academy of Marketing Science*, 49, pp. 30–50. https://doi.org/10.1007/s11747-020-00749-9

Khan, H.U., Malik, H.Z., Nazir, S., and Khan, A.F. (2023). Utilizing bio metric system for enhancing cyber security in banking sector: A systematic analysis. *IEEE Access*, 11, pp. 80181–80198. DOI: 10.1109/ACCESS.2023.3298824

Kietzmann, J., Lee, L.W., McCarthy, I.P., and Kietzmann, T.C. (2020). Deepfakes: Trick or treat? *Business Horizons*, 63 (2), pp. 135–146. https://doi.org/10.1016/j.bushor.2019.11.006

Klein, D.O., and Wueller, J.R. (2017). Fake news: A legal perspective. *Journal of Internet Law*, 20 (10), pp. 5–13.

Kumar, A., and Rosenbach, E. (2019). *The truth about the Dark Web. Intended to protect dissidents, it has also cloaked illegal activity.* Finance and Development. International Monetary Fund. pp. 22–25. file:///C:/Users/HP%20User/Downloads/the-truth-about-the-dark-web-kumar.pdf (Accessed 13th June, 2024).

Martin, K.D., and Kracher, B. (2008). A conceptual framework for online business protest tactics and criteria for their effectiveness. *Business & Society*, 47 (3), pp. 291–311. https://doi.org/10.1177/0007650307299218

Murch, R.S., So, W.K., Buchholz, W.G., Raman, S., and Peccoud, J. (2018). Cyberbiosecurity: An emerging new discipline to help safeguard the bioeconomy. *Frontiers in Bioengineering and Biotechnology*, 6, pp. 1–6. DOI: 10.3389/fbioe.2018.00039

Mustak, M., Salminen, J., Mantym, M., Rahman, A., and Dwivedi, Y.K. (2023). Deepfakes: Deceptions, mitigations, and opportunities. *Journal of Business Research*, 154, pp. 1–15. https://doi.org/10.1016/j.jbusres.2022.113368

Ney, P., Koscher, K., Organick, L., Ceze, L., and Kohno, T. (2017). Computer security, privacy, and DNA sequencing: Compromising computers with synthesized DNA, privacy leaks, and more. *Proceedings of the 26th USENIX Security Symposium*, pp. 765–779. 16th to 18th August, Vancouver, BC, Canada.

Shabsigh, G., and Boukherouaa, E.B. (2023). *FINTECH Notes. Generative Artificial Intelligence in Finance: Risk Considerations.* Washington, D.C: International Monetary Fund. NOTE/2023/006 (August).

Tolosana, R., Vera-Rodriguez, R., Fierrez, J., Morales, A., and Ortega-Garcia, J. (2020). Deepfakes and beyond: A Survey of face manipulation and fake detection. *Information Fusion*, 64, pp. 131–148. https://doi.org/10.1016/j.inffus.2020.06.014

Trim, P. R.J., and Lee, Y-I. (2023). *Strategic Cyber Security Management.* Oxford: Routledge.

Walters, R. (2015). *Cyber Attacks on US Companies Since November 2014. Issue Brief.* The Heritage Foundation. No 4487 (18 November), pp. 1–6. http://report.heritage.org/ib4487

Wenger, A., and Cavelty, M.D. (2022). Conclusion: The ambiguity of cyber security politics in the context of multidimensional uncertainty. In: Cavelty, M.D., and Wenger, A. (eds.). *Cyber Security Politics: Socio-Political Transformations and Political Fragmentation*, pp. 239–266. London and New York: Taylor and Francis.

Websites

Ofcom. (n.d.). https://www.ofcom.org.uk/ (Accessed 8th May, 2024).

Online Safety Act. (2023). London: UK Government. https://www.legislation.gov.uk/ukpga/2023/50/enacted (Accessed 8th May, 2024).

Further reading

Aloqaily, M., Kanhere, S., Bellavista, P., and Nogueira, M. (2022). Special issue on cybersecurity management in the era of AI. *Journal of Network and Systems Management*, 30 (39), pp. 1–7. https://doi.org/10.1007/s10922-022-09659-3

5

SETTING THE SCENE FOR A CYBER SECURITY MANAGEMENT CONCEPTUAL MODEL AND FRAMEWORK

5.1 Introduction

Setting the scene (Section 5.2) is followed by organizational cyber security (Section 5.3) and then embracing the modelling approach (Section 5.4). Next, cyber security culture (Section 5.5) is given attention and is followed by cyber security situational awareness (Section 5.6) and organizational learning and cyber security awareness (Section 5.7). Recent cyber-attacks (Section 5.8) precede reflection and questions (Section 5.9) and last, a conclusion (Section 5.10) is provided.

5.2 Setting the Scene

There is no doubt that increased digitalization and smart ways of living will add to the quality of life but at the same time, there are vulnerabilities that need to be taken into account. The vulnerabilities are not just specific to an organization, a product or service or a network but they involve communities of people living in a specific geographical location that are dependent upon a range of services. Mathur (2019, p. 201) places this in context by suggesting that

> "cyber-infractions are becoming a global marketing concern as they not only influence U.S. economy and security but also affect consumer confidence. Thus, there is a strong need for academicians to determine how marketers can alleviate customer cybersecurity fears to successfully manage brands".

Using social network theory and dynamic capabilities theory, Mathur (2019, p. 201) establishes how media marketing capability can be used to provide insights into strategic management and marketing and thus provide marketers with a better appreciation of risk so that the organization can deploy risk mitigation strategies to better protect the company's brands and safeguard against a data breach occurring and that results in reputational damage. Although it was found that a retailer's reputation does have an

DOI: 10.4324/9781003570905-5

effect on a consumer in terms of their risk perception and how they view a particular retailer, what is important to note is that companies are likely to increase their online marketing activities. This means that in the years ahead consumers will need to get used to buying online, providing their personal data to companies and also changing their lifestyle so that they can receive delivered goods or make preparations for the safe acceptance of such goods.

At present, attention is being given to various forms of delivery such as traditional delivery modes (e.g., by air, road, rail and sea) and non-traditional modes (e.g., by drone) and this calls into question the quality of the supporting infrastructure and what is permissible by law. It also requires managers to think of the supply chain and which components are susceptible to a cyber-attack as guarding transportation networks can prove costly. Transportation is associated with critical national infrastructure and critical information infrastructure, and deliveries made by drone are common. A man-in-the-middle attack can see the operator of a drone lose control of it to someone who has intercepted the link and diverted the drone to another location. Such action can be interpreted from the perspective of an individual intent on stealing for their own advantage. For example, a thief who follows a courier and steals the package that is left unattended on the intended recipient's doorstep can be defined as similar in character to someone who intercepts a device (e.g., drone) and takes control of it with the intention of becoming the owner of it or more likely, the beneficiary of its resale. The point being made is that the concept of criminal intent is similar; however, it is just the environment and possibly the method of attack that are different. Knowing this can place the cyber security manager on guard because it has to be expected that at some point in time, an attack will be launched on the organization. The fact that those carrying out cyber-attacks are prepared to share information with fellow hackers via websites on the Dark Web is a testimony to this.

There are various approaches to developing cyber security management and strategic intelligence initiatives and a useful approach is to draw on the work of Bloom and Chatterji (2009), which requires that we think of how organizational capabilities are matched with situational contingencies in order to establish the scale of social impact. By linking such an approach with cyber security provision and a collectivist and community-driven approach, it should be possible to extend the threat model view into a community-oriented view. The logic of this approach is that it is possible to take what is essentially an initiative to enhance organizational performance and carry it over into society by suggesting that the main outcome will resonate with and permeate through society. This can be achieved by using the approach outlined by Nardini et al. (2022, p. 256), which makes clear how a T-shaped scaling framework can be used to integrate insights from the extant literature and collect data. There are a number of scaling frameworks available (Bloom and Smith, 2010); however, managers in various business functions that have a knowledge of cyber security and are indeed responsible for integrating aspects of cyber security into their day-to-day operations will be expected to contribute more fully to cyber security management, especially from the perspective of alliance building (e.g., interpreted as a partnership arrangement). Indeed, the approach used by Westley et al. (2014, p. 237) referred to as "scaling out" (e.g., wide geographical coverage) and "scaling up" (e.g., the institutional roots of the problem) can be considered useful as regards this.

The logic of such an approach is that it allows the cyber security manager, the risk manager and the IT manager to work closely with the head of security and various strategists who are charged with devising a strategic approach to cyber security problem-solving. Second, the approach used, because it is underwritten by policies and programmes and specific guidance is followed (e.g., manuals detail what is to be done and which person to report to), makes known how senior intelligence officers based in the private sector can work with their counterparts in the public sector and can engage with external researchers (e.g., government agencies involved in applied research or university research groups) and develop and test stakeholder scenarios that result in cyber security policy. Although this approach appears rather in-depth, the point being emphasized is that the security–intelligence interface works best when it is fused into a collectivist cyber threat intelligence policy and strategy. The argument being that if an integrated organizational cyber security strategy is developed, then it makes staff throughout the organization's supply chain more aware of the need for continual security and the upgrading of security and how a security culture is to be established with partner organizations and how such a culture is to be maintained. The key point to note is that a strengthened cooperative arrangement between senior managers will lead to a more effective dialogue with law enforcement personnel (e.g., government agency representatives) and more responsive policy changes that become enforced by law.

5.3 Organizational Cyber Security

Downsizing has, over the years, resulted in flat organizational structures and an emphasis on employees utilizing facilitating technology, often in collaboration with staff in partner organizations (e.g., co-designed software packages, e-procurement tools and customer databases), without adequate support from in-house IT staff/security staff. This raises an important question: How can senior managers engage safely and securely with technology in order to share information with their colleagues and individuals in partner organizations, knowing that the networks in place operate 24 hours a day and traverse different time zones? Placing emphasis on eradicating organizational vulnerabilities through cyber security awareness and threat detection is admirable; however, cyber security awareness needs to contribute also to the development and maintenance of a security culture that guards against an employee making an error of judgment in relation to a phishing email or scammer telephone call that attempts to seek access to a password that allows a threat actor to take control of the organization's computer(s) and hold the organization to ransom.

What is worrying senior managers is that those responsible for cyber-crime use more than one approach to achieve their goal, and an organization's vulnerable employee(s) (e.g., somebody with a gambling addiction that needs money) or a subcontractor that is known to cut costs by using cloned/counterfeit software may present the biggest risk in terms of being the weakest link through which an attack can be made. In some cases, matters are made more complicated by the actions of employees who are not as security conscious as they should be and this creates an opportunity for those involved in social engineering attacks to have more attack options available to them. Davis (2007, p. 181) is aware of the issues and challenges and is of the view that social engineering can be defined in terms of "an enemy who manipulates or uses psychological tricks to gain the confidence of an authorized network employee relying on the natural human tendency to trust and help others". Davis (2007, p. 181) is aware that there may be internal, disgruntled enemies within the organization that constitute a risk, but an external enemy is likely to deploy social engineering to gain private information from internal staff that can then be used against the organization. Knowing this requires the cyber security manager to think of how best to monitor internal staff without offending them and at the same time gain their confidence so they cooperate and report incidents that suggest the organization may be at risk. If an organization is experiencing a high turnover of staff or is reliant on short-term employees, then it may be that an external threat actor knows this and is waiting to exploit an emerging vulnerability.

Woodruff (Morgan et al., 1998, p. 354) has made reference to the fact that organizational learning is an important contributor to customer value, which can be achieved through a commitment to providing a high-level customer service that is enhanced through adequate attention to security and the protection of customer data. However, organizational learning can also be used to underpin staff's commitment to security as training and staff development programmes can be used to guide employees into how to be compliant. Such programmes can be focused on changing an individual's behaviour and updating them vis-à-vis organizational policy. This it can be argued is to be viewed from the perspective of organizational sustainability and the fact that should an organization be subjected to an intense and debilitating cyber-attack, it is quite possible that reputational damage will result and require an investigation into how governance and compliance are managed.

5.4 Embracing the Modelling Approach

Referring to the strategic marketing approach, mathematical frameworks such as the one produced by Rust and Zahorik (1993) can help marketers quantify matters and are useful in the sense that they allow marketing managers to assess the value of customer satisfaction and link back to how an organization achieves its objectives and how employees are rewarded for their efforts. The mathematical framework outlined by Rust and Zahorik (1993) allows senior marketing managers to think in terms of developing a marketing strategy bearing in mind customer satisfaction and customer retention. It also focuses attention, through time, on market share and profitability and places customer satisfaction within a strategic context. This is useful because as Schweidel et al. (2008, p. 93) have noted, formal modelling frameworks allow managers to evaluate the effectiveness of marketing activity. They can also be used for abstract thinking and, in a collectivist organizational culture, where peer group decision-making takes centre stage, can provide a holistic appreciation of business-to-business and business-to-consumer relationship building, how intra-organizational and inter-organizational networks shape the organization's business model and how emergent strategies are likely to develop. So, organizational learning can be interpreted from the perspective of how networks evolve and develop and how an organization's business model should be reconfigured. Accepting that business models change through time, managers can view the change process as adaptive and gradual or transformational and rapid (Dolan et al., 2006, p. 63), depending on the organization's internal situation and the forces at work in the environment in which the organization competes. What should be noted is that building cooperative relationships takes time and is dependent upon the chemistry of the people involved. This highlights the need for senior managers to ensure that the organization's value system is malleable and able to absorb change. In addition, relationships are moulded through time and follow a certain process "beginning with small exchanges and moving to higher levels of exchange as partners fulfil their obligations" (Kranton, 1996, p. 216). Hence, an organization's security culture needs to be developed through time and viewed as contributing to the integration of security intelligence activities (Trim and Lee, 2023).

Lawrence et al. (2005) suggest that those involved in organizational learning need to consider the political dynamics within the organization and Ouchi (Rousseau et al., 1998, p. 396) suggests that trust is "the result of deep dependence and identity formation". Hence, trust-based relationships are considered vital with respect to building cooperative relations among partner organizations and marketers need to take into account emotional commitment (Hennig-Thurau, 2004, pp. 465–466), which is necessary for motivation and collective efficacy (Wilderom, 1991, p. 13). Should managers be responsive in the ways outlined, they will be able to devise a collectivist enterprise risk management cyber threat model that is reinforced through strategic intelligence that is further enhanced through university and government collaboration and the utilization of AI technology.

Trim and Lee (2021, p. 5) have looked at how cyber security threats have been researched and how solutions have been applied and are of the view that:

"Various types of cyber security models have been developed over the years and it is interesting to note that they have covered a number of fields of enquiry and various industries, and have been of a quantitative or conceptual nature".

Trim and Lee (2021, p. 5) advocate that the modelling of phenomena is well worthwhile because managers gain insights and in-depth knowledge into various security issues and can develop the knowledge needed to better understand how the computer networks and information systems in place should be managed. They also argue that the modelling approach can be viewed as holistic in orientation and can be linked with a social science-oriented approach that enables managers to better understand how people interact at work. This view can be extended to include interactive relationships with supply chain members and marketing channel members and can be linked back to the organization's value system. In other words, if senior management does not provide appropriate leadership in the way of governance, then staff are unlikely to be compliant. If this is the case, then the risk of a data breach is possibly higher than it should be and action needs to be taken to ensure that staff are sufficiently cyber security aware.

Trim and Lee (2021) are firm in their belief that organizations need to develop a cyber security culture as this will provide a foundation for translating cyber security knowledge into an appropriate cyber security model. However, managers may need convincing. Hence, the following question can be posed: How useful are cyber security models and frameworks? Trim and Lee (2021, p. 13) maintain that models can be used to ensure that managers develop a comprehensive understanding of what cyber security involves and what role cyber security specialists play. They underpin this view by saying that managers need to draw on intra-organizational and inter-organizational support in order to reduce risk. This line of argument seems logical because the nature of cyber-attacks suggests that a comprehensive cyber-attack defence system needs to be established that links the organization's cyber security objectives with government objectives. This implies that the cyber security manager needs to think of liaising with government representatives when necessary and provide support and assistance to government cyber security initiatives when required.

Being involved in enterprise risk management and contributing to cyber security policy, which is integrated into the operating procedures of various business functions, the cyber security manager can utilize their analytical skills and help form an over-arching cyber security strategy and framework that takes into account various types of risks. The advantage of such an approach is that risk assessment can be placed within a stakeholder approach to security. By placing such a framework and policy within a strategic management intelligence context, a collectivist enterprise risk management cyber threat model can be implemented across business functions, which has at its heart a risk manager.

By taking into account how organizational interdependencies give rise to vulnerabilities, managers can reconfigure the organization's business model so that the network of alliances remains robust against an attack. Vulnerabilities sometimes occur because government action stimulates market forces (Wind and Thomas, 2010) (e.g., through deregulation), which results in a set of conditions that were not previously considered. Consequently, new areas of attack open up as imposters (nonlegal entities) enter the market and remain undetected for some time (e.g., operate through websites that appear legitimate). The interdependency associated with the transfer of data, from organization to organization, is seldom viewed from the perspective of an organization's vulnerability but mostly from the stance of the actions relating to product strategy; defining unmet needs (e.g., predicting and meeting customer wants) and enhancing the quality of life of the consumer. In other words, it is a market-driven approach to business that is based on achieving a return on the assets deployed. Senior managers take calculated risks and aim to maximize profits and provide shareholders with an adequate return on their investment, which guarantees they will maintain their position within the organization. However, the cyber security management approach goes beyond immediate customer–company relations. There are internal customers within the organization's own network and also there are differing international standards to embrace that underpin day-to-day business decision-making and the complexity involved differs depending upon the type of business relationship(s) in being.

5.5 Cyber Security Culture

One of the key issues to be addressed when establishing a security culture within an organization is the communication of risk and how managers share information relating to the actions of those carrying out various forms of cyber-attack in real time. It is clear from both government and industry reports that managers need to put more time and effort into cyber security awareness and devise and implement a cyber threat intelligence strategy that counteracts the actions of those carrying out cyber-attacks because the scale of the problem is increasing. For example, cyber-attacks on US companies alone were considered to have resulted in losses in excess of US$1 trillion by late 2020 (Abraham and Sims, 2021, p. 2), and this is a reminder that urgent action is needed. This level of destruction (Shultz et al., 2005, p. 16), which is normally borne at the company level, by shareholders and, in some cases central government, and ultimately the taxpayer is not sustainable in the long run as it will increase the cost of business operations and in turn will militate against the well-being of society as organizations reduce their staff numbers and communities become impoverished due to high levels of unemployment. It is this underlying logic that is the fuel for a collectivist approach to cyber security. But is more evidence required?

The cyber-attack on the UK's Northern Lincolnshire and Goole NHS Foundation Trust in October 2016 and also the May 2017 WannaCry ransomware cyber-attack on the UK's NHS (National Audit Office, 2017, pp. 4–5) highlighted certain public sector cyber security deficiencies and resulted in a renewed call for further government and industry cooperation. Because large amounts of data are generated in the health sector through the use of service interactions involving digital channels (Brennan et al., 2021, p. 6), managers in the health sector need to remain vigilant in terms of the actions of those intent on causing maximum disruption/damage to the economy by exploiting cyber vulnerabilities.

More recently, the cyber-attack on the British Library on 28 October 2023, which witnessed the senior management refusing to pay a ransom of just over £500,000, had consequences in terms of the services provided by the institution in both 2023 and 2024. Indeed, the British Library (2024, p. 2) Cyber Incident Review reported there was hostile reconnaissance prior to the major ransomware attack, which lasted a few days. The British Library (2024, p. 2) "Learning Lessons from the Cyber-attack" report stated:

"Although the attackers encrypted or destroyed much of our server estate during the course of the attack, we have identified a server we consider likely to have been the point of entry and explore why our security measures were not sufficient…".

The British Library (2024, p. 2) staff had up to the period in question undertaken routine security assessments that included penetration tests. Although this can be considered appropriate, it is evident from the British Library (2024, p. 2) report that the criminal gang that was responsible for the attack copied and illegally removed in the order of 600 GB of files. The files included personal data belonging to users and staff. Those behind the attack, when they realized a ransom would not be paid, went ahead and placed the personal data up for sale by auction on the Dark Web. The British Library staff informed those affected that this was the case and offered advice and support where necessary.

As well as exfiltrating data and demanding a ransom, the perpetrators encrypted the library's data and systems and also destroyed some of the servers to make recovery less possible and, at the same time, cover their tracks (British Library, 2024, p. 2). The attackers hit the library where it was most vulnerable, which was the metadata that describes the items in the library collection. The time period needed to rebuild the infrastructure affected was spread over a number of months and this meant that certain library services were suspended for some time. There is no doubt that the cyber-attack on the British Library caused much disruption, and some bystanders would pose the question of why was the library the target of a ransomware attack. There are a number of possible answers that have to do with the budget the library receives and the fact that it can be considered a national asset and any disruption caused would have a knock-on effect in terms of the research community, in particular. Possibly, those behind the attack considered that the library was an easy target or possibly they were merely testing their attack capability.

Possibly, the library was deemed a target because it was well known to the public and an attack on the library that made it non-operational would result in word-of-mouth and cause fear among people. When people feel afraid, they consider how vulnerable they are. For example, people may start to think of the school where their children are educated or the hospital where they seek help in the case of an emergency being a possible future target and this may cause more concern.

The effectiveness of this cyber-attack and the response from the senior management team at the British Library brings to the fore the type of security culture that is in existence at the institution. Senior management at the British Library (2024, p. 12) implemented a Respond, Adapt and Renew policy. The Respond phase involved immediate crisis management; the Adapt phase was planned for a six-month period, the objective being to identify and implement interim solutions that would restore services, internal processes and partnerships and the final Renew phase was planned for 18 months and the objective was to "create a new resilient infrastructure and deliver permanent solutions, either by upgrading or adapting existing systems or delivering new ones where necessary" (British Library, 2024, p. 12).

The British Library's (2024, p. 15) renewed infrastructure will ensure that a best practice approach is in covering network design and proper segmentation; a commitment to cloud for development, application and virtualization; a best practice role-based-access control setup that relates to domain and storage services; a robust and resilient backup service that covers the collection of items; a holistic and integrated security approach covering the whole organization that is security focused (e.g., improved incident response, detection and remediation); much improved multifactor authentication (MFA) on-premises capabilities and third-party network access via Privileged Access Management (PAM). In addition, the British Library (2024, p. 15) is committed to improving cyber incident event reporting and enhancing vulnerability management; ensuring that the policies, processes and standard operating procedures to govern and manage the IT lifecycle are clearly defined, embedding security in the IT lifecycle; adhering to compliance policy that is governed by standards and frameworks and having firmer governance structures in place that are aimed at delivering security-enabled applications that are needed on an ongoing basis.

Institutions are prone to cyber-attacks and various UK universities have been targeted. The universities of Cambridge, Manchester and Wolverhampton were targeted by the Anonymous Suda hacker group and suffered disruption of services. It is thought that the attacks were politically motivated. The INC Ransomware is known to have carried out an attack on Cambridge University Press & Assessment (CUPA) that affected their email system and other UK universities have been attacked including the universities of Hertfordshire, Newcastle, Northampton and Portsmouth. The ransomware was thought to be the motive. Furthermore, attacks on institutions of higher education have involved phishing attacks, the use of malware, ransomware and DDoS. Universities outside the UK have also been attacked and some are thought to have paid ransoms in the order of a couple of hundred thousand dollars. There are various reasons as to why a university is attacked and these include: The leadership model in place; the known resources of the institution and the personal data of students that can be exploited.

In order to promote cyber security best practices, senior managers need to establish a security culture that is underpinned by an intelligence-oriented organizational value system, which ensures that a strategic cyber intelligence focus is evident. Trim (2004, 2005) and Trim and Lee (2010) are of the view that senior managers need to devise and implement an effective cyber security strategy that is grounded within the strategic marketing school of thought (Aaker, 1992); if that is, the organization is to effectively deal with the myriad of cyber-attacks and, at the same time, harden the organization, making it resilient and able to withstand a coordinated and prolonged cyber-attack. The emphasis on marketers working in tandem with the cyber security manager and the risk manager shows that playing a central role is determined by the fact that staff have the knowledge and skills to collect, analyse and interpret data that is market oriented but also underpinned by a wider set of conditions that mean a wider view of situational awareness can be drawn on to help senior management devise an integrated organizational cyber security strategy that is integrated into the business model of partner organizations. Integration can only be effective provided that the enterprise risk management cyber threat model in place is co-owned and co-managed and is updated through time.

Building and maintaining trust-based relationships with external partners (in both business and government) is key to achieving long-term, sustainable working relationships and maintaining credibility within the industry and with various publics. The development of internal trust (brought about and reinforced through leadership and teamwork) needs to be viewed alongside the development of external trust, which sustains relationships with supplier organizations, joint venture partners and customers (Huff and Kelley, 2005, p. 97). Han et al. (2008) suggest that relationship building is in fact associated with structural bonding, which comes about through the exercise of trust. Drawing on their research findings, Suh and Kwon (2006, pp. 198–199) state:

> "It is safe to say that the success of [the] supply chain rests on the degree of trust that the supply chain partners believe is in the partnership. Many supply chain tools presuppose that each partner behaves in a manner consistent with expectation based on trust".

Suh and Kwon (2006, p. 199) further elaborate by mentioning collaborative planning, forecasting and replenishment (CPFR) and make reference to the sharing of information, which brings out the need for trust-based working relationships to be formed and maintained through time.

5.6 Cyber Security Situational Awareness

Situational awareness and analysis are a formal process that involves both qualitative and quantitative analyses of an organization's environment. Of key interest are risk in relation to vulnerability and impact in relation to sustainability. As regards cyber security situational analysis, it is important that the cyber security manager works within a routine to establish best practices because interconnectivity means that it is not realistic to analyse the organization in isolation. Indeed, it is essential that supply chain partners are brought into the equation because an impact will have a knock-on effect within the industry. Researchers at Carnegie Mellon University (2016, p. 4) have provided a useful introduction to what situational awareness involves and indicate that it provides an organization with "an understanding of its critical service's operating environment and the environment's impact on the operation of the critical service". This is important because stakeholders need to have an accurate and up-to-date understanding of the organization's projected future state of a critical service provision (Carnegie Mellon University, 2016, p. 4). Bearing this in mind, the cyber security manager will need to familiarize themselves with the operating environment and know how the assets and other services are affected and in turn affect other high-value physical and cyber processes (Carnegie Mellon University, 2016, p. 4). This is achieved through staff undertaking situational awareness that unearths a common operating picture relating to the actions needed to prevent the disruption of a critical service or the restoration of a service should an incident occur (Carnegie Mellon University, 2016, p. 4).

Underpinning the approach is a clear commitment to risk management (Carnegie Mellon University, 2016, p. 5): "Risk management is the foundation for eliciting situational awareness requirements and the lens through which situational awareness information is interpreted and communicated". This said, it can be suggested that risk management involves a number of processes and is encompassed within the situational awareness process as the objective is to provide information relating to the management of an asset(s) (Carnegie Mellon University, 2016, p. 5). By highlighting the vulnerabilities evident, it should be possible to identify potential risks and ensure that the critical service performs as expected (Carnegie Mellon University, 2016, p. 5) as the vulnerabilities identified are rectified. There is a clear link here with business continuity planning and the fact that the cyber security manager and their colleagues need to ensure that the organization is resilient means that it is able to withstand the cyber-attacks it encounters.

From the above, it is clear that risk management is linked with resilience, and simulation exercises prove helpful in terms of allowing staff to learn from past events and gauge the projected future state of a critical service (Carnegie Mellon University, 2016, p. 15). Learning from real-world case examples will help cyber security managers and their colleagues to devise contingency plans that can be implemented when an impact momentarily prevents an organization from functioning normally. The main point to note is that if an incident does occur, then the disruption caused is minimized and the organization is able to recommence trading as soon as possible.

On reflection, situational awareness and analysis represents a complex and necessary activity that feeds into the organization's strategic intelligence operation. For example, those who undertake situational awareness need to collect, analyse and communicate their findings to their peers and include a broad range of aspects in their analysis such as economic, social, political and geographic events so that the assessment made is thorough (Carnegie Mellon University, 2016, p. 36) and senior management are not caught out by a surprise event.

Cyber-attacks on supply chain members are common practice and to prevent such attacks from causing damage, managers need to develop and contribute to cyber security situational awareness and advise senior managers in terms of the different types of cyber-attacks that hackers deploy (Esteves et al., 2017). They also need to make the types of attack known to employees through various internal marketing vehicles (e.g., inter-company conferences, training seminars, workshops and various newsletters and company gatherings/functions). This is important because staff are not always up-to-date or able to update their knowledge and skill base in order to identify a spurious email phishing attack as some URLs and logos look genuine. The reason why this is considered important is because (i) the organization's internal security may be dysfunctional and uncoordinated (e.g., the latest software security is not comprehensive/deployed); (ii) external advice and support may not be available during an attack and (iii) government policy may not be as effective as it should be in guarding against certain types of attack on critical national infrastructure. As regards current, ransomware attacks, it can be noted that even if a ransom is paid it does not guarantee that the organization will be given access to its data, computers and networks because advanced ransomware software is designed to automatically delete files. To guard against a vulnerability being exploited, senior managers need to have in place an appropriate, collectivist enterprise risk manage-ment cyber threat model that ensures that all identified cyber threats are placed in a risk register so that relevant stakeholders are aware of the current issues and challenges being confronted with and how staff in the organization prioritize the separate risks. It also needs to be made clear as to how the identified potential threat(s) will be eradicated. Again, this focuses on cyber security awareness and the research undertaken in this area has done much to focus the minds of marketers (Trim and Lee, 2019) but it is only part of the strategic marketing approach to the problem. The emphasis has to be on linking more firmly marketing operations with finance (e.g., payment systems) and technology (e.g., networks and websites) and ensuring that each aspect of the organization's business operations is secure.

Various conceptual models have been developed over time that can be used in conjunc-tion with other models and frameworks to provide senior managers with insights into how to devise information-sharing policies with cooperative partner organizations. By drawing on various types of intelligence, appropriate intelligence systems can be devised that incorporate marketing decisions (Jagetia and Patel, 1981, p. 101), which can prove helpful in terms of countering espionage (Pearce, 1971, p. 23). To fully appreciate how staff in partner organizations can produce a collectivist enterprise risk management cyber threat model, it is necessary to look at how organizational learning is utilized to share information at various levels in a partnership arrangement.

5.7 Organizational Learning and Cyber Security Awareness

Organizational learning is known to contribute to cyber security awareness through a strategic cyber security management strategy by ensuring that the development and utili-zation of knowledge occur through the process of transformational leadership (Trim and Lee, 2023, p. 73). Understanding how employees absorb information and knowledge while undertaking intelligence and planning activities allows senior managers to devise and implement appropriate cyber security awareness training programmes that increase an employee's strategic intelligence skill base and at the same time establish a collectivist security culture. The emphasis is to ensure that risk assessment and risk analysis are viewed as a shared responsibility and manifest in an inter-company integrated cyber secu-rity strategy. For this to be the case, managers are required to become better acquainted with other fields of learning such as psychology because of the growing influence of the Internet and what is known as cyberpsychology (Barak and Suler, 2008, pp. 7–8). Within the broad context of cyberpsychology, managers need to familiarize themselves with new forms of buyer behaviour and the different forms of deception (illegal acts) that are deployed by those out to gain an advantage through illegal means such as implementing online scams, hijacking a company's website and impersonating a company employee to steal sensitive data.

Pearce (1976) has emphasized that control, as well as policy and strategy, is a key factor as regards intelligence work and, with respect to organizational intelligence systems, Brockhoff (1991, p. 93) suggests that an organization's information system may not be as comprehensive as required and because of this managers need to be more involved in the risk management process than they are and think in terms of developing a model(s) for intelligence gathering (Zinkhan and Gelb, 1985). However, managers need to reflect on the fact that mathematical models, although they can replicate relationships involving variables, and involve complex reasoning, may be beyond what the model can do (Mentzer and Gandhi, 1993, p. 112). This highlights the need for managers to draw on information held by partner organizations and to consider how to use AI to better effect. The sharing of confidential and sensitive data and information is perceived as beneficial to partner organizations and places emphasis on managers developing and maintaining trust-based relationships with business and knowledge providers across industry sectors. AI is, it can be argued, a game changer and it is likely that new threat detection systems will emerge in future years.

Being aware of the skills required for staff to undertake a range of cyber security duties is an important attribute and one that the cyber security manager needs to take cognizance of. It is at this point that reference needs to be made to the role played by the training manager and how training support can help staff gain the skills they need to take on and outthink those intent on causing the organization harm. As well as having technical knowledge, it is important to realize that staff also need to be able to think strategically and this means helping to set or provide support for the formation of strategic objectives that help them to achieve the organization's cyber security objectives (Trim and Lee, 2023, p. 191). The learning organization concept is well established and can help senior managers devise and implement policies and strategies that are aimed at integrating the structures and mechanisms existing in partner organizations into a strategic organizational configuration. Combining cyber security training programmes with cyber security staff development programmes is logical because it can help raise cyber security awareness, establish a cyber security culture within the organization's security culture and raise the cyber security skill base of employees thus helping to close cyber security knowledge gaps.

As well as preparing staff to be able to identify and deal with external threats, it is necessary for the cyber security manager and the training manager to think of how the insider threat may emerge or be played out. The potential threat from insiders sometimes goes undetected and because of this, the damage caused can be extensive. Often, an insider plans meticulously on how to cover their tracks and disguise their actions and are well able to abide by their time. Working sometimes with a criminal syndicate, they find ways to exploit an organization's main vulnerability and have no emotion in terms of the effect an impact will have on the people they work with and are close to. Monitoring employee behaviour is sensitive, however, and often viewed from a trust-building perspective. However, staff can be monitored in ways that do not raise ethical concerns. For example, if a member of staff is continually accessing databases that they do not have security clearance to access, then questions relating to the organization's level of security can be raised but also questions should be asked in terms of why a particular member of staff wants to access the type of information they are seeking if it is not within their day-to-day operations. So, an insider's ability to deceive or engage in deceptive behaviour is something that human resource management personnel need to be aware of. But it goes deeper than this. Knowing how an employee relates to other employees is important from several perspectives. These include how they monitor the threat environment and make their findings known to their colleagues, how much help they are prepared to provide to their colleagues and what they expect to receive from colleagues in return for providing up-to-date information. Some individuals are prepared to be benevolent and provide information on the understanding that they believe it is beneficial to the organization. Those who are more self-centred and hedonic may well have a different attitude and be motivated by different personal objectives. What needs to be noted is that those members of staff who are out to exploit information for their own advantage may also be prepared to behave in a deceptive manner.

Senge (1999, p. 14) provides useful insights into what a learning organization is by explaining that a learning organization is an organization "that is continually expanding its capacity to create its future". To achieve this, senior management must ensure that there is an appropriate culture in place so that employees gain "the knowledge and skill they need in order to undertake their duties in a systematic and logical manner, and thus improve the organization's way of doing business" (Trim and Upton, 2013, p. 172).

It is useful to consider why the cyber security manager should be directly involved in and committed to helping to establish a learning organization culture. Some critics suggest that the cyber security manager is more concerned with the technicalities of cyber security and that organizational learning is the priority of the training manager and staff in the human resource management function. Really, organizational learning is concerned with the development of knowledge and the cyber security manager is very much concerned with how knowledge in the way of finding solutions to new cyber security problems can be translated into effective organizational policy.

Trim and Lee (2007, pp. 335–336) add to this by suggesting that senior managers need to understand that the concept of organizational learning, if managed in an incremental and proactive manner, will bring about organizational change in the way expected. Change can be achieved by institutionalizing the learning process and, in addition, empowering people to both take and seek responsibility. Trim and Lee (2023, p. 198) are clear about the benefits of organizational learning and the fact that employees need to take responsibility for their personal development because to do so is proactive and can be associated with cyber security knowledge development.

As regards critical infrastructure, the Four-Pillar Model of Critical Information Infrastructure Protection advocated by Suter (2007, pp. 1–4) is considered relevant as it takes into account: (a) Prevention and early warning; (b) detection; (c) reaction and (d) crisis management. Whether the cyber threat is defined in terms of the organization, the organizational partnership in which the organization functions, critical infrastructure or a combination of all three, the cyber security manager will be required to have a strategic intelligence perspective and threat identification and threat solution are paramount. Reflecting on this, it can be suggested that the cyber security manager needs to leverage their cyber security management knowledge and undertake a strategic intelligence analysis of the cyber threat environment that is aimed at identifying current and future threat actors and their associations. Aaker and McLoughlin (2010, p. 93) provide guidance regarding how a manager needs to think in terms of strategy formulation and suggest that attention needs to be given to: (i) What a strategic uncertainty is related to and how it impacts the business and (ii) the immediacy of a strategic uncertainty and what it is related to.

Ahmad et al. (2020, p. 948) acknowledge the role that organizational learning plays and state that

"Organizations that continuously evaluate the quality and utility of intelligence about the threat environment improve their overall organizational security strategy, processes, and tactics. In doing so, organizations develop a comprehensive knowledge base of profiles on attackers and associated attack scenarios".

Ahmad et al. (2020, p. 948) continue this line of argument by suggesting that developing a knowledge base is key with regard to the transformation of security strategy, which involves a number of factors including security technologies and training protocols, policies and procedures.

Scenario analysis is considered useful in terms of developing an understanding of the motives behind cyber-attacks and what needs to be done in order to limit the damage inflicted on the organization should the attack prove successful. By holding regular scenario training exercises, an employee's knowledge base can be built up over time and they can develop the confidence to assume higher levels of responsibility. The key point to note is that scenario exercises test an individual's knowledge of a subject and get them to think through the consequences of their actions. In some instances, a manager may need to take a calculated risk and authorize a certain action knowing that it will have consequences of some kind.

5.8 Recent Cyber Attacks

Knowing how to prepare for a cyber-attack and actually responding to a cyber-attack is important. The response, in real-time, needs to be effective. The BBC reported on 3 April 2024 (Ashe, 2024) that Leicester City Council was the target of a ransomware attack on 7 March 2024 and as a result its telephone and computer systems were affected. Those behind the ransomware incident shared about 25 documents online that contained confidential information relating to people's rent statements, aspects of council housing and information relating to passports, for example, but later on, the attacker released a larger batch of documents. On 1 June 2024, it was reported by the BBC (Adams, 2024) that a school in Essex had encountered a ransomware attack that compromised its IT system and that the lessons of some school children had been affected. On 1 June 2024, the *Independent* (Wise, 2024) reported that previously employed staff working for the Santander Bank as well as the bank's customers in Spain, Chile and Uruguay had had their personal data stolen and that the information was available for purchase on the Dark Web.

On 4 June 2024, the BBC (2024) reported that a cyber-attack on a number of hospitals in London, which included King's College Hospital, Guy's and St Thomas', the Royal Brompton Hospital and the Evelina London Children's Hospital, resulted in the suspension of primary care services and, as a consequence, operations had to be cancelled and those in need of emergency services had been sent to other hospitals for treatment. The target of the attack was a company called Synnovis, which was a provider of pathology services. Blood transfusions were hit and so too were the availability of test results. It was also reported that the cyber-attack, which meant that hospital staff could not connect to the main server, had also affected general practitioner (GP) services across parts of the area including Bexley, Greenwich, Lewisham, Bromley, Southwark and Lambeth. A ransomware cyber-attack was cited as the cause of the problem.

It is useful at this juncture to establish which type of cyber-attack is most commonly occurring. The threat report produced by ENISA (2023, p. 4) pays attention to this and DDoS and ransomware attacks are at the top of the list followed by social engineering attacks, data-related threats, information manipulation and malware. It is also evident that threat actors are placing emphasis on professionalizing their as-a-service programmes, are using unique methods to infiltrate environments and are also putting pressure on their victims via extortion methods (ENISA, 2023, p. 4). ENISA (2023, p. 4) also makes it known that public administration is being increasingly targeted and so are individuals and the following sectors – health, digital infrastructure and manufacturing, finance and transport. It is also apparent that state-nexus groups remain committed to remaining undetected and are trojanising known software packages; cyber criminals are increasingly targeting cloud infrastructures; geopolitical motivations and increased extortion operations do include ransomware attacks but are also linked with other types of attacks and social engineering attacks have increased enormously with AI emerging but phishing attacks are still prominent (ENISA, 2023, p. 4).

ENISA (2023, pp. 20–21) has identified four categories of cybersecurity threat actors: They are *state-nexus threat groups*; *cybercriminals*; *hackers-for-hire* and *hacktivists*. ENISA (2023, pp. 20–21) has described each group as follows: *State-nexus threat groups* are associated with what is known as APTs and are generally well funded. Associated mainly with espionage, they target both states and organizations. *Cyber criminals* are motivated by financial gain and are opportunistic and indiscriminate in their approach. They often use social engineering and other attack methods and are increasingly seeking ways to collaborate with other criminals. *Hackers-for-hire* actors are known to provide services to state-nexus groups and are known to engage in Ransomware-as-a-Service (RaaS), for example. *Hacktivists* have a different set of objectives and are motivated to disrupt through hacking activities to highlight political or social change. It is suggested that *Hacktivist groups* can be influenced by state-nexus groups vis-à-vis information manipulation and interference (e.g., intrusion campaigns).

5.9 Reflection and Questions

In order to devise a cyber security management conceptual model and framework, the senior management needs to utilize organizational learning to help establish a cyber security culture that underpins cyber security awareness. The modelling approach, whether conceptual in orientation or mathematically derived, can be used to establish a model and/or framework within which cyber security situational awareness occurs. Because the organization's cyber security policy is to some degree influenced by staff in partner organizations, it can be suggested that an analytical approach needs to be taken that firmly incorporates cause and effect. In other words, the cyber security model and framework

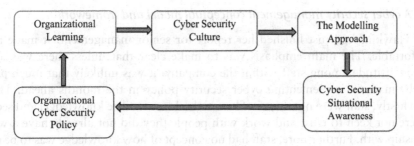

FIGURE 5.1 Cyber security model and framework process.

process is formally defined, is based on and incorporates a set of realistic and measurable objectives and is under the direct control of senior management. Please consult Figure 5.1.

Cyber-attacks are on the increase and ransomware, which involves the payment of money (normally in the form of bitcoins), is coupled with the sale of personal/private information if the fee demanded is not paid. As senior managers and entrepreneurs utilize technology to find new ways of doing business and implement new business models that guarantee efficiency, cyber criminals work hard to spot opportunities that will yield them an advantage. Because senior managers are placing more emphasis on establishing how technology can be utilized to share information with their colleagues and individuals in partner organizations, the networks used are targeted and become vulnerable to attack. Embracing the modelling approach has its advantages but it is essential that a cyber security culture is established that is reinforced through situational awareness and analysis and organizational learning. This is because much can be learned from individual cyber-attacks, and common problems can be resolved by involving staff in partner organizations that reflect on issues involving drawing on an organization's memory.

Question 1: Why is it important for an organization to have a security culture?
Question 2: How can senior management establish a cyber security culture?
Question 3: What does the cyber security manager need to take into account when thinking of deploying the modelling approach?

5.10 Conclusion

What has emerged over the years and remains firmly accepted is a belief that whatever cyber security strategy is implemented will need to be revised through time. This is because the upper hand is in fact with those carrying out cyber-attacks. Counteractive cyber security attack policies and strategies are in place to defend against continual attacks, but more needs to be done to make an organization secure. As new business models evolve, so too do the opportunities for attack and it is because of this that senior management need to consider making security a shared responsibility. This means thinking of ways to motivate staff to adopt a proactive cyber security stance and, in addition, establish new ways to work that involve sharing information. New work practices should be embedded in the organizational learning approach and the transformation management approach and should facilitate best practices through teamwork involving staff in partner organizations.

Case 5: A cyber security management conceptual model and framework

Angela Hawkins had just finished her report for senior management. It made reading uncomfortable. The main emphasis was to make clear that unless there was a major change in attitude among staff within the company, it was unlikely that much progress would be made in implementing cyber security policy in the months ahead. This was because firstly, staff were not aware of how to build and utilize knowledge; and secondly, staff were not keen to trust and work with people they did not already have a working relationship with. Furthermore, staff had no concept of how knowledge was to be created and shared for the benefit of other members of staff. On occasion, staff seemed to react to the policies implemented and were very negative about future policies. A blame culture was evident, and because of this, a high percentage of the staff were unhappy about the work environment.

Some staff considered that they were sufficiently aware of the cyber security issues the organization was confronted with and had informed senior management about organizational vulnerabilities from time to time. Unfortunately, staff were informed that security was under the control of the security manager, and he would take responsibility for all eventualities. The security manager was very good at physical security and was seen constantly walking around the building; however, he had limited knowledge of computer systems and networks and was not keen to develop his knowledge of how the systems in place worked and were managed. The idea of a collectivist cyber threat intelligence policy and strategy appealed to staff, but nobody had an idea of how it would be implemented. Yes, such an approach would be well integrated into the company's cyber security strategy, but could it be integrated into the company's supply chain? If yes, who would do this? And who would provide the necessary support?

Angela Hawkins considered that the company's security policy needed to be upgraded. If it was upgraded successfully, then cooperation among staff would be strengthened. As a result, a focal point would be achieved for establishing a security culture, and cyber security could be at its centre. Having talked about this with Mr. Smith, the security manager, she realized that he was part of the problem because he was not over-enthusiastic about the idea and downplayed what she was suggesting.

Restructuring within the organization had created a number of challenges and some employees were waiting to be transferred to other departments. Hence, the staff were not as focused on security as they should be. They were more focused on their immediate work and how they would fit in with the major change that was occurring. It was clear that in order to establish an appropriate cyber security knowledge base, senior management needed to get staff to think outside their immediate activities and embrace the cyber security management approach. As regards changing the mindset of staff, Angela realized that she had to work with Mr. Smith and get the employees to think in terms of using their integrity and being rewarded for it and, in certain instances, they needed to be benevolent and not ask for an immediate reward. In addition, senior management needed to promote the stakeholder approach and make sure that staff in partner organizations were of the same mindset. This was to prevent resistance to change and stop the infighting that had evolved through time.

Having looked in-depth into the development of cyber security models, Mrs. Hawkins considered that it was possible to devise and implement an industry-specific cyber security model that linked the computer networks and information systems. She considered this would underpin the holistic approach to security. The main advantage of this is that it would allow risk management to be framed in the context of international standards that embraced and underpinned the day-to-day business decision-making process.

Another area that needed greater attention was situational awareness. Mrs. Hawkins considered that companies in the industry were defensive in their approach and attention needed to shift to anticipating an attack. This was so that management could identify how threat actors were changing their approach, how they were being motivated and how they were gearing up for the next level of attack. More had to be done in terms of linking the organization's analysis with alternative sources of situational analysis as found in government reports and highly specialized reports produced by specialist cyber security consultancies. This she considered worthwhile and would provide a broader view of critical infrastructure and the role that critical infrastructure played. By studying the latest types of cyber-attack, it was expected that guidance could be drawn on and the knowledge gained could be used to establish an intelligence function. A number of questions surfaced that needed attention.

Question 1: How could the values of employees be aligned with the organizational values in place so that staff considered cyber security to be at the heart of security?

Question 2: How can senior management establish a cyber security culture that incorporates security awareness; risk communication and information sharing?

Question 3: Which factors should the cyber security manager include when undertaking situational awareness?

References, websites and further reading

Aaker, D.A. (1992). *Strategic Market Management*. Chichester: John Wiley & Sons.

Aaker, D.A., and McLoughlin, D. (2010). *Strategic Market Management*. Chichester: John Wiley & Sons Limited.

Abraham, C., and Sims, R.R. (2021). A comprehensive approach to cyber resilience. *Sloan Management Review*, 63, pp. 1–4.

Ahmad, A., Desouza, K.C., Maynard, S.B., Naseer, H., and Baskerville, R.L. (2020). How integration of cyber security management and incident response enables organizational learning. *Journal of the Association for Information Science and Technology*, 71, pp. 939–953. DOI: 10.1002/asi.24311

Barak, A., and Suler, J. (2008). Reflections on the psychology and social science of cyberspace. In: Barak, A. (ed.). *Psychological Aspects of Cyberspace: Theory, Research, Application*, pp. 1–12. Cambridge: Cambridge University Press.

Bloom, P.N., and Chatterji, A.K. (2009). Scaling social entrepreneurial impact. *California Management Review*, 51 (3), pp. 114–133.

Bloom, P.N., and Smith, B.R. (2010). Identifying the drivers of social entrepreneurial impact: Theoretical development and an exploratory empirical test of SCALERS. *Journal of Social Entrepreneurship*, 1 (1), pp. 126–145. DOI: 10.1080/19420670903458042

Brennan, D., Dhruv, G., and Hamilton, S. (2021). The future of marketing analytics and public policy. *Journal of Public Policy & Marketing*, 40 (4), pp. 447–452. DOI: 10.1177/07439156211042372

British Library. (2024). *Learning Lessons from the Cyber-attack: British Library Cyber Incident Review*. London: The British Library (8th March).

Brockhoff, K. (1991). Competitor technology in German companies. *Industrial Marketing Management*, 20 (2), pp. 91–98.

Carnegie Mellon University. (2016). *CRR Supplemental Resource Guide. Volume 10: Situational Awareness Version 1.1*. Pittsburgh, PA: Carnegie Mellon University. file:///C:/Users/HP%20User/Desktop/CRR_Resource_Guide-SA_0.pdf (Accessed 7th June, 2024).

Davis, B.J. (2007). Situational prevention and penetration testing: A proactive approach to social engineering in organizations. In: Merkidze, A.W. (ed.). *Terrorism Issues: Threat Assessment, Consequences and Prevention*, pp. 175–188. New York: Nova Science Publishers, Inc.

Dolan, S.L., Garcia, S., and Richley, B. (2006). *Managing by Values*. Basingstoke, Hampshire: Palgrave Macmillan.

ENISA. (2023). *ENISA Threat Landscape 2023*. Athens: European Union Agency for Cybersecurity (ENISA), (October). DOI: 10.2824/782573

Esteves, J., Ramalho, E., and De Haro, G. (2017). To improve cybersecurity, think like a hacker. *Sloan Management Review*, 58 (3), pp. 71–77. http://mitsmr.com/2mXYJdD

Han, S-L., Kim, Y.T., Oh, C.Y., and Chung, J.M. (2008). Business relationships and structural bonding: A study of American metal industry. *Journal of Global Academy of Marketing Science*, 18 (3), pp. 115–132.

Hennig-Thurau, T. (2004). Customer orientation of service employees: Its impact on customer satisfaction, commitment, and retention. *International Journal of Service Industry Management*, 15 (5), pp. 460–478. https://doi.org/10.1108/09564230410564939

Huff, L., and Kelley, L. (2005). Is collectivism a liability? The impact of culture on organizational trust and customer orientation: A seven-nation study. *Journal of Business Research*, 58 (5), pp. 96–102.

Jagetia, L.C., and Patel, D.M. (1981). Developing an end-use intelligence system. *Industrial Marketing Management*, 10 (2), pp. 101–107. https://doi.org/10.1016/0019-8501(81)90003-1

Kranton, R.E. (1996). The formation of cooperative relationships. *The Journal of Law, Economics & Organization*, 12 (1), pp. 214–233. https://doi.org/10.1093/oxfordjournals.jleo.a023358

Lawrence, T.B., Mauws, M.E., and Dyck, B. (2005). The politics of organizational learning: Integrating power into the 4i framework. *Academy of Management Review*, 30 (1), pp. 180–191. https://www.jstor.org/stable/20159102

Mathur, M. (2019). Where is the security blanket? Developing social media marketing capability as a shield from perceived cybersecurity risk. *Journal of Promotion Management*, 25 (2), pp. 200–224. DOI: 10.1080/10496491.2018.1443310

Mentzer, J.T., and Gandhi, N. (1993). Expert systems in industrial marketing. *Industrial Marketing Management*, 22 (2), pp. 109–116. DOI: 10.1016/0019-8501(93)90036-7

Morgan, R.E., Katsikeas. C.S., and Adu, K.A. (1998). Market orientation and organizational learning capabilities. *Journal of Marketing Management*, 14, pp. 353–381.

Nardini, G., Bublitz, M.G., Butler, C., Croom-Raley, S., Escalas, J.E., Hansen, J., and Peracchio, L.A. (2022). Scaling social impact: Marketing to grow nonprofit solutions. *Journal of Public Policy & Marketing*, 41 (3), pp. 254–276. DOI: 10.1177/07439156221087997

National Audit Office. (2017). *Investigation: WannaCry Cyber Attack and the NHS*. HC 414 Session 2017–2019. London: National Audit Office.

Pearce, F.T. (1971). INTELLIGENCE: A technology for the 1980's. *Industrial Marketing Management*, 1 (1), pp. 11–26.

Pearce, F.T. (1976). Business intelligence systems: The need, development, and integration. *Industrial Marketing Management*, 5 (2/3), pp. 115–138. https://doi.org/10.1016/0019-8501(76)90035-3

Rousseau, D.M., Sitkin, S.B., Burt, R.S., and Camerer, C. (1998). Not so different after all: A cross-discipline view of trust. *Academy of Management Review*, 23 (3), pp. 393–404. https://doi.org/10.5465/amr.1998.926617

Rust, R.T., and Zahorik, A.J. (1993). Customer satisfaction, customer retention and market share. *Journal of Retailing*, 69 (2), pp. 193–215. https://doi.org/10.1016/0022-4359(93)90003-2

Schweidel, D.A., Fader, P.S., and Bradlow, E.T. (2008). Understanding service retention within and across cohorts using limited information. *Journal of Marketing*, 72 (1), pp. 82–94. DOI: 10.1509/jmkg.72.1.082

Shultz, C.J., Burkink, T.J., Grbac, B., and Natasa, R. (2005). When policies and marketing systems explode: An assessment of food marketing in the war-ravaged Balkans and implications for recovery, sustainable peace and prosperity. *Journal of Public Policy & Marketing*, 24 (1), pp. 24–37. DOI: 10.1509/jppm.24.1.24.63897

Senge, P.M. (1999). *The Fifth Discipline: The Art & Practice of the Learning Organization*. London: Random House.

Suh, T., and Kwon, I-W.G. (2006). Matter over mind: When specific asset investment affects calculative trust in supply chain partnership. *Industrial Marketing Management*, 35 (2), pp. 191–201. DOI:10.1016/j.indmarman.2005.02.001

Suter, M. (2007). *A Generic National Framework for Critical Information Infrastructure Protection (CIIP)*. (August). Zurich, Switzerland: Center for Security Studies.

Trim, P.R.J. (2004). The strategic corporate intelligence and transformational marketing model. *Marketing Intelligence and Planning*, 22 (2), pp. 240–256. DOI:10.1108/02634500410525896

Trim, P.R.J. (2005). The GISES model for counteracting organized crime and international terrorism. *International Journal of Intelligence and Counter Intelligence*, 18 (3), pp. 451–472. DOI: 10.1080/08850600590945425

Trim, P.R.J., and Lee, Y-I. (2007). Placing organizational learning in the context of strategic management. *Business Strategy Series*, 8 (5), pp. 335–342.

Trim, P.R.J., and Lee, Y-I. (2010). A security framework for protecting business, government and society from cyber attacks. In: *5th IEEE International Conference on System of Systems Conference (SoSE): Sustainable Systems for the 21st Century*. Loughborough: Loughborough University (22nd to 24th June).

Trim, P.R.J., and Lee, Y-I. (2019). The role of B2B marketers in increasing cyber security awareness and influencing behavioural change. *Industrial Marketing Management*, 83, pp. 224–238. https://doi.org/10.1016/j.indmarman.2019.04.003

Trim, P.R.J., and Lee, Y-I. (2021). The global cyber security model: Counteracting cyber attacks through a resilient partnership arrangement. *Big Data and Cognitive Computing*, 5 (3), pp. 1–17. https://doi.org/10.3390/bdcc5030032

Trim, P.R.J., and Lee, Y-I. (2023). *Strategic Cyber Security Management*. Oxford: Routledge.

Trim, P.R.J., and Upton, D. (2013). *Cyber Security Culture: Counteracting Cyber Threats through Organizational Learning and Training*. Farnham: Gower Publishing.

Westley, F., Antadze, N., Riddell, D.J., Robinson, K., and Geobey, S. (2014). *The Journal of Applied Behavioral Science*, 50 (3), pp. 234–260. DOI: 10.1177/0021886314532945

Wilderom, C.P.M. (1991). Service management/leadership: Different from management/leadership in industrial organisations? *International Journal of Service Industry Management*, 2 (1), pp. 6–14. https://doi.org/10.1108/09564239110002332

Wind, Y., and Thomas, R.J. (2010). Organizational buying behaviour in an interdependent world. *Journal of Global Academy of Marketing Science*, 20 (2), pp. 110–122. https://doi.org/10.1080/12297119.2010.9730184

Zinkhan, G.M., and Gelb, B.D. (1985). Competitive intelligence practices of industrial marketers. *Industrial Marketing Management*, 14 (4), pp. 269–275. https://doi.org/10.1016/0019-8501(85)90019-7

Websites

Adams, L. (2024). A school has declared a "significant critical incident" after it was targeted in a cyber-attack. *BBC Website*, 1st June. https://www.bbc.co.uk/news/articles/cl44877v7xxo (Accessed 3rd June, 2024).

Ashe, I. (2024). A cyber-attack on a city council has left a number of street lights lit day and night. *BBC Website*, 3rd April. https://www.bbc.co.uk/news/uk-england-leicestershire-68881057 (Accessed 3rd June, 2024).

BBC. (2024). Critical incident over London hospitals' cyber-attack. *BBC News*, 4th June. https://www.bbc.co.uk/news/articles/c288n8rkpvno (Accessed 5th June, 2024).

Wise, A. (2024). Santander staff and customer data stolen in major cyber attack. *The Independent*, 1st June. https://www.independent.co.uk/business/santander-staff-and-customer-data-stolen-in-major-cyber-attack-b2554720.html (Accessed 3rd June, 2024).

Further reading

Nonaka, I., and von Krogh, G. (2009). Tacit knowledge and knowledge conversion: Controversy and advancement in organizational knowledge creation theory. *Organization Science*, 20 (3), pp. 635–652. DOI: 10.1287/orsc.1080.0412

Martin, K.D., and Kracher, B. (2008). A conceptual framework for online business protest tactics and criteria for their effectiveness. *Business & Society*, 47 (3), pp. 291–311. https://doi.org/10.1177/0007650307299218

Pirson, M., and Malhotra, D. (2011). Foundations of organizational trust: What matters to different stakeholders? *Organization Science*, 22 (4), pp. 1087–1104. DOI: 10.1287/orsc.1100.0581

6

PARTNERSHIP IN THE CONTEXT OF CYBER SECURITY

6.1 Introduction

The chapter starts with challenges and issues in relation to critical infrastructure (Section 6.2) and continues with attacks involving social media networks and platforms (Section 6.3). Areas of cyber security threat awareness (Section 6.4) is followed by Open-Source Intelligence (OSINT) (Section 6.5) and the need for partnership (Section 6.6). Next, smart cities (Section 6.7) is followed by reflection and questions (Section 6.8) and then a conclusion (Section 6.9) is provided.

6.2 Challenges and Issues in Relation to Critical Infrastructure

Makrakis et al. (2021, p. 165295) are of the view that an Industrial Control System (ICS) is composed of two separate domains: IT, which constitutes the service element (workstations, servers and databases) that support all the business operations, and Operational Technology (OT), that relates to the operational aspects (hardware, software and networking aspects) of the machinery in use. To understand the level of risk within critical infrastructure, it is necessary to have a knowledge of the configuration of the different subsystems and how the different critical assets are to be protected from attack. For example, computer-based systems are linked to various networks, and computer apps (e.g., application programs) allow a certain function to be undertaken and can be found on various types of platforms.

When considering connectivity generally and how networks are configured, it is useful to think of both critical national infrastructure and critical information infrastructure and the functioning of SCADA (Supervisory Control and Data Acquisition) systems. SCADA systems are at risk because they control the supply of a range of services from electricity supply to the supply of water. As well as attacks being carried out by outsiders, insiders and criminals/hacktivists/script kiddies, according to Makrakis et al. (2021, p. 165301), industrial espionage actors, cyber-terrorists and nation-state actors possess the knowledge to carry out targeted attacks by launching/activating malicious code that

DOI: 10.4324/9781003570905-6

inflicts damage on ICSs. Makrakis et al. (2021, pp. 165301–165310) make reference to successful malware attacks known as Stuxnet, which utilized compromised certificates and spread malicious code to other workstations; Duqu, which is known to gain access and leak information; Shamoon, which wipes hard drives; Havex, known as a backdoor malware that infects and then modifies thus deepening the attack; BlackEnergy (BE) referred to as a botnet/DDoS tool that relies on in-depth reconnaissance over a period of time before the attack is launched; Industroyer/CrashOverride, known also as an intrusion device that relies on phishing attacks; Triton/Trisis/HatMan, which is known to disrupt the safety mechanisms of the controllers; VPNFilter is known to carry out reconnaissance and infect systems; WannaCry, reported on extensively is known to be a crypto worm-based attack that focuses on MS Windows computers; NotPetya, which is a cryptoworm based attack that focuses on MS Windows–based hosts and DarkSide ransomware has been used to disable a company's IT networks, an example being Colonial Pipeline, whose management were asked to pay a ransom for decrypton keys that would then allow the company's systems to be restored. Understanding how such attacks can penetrate organizational defences is key, but the cyber security manager also has to be aware of how such attacks can be operationalized. For example, it is through downloading a document via a database or possibly as a result of a member of staff accessing a website that they should have avoided. Knowing whom to draw on for assistance in real time is a key component of defence and can be considered an aspect of strategic intelligence planning and foresight. This is because forward planning allows contingency plans to be devised that can be implemented during a crisis. Should a crisis not be resolved quickly, it is likely to become an emergency and then, if the situation escalates, a disaster with cascading effects.

The cyber-attack on critical national infrastructure can be highly disruptive as indeed was the cyber-attack on Ukraine's power system in December 2015. Apparently, the cyber-attack started with the malware being installed via phishing emails and this happened a number of months in advance of the main attack (Sun et al., 2018, p. 46). This allowed those carrying out the attack to monitor the operations of the power grid, which was the main target, and it seems that during this reconnaissance period, the activities of the attack went undetected. According to Sun et al. (2018, p. 46), on the day of the attack, "human machine interface (HMI) was hijacked and used by the attackers to remotely open a number of circuit breakers which directly cut power to the customers". By successfully compromising the telephone system and communication network via a DoS attack, those instigating the attack prevented customers from being able to inform the call centre that they were experiencing problems with their electricity supply and, in addition, the malware on the HMI deleted software so that the operators were unable to establish the extent of the power disruption (Sun et al., 2018, p. 46). So, it was clear that the well planned, targeted attack had been executed according to specific instructions and the focus of the attack was to maximize the damage caused to the community. By prolonging the recovery period and ensuring that the restoration of the power supply took longer than expected, the harm caused through disruption was maximized.

The above example only brings out the key points and it is useful to reflect on what the possible consequences of such a cyber-attack might be. A power outage during the busiest part of the day is likely to affect people travelling to work and will possibly delay schools opening to admit their pupils or the schools affected may demand that parents collect their children early and take them home. As well as businesses and homes being unable to function because of a loss of power, supermarkets may not be able to remain open because a loss of power means that their refrigerated facilities do not operate as normal, and this may result in spoiled produce. Although hospitals, like other organizations, have backup power supplies, hospital theatre managers may need to cancel operations and push back those waiting for treatment which means an extended waiting list emerges. A power cut may affect traffic lights used on roads and a loss in power may cause the traffic lights to fail and this may result in a number of accidents. Because all these events occur at the same time, it can be assumed that the emergency services will be at full stretch and some of the emergency situations will not be catered for. The media companies engaged in live reporting may not have full facts and may to some degree cause further harm by misreporting the situation which causes panic and further disruption as people act in a way that is unexpected.

Although safeguards are in place to protect against cyber-attacks, it is clear that those implementing attacks are studying how those involved in making the systems secure are in fact doing so. Furthermore, those who instigate the attack may not work in isolation but may in fact share their knowledge and information with those of similar minds who are based in different countries. The international standards in place have done much to ensure that companies operate in a certain way but at the same time, the information in a specific standard is available to those who carry out such attacks.

6.3 Attacks Involving Social Media Networks and Platforms

Web-based platforms such as Facebook, LinkedIn, Instagram, TikTok, Twitter and YouTube have become well established as information providers and vehicles through which consumers can obtain and exchange information with a range of individuals, both corporate and personal. However, they are known to be a target for the spread of false information, some of which emanate from state actors. Thuraisingham (2020, p. 1116) is aware of this and, referring to social media systems, states that malicious software may be used to "change the contents of the messages posted. Such software could also create fake profiles that would then post false information. The images and video contents posted on social media could also be subject to attacks".

Before progressing, it is useful to consider how criminals use social media to achieve their goals. Goodman (2016, p. 150) provides us with such evidence and indicates that in 2010, local criminals in Nashua, New Hampshire, USA:

> "turned to Facebook to determine when victims were away from their homes. Nashua police discovered that this crime ring checked Facebook updates of their victims before carrying out more than fifty break-ins and stealing nearly $200,000 in property during their burglary spree.............."

Goodman (2016, p. 150) provides a further example and states that in 2011, a study was conducted relating to convicted burglars who had been operating in the U.K., which suggested that 78% had used various social media sites (e.g., Facebook, Twitter and Foursquare) to monitor messages before they selected a specific home to burgle. Goodman (2016, p. 150) also reported that the UK burglars used Google Street View to carry out scoping of the property prior to executing their plan. The reason for this was to devise possible escape routes so that they would be able to flee from the scene of the crime and make their getaway.

Thakhur et al. (2019, pp. 43–45) suggest that criminals are well able to use social media in order to carry out social engineering attacks that are focused on information gathering, recruiting insiders, running scams and managing cyber bullying campaigns. Issues of concern such as identity personalization and identity deception (van der Walk et al., 2018) are constantly surfacing and users of social media need to pay greater attention to how they can remain safe interacting online. Most social media users consider that they are operating within a well-regulated environment and that the platform provider has their interest in security at heart. What needs to be understood is that those intent on deceiving, whether it is to steal sensitive information by befriending someone or manipulating a situation to take advantage of somebody, have planned and coordinated and undertake it at a time when people are vulnerable and less aware of the threat they face.

It is clear that the cyber security manager, working with the IT manager, the risk manager and the security manager, need to know how AI can be used to detect and protect against the manipulation and fabrication of information. It is accepted that people through their interaction and posts on social media can spread false rumours by misinterpreting information and events. However, although ML techniques are being used to detect malicious software (Thuraisingham, 2020, p. 1117), detecting fake news and who is behind the made-up stories that surface is not a straightforward task. Often, privacy issues surface and need to be dealt with but there are ideological concerns as well. Some state actors are known to have access to vast resources and can play out a continuous game whereby prominent people in society are attacked and discredited and politicians are placed in compromising situations. For example, a deepfake video appeared on Facebook in the Summer of 2019 showing the Democratic Speaker of the House of Representatives, Nancy Pelosi, slurring while talking and appearing drunk (The Sunday Times, 2019, p. 17). There have been other such examples, a number of which have been aimed at politicians and celebrities in society. The Sunday Times (2019, p. 14) reported:

> "Today, deepfake development is a cottage industry. According to Deeptrace Labs, more than 100,000 people spread across 20 known deepfake forums are toiling away, day in, day out, uploading code libraries for free, allowing others to tweak, improve and share algorithms that are, at an astounding speed, getting better at automatically crafting faked videos".

According to The Sunday Times (2019, p. 14), portals exist whereby custom deepfakes can be purchased for as little as US$3 and all that is needed is 250 pictures of the chosen person and, also, customized voice-cloning is available that costs US$10 for every 50 words.

The actions of such perpetrators and those affected must be viewed in terms of the psychological dimension. For example, continued targeted pressure on an individual is likely to result in some sort of human failure that can cause embarrassment to the person concerned and this can affect their career and personal life. However, an attack on an individual not only causes harm to them and their family, but if they occupy a high position in society, it can also cause discontent and confusion among the public and the community. Corporate staff can also feel the brunt of those out to cause harm as they are targeted with the intent of being exploited in some way and this has psychological damage associated with it. Corporate staff have been targeted by activists and received criticism that has forced them to take responsibility for a situation that may not have been of their making. Attacks can be timed to coincide with business negotiations and can be aimed at disrupting business partnerships. Sometimes, social media is used as a vehicle to orchestrate identity theft and is now receiving attention.

There are ways to guard against identity theft. Staff should be told not to divulge personal information such as social security numbers and bank account details; they should not send personal or confidential information via text messages or through emails; they should avoid responding to phishing emails and they should not place their details in an online form (Thakhur et al., 2015, p. 310). Because people get targeted on a regular basis, it is easy to overlook something and fall victim to a scam. If this is the case, the employee needs to report it immediately to the IT manager and security department as well as their line manager and be honest about what has been done and when it was done. It is better to have full information as soon as possible as opposed to having bits and pieces of information over a long period of time. This is because if the full extent of what has happened is not made clear early on, the ramifications could be even more serious. This brings to attention the need for a clear and well-documented internal security policy and how such matters are reported and to whom. Having a well-defined security policy in place is beneficial in terms of establishing and maintaining a security culture.

6.4 Areas of Cyber Security Threat Awareness

The cyber security manager is well aware of the need for vigilance in terms of how those orchestrating cyber-attacks are developing their knowledge base, who they are in contact with and the sorts of skills they are hiring. This means due care and attention need to be given to both current and future investments in cyber security. For example, there have been discussions about the usefulness of biometrics because it is known that fingerprint scanning has limitations and cyber criminals can find ways to exploit such technology. Biometrics has been defined as the "physiological and/or behavioral characteristics used for automatic recognition of an individual" (Arteche et al., 2022, p. 1059). Biometric authentication is known to be costly and requires much thought in terms of keeping it secure. Voice recognition, along with fingerprint and retina recognition, has been used by companies to restrict access to people's data and to safeguard transactions and entry to buildings and sensitive areas. However, an attack from a malicious third party can do untold damage as Arteche et al. (2022, p. 1063) indicate. For example, there is the direct attack, which sees the biometric technology as the entry point, and indirect attacks, which is when access is gained on a system through other means. Arteche et al. (2022, p. 1063) go on to explain that

> "Direct attacks often involve spoofing and alteration while indirect attacks include phishing attacks, malware injection, and circumvention. Spoofing attacks involve gaining an invalid and unauthorized access to biometric mobile applications by presenting a fake biometric feature or trait such as face mask, silicon finger etc."

Cyber security is undergoing a transformation and although facial recognition will develop extensively within the next decade, it can be suggested that security is reinforced at present through encryption and is moving towards two-factor authentication and authorization (Khan et al., 2023, p. 80182). Blockchain technology, because it involves a distributed, decentralized ledger, can be considered an influential innovation as it allows a set of transactions to be incorporated into a central ledger and this can be considered robust as the data in the central ledge should be safe from manipulation and modification as the data is encrypted and then decrypted (Aggarwal et al., 2022, pp. 3312–3313). The blockchain concept has the main advantage of eliminating human error and has the added benefit of restricting access to the data and information in the ledger because the end user has their own encryption keys (Bansal et al., 2020, p. 264). However, Madnick (2019) has claimed that blockchain technology is not as secure as was first thought and vulnerabilities do exist that need to be eradicated.

Writing on the risks of the blockchain, Konig et al. (2020, p. 121) state:

"In the world of cryptocurrencies, wallets are used to store cryptographic keys of the users. Research shows that there has been a multitude of attacks directed at wallets and a lot of money has been stolen by stealing or deleting keys".

Konig et al. (2020, p. 121) are of the view that an attacker can access a victim's private key(s) and once this is achieved, can generate new transactions and thus spend the victim's money. The question posed is how can an attacker steal the keys? Konig et al. (2020, p. 121) indicate that it is possible to compromise a client's software and make reference to Bitcoin Core v0.15, which contained a vulnerability and as a consequence, an attacker was able to assume ownership of the victim's wallet.

It is obvious that cyber security covers a broad and growing area of interlinked subject areas, and that cyber security needs to be thought of as multidisciplinary in nature. In June 2024, the UK government's stance in relation to cyber threats and international peace was made known by Ambassador Barbara Woodward, Permanent Representative to the UN, during a UN Security Council meeting on cybersecurity. Woodward (2024) is of the view that there are three noticeable trends of importance to the UK that are also of relevance to the international community. The first is the increase in ransomware, which is known to disrupt government functions and also hinder public service provisions. The second is the use of AI systems and because of this more needs to be known about how cyber threats will change because of the actions of malicious and irresponsible actors and their intention to exploit vulnerabilities in AI systems. The third area of concern is how malicious and irresponsible actors will take advantage of the opportunities in the growing market for advanced cyber intrusion capabilities.

Woodward (2024) has also made reference to the fact that more effort must be put into raising awareness in relation to possible cyber threats and has flagged the use of malicious cyber activities in relation to obtaining cryptocurrencies that fund illegal weapons programmes. Also flagged for attention is the risk of disinformation and the effect it can have on international peace and security. Woodward (2024) makes clear that the UK government will uphold the UN Framework for Responsible State Behaviour and suggests there is a real need for countries to work together to achieve capacity-building and public–private partnerships in the area of cyber security.

Reflecting on such comments motivates the cyber security manager to think more deeply about the consequences of not doing enough, both to protect the organization and at the same time contribute to government policy that makes the world more secure. But to have an all-round appreciation of the type of cyber threats that are evolving and how cyber-attacks are implemented requires both an all-round appreciation of what is happening in the real world and how the organization's memory should be up-to-date to both store and utilize such knowledge. Monitoring the cyber landscape and being able to predict how cyber-attacks materialize can be argued as a necessity. One way this can be done is through OSINT.

6.5 Open-Source Intelligence (OSINT)

Odom (1997, p. 404) suggests that the term "national security" has over the years been expanded from purely a military affairs perspective into all aspects of public policy and because of this attention needs to be given to the degree to which civil government is to be included in national security policymaking. It can be argued that cyber-attacks, some of which are initiated by state actors, are falling more into the technology-military domain and drawing more on a higher level of cyber skill. In order to understand this, the cyber security manager needs to engage fully in OSINT.

According to Pastor-Galindo et al. (2020, p. 10282), OSINT involves

"the collection, processing and correlation of public information from open data sources such as the mass media, social networks, forums and blogs, public government data, publications, or commercial data. …. together with the application of advanced collection and analysis techniques, OSINT continuously expands the knowledge about the target".

There are various means by which data and information can be collected, sorted, analysed, interpreted and disseminated. Various software programs exist to pick up lead words and sentences, and in some cases, intelligence officers leverage the help of staff in partner organizations. In addition, some governments provide structured intelligence for use by commercial organizations, and intelligence, security and law enforcement staff leave the public sector to take up employment in private companies thus taking their skills with them. They bring with them knowledge of how to make links within patterns of data and information, and nowadays, staff are utilizing AI to not only analyse data but also to look for associations and indicators that suggest that possibly an occurrence is going to result in a certain outcome or have a certain impact.

There are a number of issues to be aware of regarding data and information derived from open sources. For example, Pastor-Galindo et al. (2020, pp. 10284–10285) suggest that there are issues in relation to the complexity of data management, information that is unstructured, the rise of misinformation, the unreliability of data sources and legal and ethical factors that surface from time to time. The cyber security manager needs to be aware of this when they seek the help of in-house staff or commission external intelligence providers to analyse a problem. Being able to establish the quality of data/information is essential and so too is knowing how to access data and information on a continual basis. For example, social media networks have large quantities of data and information; however, the quality of it varies enormously in terms of accuracy and completeness. Often, snippets of data/information are available and although ways can be found to fill the gaps and establish a holistic view of a subject, often noise occurs in the way of misinformation and distortion and sometimes through rumour.

When planning to use OSINT, it is useful to adopt the approach outlined by Patton (2010, p. 139), which involves distinguishing the intelligence cycle from the critical thinking process. This is because the critical thinking process includes additional steps. For example, the intelligence cycle is made up of five main actions: planning and direction, collection, processing, analysis and production and dissemination (Patton, 2010, p. 139). The critical thinking process is in fact composed of eight steps: purpose, question at issue, information, interpretation and inference, concepts, assumptions, implications and consequences and point of view (Patton, 2010, p. 139). RAND (Williams and Blum, 2018, pp. 13–14) takes the four-step operation cycle approach which is composed of collection, processing, exploitation and production and translates it into acquisition and retention (collection – step 1); translation and aggregation (processing – step 2); authentication, evaluating credibility and contextualizing (exploitation – step 3) and classification and dissemination (production – step 4).

The main advantage of such approaches is that they can be adopted by partner organizations and consequently, a more in-depth analysis and interpretation can manifest. This is because staff in partner organizations can also draw on data and information sources from suppliers and channel partners, and by combining their intelligence activities, a more rounded view of a problem can be arrived at resulting in network members sharing information relating to current and future cyber-attacks and threats.

Glassman and Kang (2012, p. 674) are of the view that "recent developments of the Internet/Web have created new roles for human–computer symbiosis in information relationships, actually augmenting human intelligence in dynamic problem solving". It is recognized that those responsible for intelligence work assume responsibility for the quality of data/information that is collected and are experts at knowing how it is to be utilized within the constraints imposed. For example, data and information that is decoded and becomes sensitive information is unlikely to be circulated generally among partner members, unless there is a good reason to do so. Bearing in mind that the data/information analysed is used to predict an event, it has to be viewed from the perspective of validation. Issues such as its reliability and generalizability also have to be considered. Although during the analysis stage, the unknowns are filtered out, it has to be said that errors can occur and are likely to result in missed signals in the data. This can occur due to excessive noise and people being overworked or too thinly spread. As well as cyber-attacks being launched against an organization, attacks are also aimed at individuals. Hence, chat and other forms of communication need to be viewed from the perspective of preventing cyber bullying from occurring and having a detrimental effect on the organization. Cyber bullying involves much unpleasantness and manifests in aggressive messaging and the release of embarrassing photographs (Law et al., 2012, p. 668) that can do psychological harm to those affected.

6.6 The Need for Partnership

It can be noted that: "Digital technology makes it possible for large volumes of information to be stored in easily searchable formats. As a result, more information is readily accessible to today's 'information consumer' working within the digital environment" (Wonders et al., 2012, p. 250). Very rarely do managers ask questions about the safe storage of data and information and managers normally have limited knowledge of cloud computing and what it involves. Too often, the cost of data storage is given precedence over data security and few risk assessments take into account the possibility of the financial vulnerability of the cloud provider. However, a collectivist enterprise risk management cyber threat model can help managers to determine what sensitive data if any is to be placed in the cloud. Should data be placed in the cloud, then the associated risk factors will need to be listed in the risk register and an explanation provided so that the stakeholders can see how the risk is mitigated.

It can be noted that in situations of high perceived risk, people deploy a risk-reducing strategy based on behavioural choices, which lowers their vulnerability to what are regarded as potentially negative outcomes (Cho and Lee, 2006, p. 119). Managers will, therefore, need to trade off cost versus the degree of security that is considered appropriate, and may think of ways to make the organization less vulnerable by sharing business operations with relevant partner organizations. An integrated risk policy can help organizational staff devise an effective risk mitigation policy that takes into account issues such as cyber insurance. This does, however, call into question cyber security policy and what the role of the risk manager is. It also highlights the issue of adequate cyber insurance cover. For example, it may be possible for an organization to take out a cyber insurance policy so that if a cyber-attack is launched on the organization, its infrastructure and business operations are protected through adequate insurance cover. However, if repeated attacks are made on an organization, it may not be possible for the organization to maintain its insurance cover due to escalating insurance premiums.

A successful partnership requires coordination, governance and reinforced cooperation (Rese, 2006, p. 74). These are all outcomes of organizational learning intervention. Hence, a cooperative partnership can be interpreted from the perspective of mutuality, which occurs at all levels within a partnership arrangement (Wucherer, 2006, pp. 91–92). This requires senior managers to think in terms of integrated solutions (cooperation between internal business units and departments); however, it is essential that end users and stakeholders of various kinds including research institutes and government agencies are included in the process (Windahl and Lakemond, 2006, pp. 816–817) because of the need to scale wide and deep and extend the scope to ensure that the solutions are community focused (Nardini et al., 2022). A question to be addressed, however, is: What type of information do organizational representatives need to make available to stakeholders? To answer this question, senior managers need to engage with community groups of importance and include them in the risk-sharing process as they can provide support that encourages senior managers to adopt an inter-organizational risk management strategy that is viewed as co-owned. This adds weight to the argument that a strategic intelligence approach is useful in terms of enhancing cyber security provision because it couples cyber security–related risk with other forms of organizational risk. For example, outsourcing may be considered cost-effective, but it may have associated vulnerabilities in terms of the security of sensitive data (e.g., an outsourced online customer support service is subcontracted out to a second-tier service provider). It may also link with and incorporate other forms of risk such as country risk, political risk and/or economic risk or environmental risk, for example. To this can be added technology risk and any other variant of risk (e.g., social) that is considered influential in some way and which needs to be placed in the context of a risk assessment.

The risk associated with an operational activity may increase as the organization becomes more vulnerable as a result of non-organizational staff (those employed by a subcontractor) undertaking certain tasks on behalf of the company and gaining access to the organization's confidential passwords and data (e.g., client list, contracts and future plans). Because external organizations and cloud providers are increasingly being used to store confidential data, more attention needs to be given to how the employees of such organizations, subcontract their services. This raises an additional question: Who has access to the organization's intelligence (e.g., AI-produced reports)? In addition, staff from subcontracted external organizations may inadvertently introduce inappropriate software that contains malware into the organization's computer system and network as they cut costs to ensure profitability. Again, reference to untrustworthy software can be made in the risk register(s). Hence, there needs to be a policy in place for linking CTI with strategic intelligence, and to be effective, a senior manager (e.g., cyber security manager) needs to work alongside the organization's risk manager, and report back to senior management (e.g., the chief information/security officer).

A resilient organization will, we argue, have adequate security in place, but it does not mean that it will withstand a sophisticated cyber-attack. CTI is based on having appropriate cyber security knowledge that feeds into a collectivist enterprise risk management cyber threat model, however, as Fahy et al. (2005, p. 2) state: "Enterprise Governance is based on the principle that good governance alone cannot make an organisation successful". Hence, senior managers need to think deeply about how a strategic collectivist CTI policy and strategy framework can be developed and implemented among partner organizations, if that is, security is to be intensified throughout the supply chain. The logic of this is that security is viewed as an investment as opposed to a cost.

Bearing the above in mind, we are of the view that senior managers can use the organizational learning approach to provide organizational interventions to reinforce the security in place. An open and transparent style of communication will, we argue, reinforce the need for continual learning and will encourage staff in partner organizations to adopt a proactive, adaptive and risk-sharing approach to doing business. Referring to the role that organizational culture plays, McAuley (2004) suggests that there is a need to be politically aware so that it is possible to maximize the gains expected. Additionally, staff need to be able to play a key role in the relationship-building process (Hingley, 2005, pp. 66–75). With respect to organizational vulnerability, Sheffi (2005) is right to suggest that ways need to be found to reduce an organization's level of risk, and this can be done through the stance of "mutual market responsibility" (Walters, 1979, p. 214). An integrated intelligence systems approach that relies upon up-to-date intelligence can be implemented that incorporates an ethical approach to data collection and usage (Carrigan and Kirkup, 2001, pp. 415–435). Furthermore, new approaches can be found to undertake foresight planning based on CTI and analysis. This can be considered relevant because it allows managers to think in terms of connectivity and the move to smart living.

6.7 Smart Cities

Lim and Taeihagh (2018, p. 1) have reflected on the fact that the United Nations (UN) has predicted that by 2050, something like two-thirds of the world's population will be found in cities. This is a staggering number, and it calls into question a number of issues regarding security and the quality of life. Indeed, as regards transportation, there is a view that autonomous vehicles, which are associated with reduced emissions and energy consumption and are considered to have less impact in terms of environmental degradation, may have security issues that need attention. An autonomous vehicle has been defined by Raiyn (2018, p. 325) as "a vehicle that can operate under its own power". Autonomous vehicles are viewed as having potential risks and these risks are in different forms. It has been suggested that legislation needs to be introduced to ensure data is protected and privacy is evident. For example, Lim and Taeihagh (2018, p. 9) report that those who own an autonomous vehicle or are the lessee of it need to be informed about the "collection, transmission, retention, and use" of data that is generated by the vehicle. This is the case in the United States and a law is in place to ensure this. In addition, laws are required to ensure that the data obtained and stored in an autonomous vehicle can be destroyed once the owner decides to sell it. It is useful to make reference to the fact that because autonomous vehicles are reliant on the use of sensors, as well as high-definition maps and other data/information sources, a lot of personal information is made use of and it is this that the user will want to maintain control over (Taeihagh and Lim, 2019, pp. 112–113). Laws are in place to protect and shield the user from data disclosure; however, if the user sells the autonomous vehicle, they may forget to delete the data recorded to date. This has been the case when a computer is at the end of its life, and it is handed over for recycling. Sometimes, the owner forgets to clear the data stored on the computer and those receiving it can, should they wish, see the data that is stored on the computer's hard drive. From a security perspective, the question to be posed is: Who would want to utilize such data? In addition, what is the purpose of utilizing such data? There are all sorts of reasons as to why criminals would want to obtain such data. The data is unique to the individual concerned and will provide a basis for profiling their lifestyle, where they go and who they meet and spend time with. If the computer has also been used for business, then really sensitive data such as banking details and contract information may be stored on the computer. Such intelligence could be used for the purpose of social engineering and also gaining the person's confidence so that they let an unknown person into their orbit as they consider that they are someone they have something in common with. Identity theft is also an issue and one that needs to be viewed seriously because it can take years to overcome issues such as a bank loan being taken out fraudulently in somebody else's name. What this highlights is that any device that stores data and information presents a risk if the data/information is not erased and the device falls into the hands of the wrong person.

It is important to note that autonomous vehicles have the capability to communicate with other autonomous vehicles via onboard sensors and this also allows them to share information (Raiyn, 2018, p. 325) and because of this they may be at risk because an attacker can modify the programming code. This is normally done at the design and implementation stage. Possibly, the greatest worry is that a cyber-attack on an autonomous vehicle, especially if it is a cargo vessel out at sea, may involve an attack on its global navigation satellite system but it is also possible that an attack will be made on the autonomous vehicle's wireless communication system (Raiyn, 2018, pp. 326–327).

Taeihagh and Lim (2019, p. 107) make known that autonomous vehicles have the potential to reduce the number of incidents/accidents associated with people as humans are prone to errors; however, they indicate that "the elimination of human error does not imply the elimination of machine error". Strict laws are in place that regulate the use of autonomous vehicles and more can be expected. Manufacturers will be expected to adhere to international standards and there will be specific regulatory controls in place relating to product liability, but this will not eliminate every aspect of risk. Indeed, it can be expected that those who buy an autonomous vehicle for reuse or renting out will need adequate insurance because as well as the performance of the autonomous vehicle, there is the issue of risk associated with an attacker taking possession of it and the consequences of such intervention (e.g., accident and damage). This is especially the case as regards driverless cars.

So, what is emerging is a view that cyber security needs to be placed in a broader context and that ways need to be found to integrate the different forms of cyber security into a holistic and integrated view of cyber security. This means more thought needs to go into establishing the motivations behind an attack and understanding the consequences of such attacks (Linkov et al., 2019, p. 3). The cyber security manager can ensure that systems are in place to prevent social engineering attacks to gain information and also the passwords in place are robust and well protected. More importantly, a system needs to be in place to help safeguard the passwords used and constant monitoring of password policy is advised. This will do much to eliminate human vulnerabilities, but it is not enough. Hence, risk assessment and threat modelling can be justified in terms of establishing how an attacker might target and launch an attack on an autonomous vehicle (Kim et al., 2021, pp. 11–14). A risk assessment needs to be formally defined and include (Kim et al., 2021, p. 11): The identification of threats and security requirements, an evaluation of the risks and the prioritization of the security requirements vis-à-vis what is termed acceptable risk. Testing organizational procedures through training exercises and the use of scenario analysis proves helpful as regards establishing what vulnerabilities may be in existence and how an attacker is likely to exploit the vulnerabilities. Evidence can be provided that helps the cyber security manager to justify the case for intrusion detection as it may involve various software usage, which can prove expensive. For example, firewalls are taken into account when risk mitigation strategies are devised and implemented, but more needs to be done. It is expected that increased attention will be given to the use of AI (especially ML and DL) (Kim et al., 2021, pp. 19–21) that will help threat detection.

With specific reference to drones (sometimes referred to as unmanned aerial vehicles (UAVs)), Vattapparamban et al. (2016, p. 217) indicate that they are prone to what is known as a man-in-the-middle attack, whereby the drone is taken over and does not perform in the way the owner/user expects. A common attack on a drone involves what is known as spoofing and this brings to the fore the way in which a drone receives communications and gives out communications with a control centre via the Global Positioning System (GPS). Vattapparamban et al. (2016, p. 218) have explained what is involved:

> "The communication links in drones include incoming signals from GPS satellites, signals notifying the drone's presence, and a two-way link between the ground station and the drone. GPS enables a drone's navigation, and due to no encryption of the signals they can easily be spoofed".

The evolving smart city concept is taking hold as people come to terms with developments in the further utilization of technology that is being stimulated by the Internet of

Things (IoT). Chen et al., 2021, pp. 2–3) are specific about the key building blocks vis-à-vis a smart city, they are: Smart energy, smart building, smart transportation, smart economy, smart healthcare, smart security, smart government, smart education, smart logistics, smart environment and smart public service. Hence, reference back to critical national infrastructure and critical information infrastructure surface and need attention. Bearing in mind the level and degree of interconnectivity, it is not surprising to learn that those involved in planning smart cities and ensuring that the services available to smart city residents have at the top of their agenda cyber security. Indeed, cyber security will in the years ahead likely become dependent and fully associated with AI and ML, and DL is expected to play a key role. For example, DL has been linked with the detection of malware, spam and fraud and is linked with intrusion detection and traffic analysis and identification (Chen et al., 2021, p. 3). Furthermore, security experts will be expected to place more emphasis on cyber security defence technologies, which they have at their disposal (Chen et al., 2021, p. 3): Firewalls (e.g., guards the data exchanged between the external network and the internal network); antivirus software (e.g., software designed to detect and eradicate malware); data leakage prevention (e.g., data is guarded and kept safe) and intrusion prevention system (e.g., attacks are prevented). Reflecting on the type of cyber threat and how it is likely to be implemented enables cyber security experts to categorize such attacks and forecast the type of impact likely to arise.

Chen et al. (2021, p. 5) provide a useful snapshot into the cyber threat landscape by suggesting that a cyber intrusion has the potential to impact a smart city infrastructure control system by paralyzing water, electricity, oil and gas supplies, and bringing transportation systems to a standstill; malware can be used to destroy and disrupt or even allow the attacker to take control of complex operating systems; spam can invade a recipient's privacy and occupy the cyber bandwidth eventually causing a website system to suffer from congestion and crash and Internet fraud has the potential to damage people's property and heighten mistrust.

It is clear from the above that planning and functioning of a smart city requires a great deal of thought. Not only do issues such as urbanization and the environment surface in the context of the quality of life but also there are immediate issues of concern regarding smart city dwellers and their everyday security. It can be surmised that as regards the day-to-day functioning of the city, great amounts of data will be held in the cloud and will need to be maintained and kept safe. Much of the data will be guarded by private companies but some will reside in the public sector domain. If the majority of the data is stored in the cloud, then again, questions relating to security and the ethics associated with putting data in the cloud will be on the agenda of senior management and indeed those who invoke the regulations governing the industry. If a smart city suffers from a man-made disaster (physical war or cyber war) or a natural disaster (earthquake, fire or flood), then possibly recovery will take time as some systems are rendered inoperable and it takes time to implement emergency services.

It is good to note, however, that governments and city planners around the world have placed great emphasis on ensuring that the smart city concept is workable and will be fit for purpose. The level of complexity involved is high as new ways have to be found to integrate technologies into a realistic and economically affordable infrastructural system. There are specific areas that cyber security experts need to put time and effort into to ensure that the systems in place are fully operational and the control mechanisms in place are not compromised. For example, Lee et al. (2019, p. 4) suggest that if hackers obtained control of CCTV, then they would be able to invade people's privacy through a four-step approach: (1) An attacker accesses the privacy, hard-coded account information relating to the smart CCTV cloud service; (2) the attacker controls the videos and thus infringes stored personal privacy; (3) the connected CCTV is then controlled remotely via the CCTV cloud and (4) the attacker releases real-time transmission of the videos downloaded by availing themselves of the cloud service and in the process infringe personal privacy.

Scenarios such as these are useful because they focus on specific types of cyber-attacks and require those involved in the development of critical national infrastructure and critical information infrastructure to think of how should a cyber attack occur, action can be taken in real time to prevent cascading effects and the situation getting out of control. Because there are a number of different suppliers of goods and services that go into the development of a smart city and support smart city living, it is essential that government representatives, planners and providers of infrastructure, think in terms of a strategic approach to sustainable partnership development (Trim and Lee, 2008, p. 223), defined as:

> "An all embracing mutually oriented mechanism that allows staff within an organization to identify, devise and implement a legal instrument that results in combined ownership, an integrated management model that is underpinned by a hybrid organizational culture, which gives rise to a clearly defined mission statement and marketing strategy".

Although partnership arrangements are composed of different stakeholders and each has their own set of objectives, it has to be remembered that complex technology is developed in partnership and that connectivity requires networks within networks. Hence, staff employed by organizations involved in providing smart city products and services need to undertake scenario planning in order to identify the vulnerabilities embedded in alternative strategies (Trim and Lee, 2008, p. 225). The logic underpinning this view is based on the fact that as technology evolves, some controllable factors mutate into uncontrollable factors because the technology changes and uncertainties become evident. Scenario analysis and planning can help senior managers to identify future uncertainties and, consequently, by implementing management action considered relevant and necessary, an uncontrollable factor can be turned into a controllable factor.

6.8 Reflection and Questions

There is no doubt that OSINT can be used to identify future cyber security–related vulnerabilities. Interestingly, the move to smart city living places much emphasis on both the production and consumption of products and services and also, the critical infrastructure that facilitates connectivity. Figure 6.1 makes this clear and, furthermore, the overall complexity means that partnerships, involving a range of network members and which are either formal or informal or both, will need to incorporate joint cyber security threat awareness activity owing to the fact that supply chain members are vulnerable to attack.

When senior managers consider investing in new technology or changing the business model and engaging more online, it has to be said that attention needs to be given to

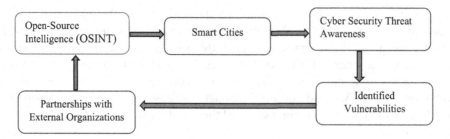

FIGURE 6.1 Partnership development to combat cyber security attacks.

how critical national infrastructure and critical information infrastructure support the computer systems, networks and computer apps used. SCADA systems are key as they underpin the linkage between organizations and their functioning, but they are targets for attack and can be disrupted in various ways. Social media is also susceptible to manipulation and false information and various social engineering ploys are used to target certain types of users. As well as individuals being harmed by attacks on social media, an attacker can set out to disrupt business negotiations as this may provide them with a specific type of advantage. Making staff aware of such actions will help senior management put a security policy in place that helps establish and maintain a security culture. Biometrics and blockchain technology are innovations to increase security but may well have vulnerabilities. Understanding which risks the organization is susceptible to will improve the management's view of the role played by CTI. The smart city concept and, in particular, the use of autonomous vehicles will raise issues and concerns about interlinked security and what needs to be done to counter possible disruptions in service provision.

Question 1: Why is it important for senior management to view partnership from a holistic cyber security perspective?
Question 2: What are the cyber security vulnerabilities associated with the smart city concept?
Question 3: How can senior management ensure that employees use social media responsibly?

6.9 Conclusion

There is no doubt that the quality of critical national infrastructure and critical information infrastructure will play a key role in determining how fast society moves to embrace the smart city concept. The smart city concept also embraces new forms of transportation involving goods and people, the use of autonomous vehicles and the supply of services, which are operated by companies utilizing blockchain technology. As cities become more compact and more dependent upon Internet services, it can be predicted that biometric forms of identification will become more commonly used. Taking these developments into account will highlight even more the role that cyber security and the cyber security manager are expected to play on a day-to-day basis. Bearing in mind the role played by connectivity, a more formalized approach to planning involving the public sector and the private sector can be expected, which will require an increased sense of cyber security awareness. By integrating cyber security provisions within a partner organization's operating system, potential cyber security vulnerabilities can be identified and rectified before any harm or damage is caused or any harm/damage that does result can be limited through swift action.

Case 6: Partnership in the context of cyber security

John Hargreaves, head of cyber security, and Georgina Wright, head of IT, were deep in discussion relating to aspects of partnership involving various organizations in the industry in which their company competed. They had focused extensively on issues relating to connectivity and had covered all aspects of critical national infrastructure and critical information infrastructure. Of key concern were SCADA systems and the fact that the countries in which the company operated were being subjected to increased cyber-attacks. Issues surfaced relating to malicious code that had inflicted damage on ICSs, and which had been reported by various governments. Cooperation between governments had increased in recent years but the increased sophistication in cyber-attacks on critical infrastructure had worried policymakers because their attention was being diverted from solving economic problems to worrying about how the damage inflicted on critical infrastructure could be limited.

Mr. Hargreaves and Georgina Wright also talked through issues revolving around the use of social media and how staff were falling victim to scamming which was widespread. There had been several stories in the media regarding the exploitation of staff and the psychological damage associated with it. Activists were known to be behind a number of attacks, and it was becoming difficult to establish if the attacks were related to a political movement, an individual and the company they worked for or a more deep-rooted cause that was aimed at destabilizing the country. The intelligence gained suggested that the cyber-attacks that had done the most damage were in fact aimed at disrupting trade between selected nations and also the sustainability of companies. It was clear that the attacks were targeted and carried out by multiple threat actors. Because of this, a comparison had to be made between distinguishing between identity theft and what was involved and actions taken to cripple a country's economy.

The biometrics policy had worked well to date, and it was suggested that partner organizations should also adopt biometric authentication as this could be applied to people working from home and using their own devices. Mr. Hargreaves had been responsible for implementing the biometrics policy within the company and was pleased with the overall results. There had been no leakage of data or information and encryption and two-factor authentication and authorization had worked well. The question remained: Could partner organizations be encouraged to implement a robust biometrics policy? Blockchain technology had also been utilized to good effect and senior management was confident that this too could be rolled out in partner organizations. But life was not that easy. Some managers based in prominent supplier companies did not know about encryption and had refused to look into its use. Although the blockchain concept had a number of advantages associated with it, various managers had considered that human error was unlikely and the systems in place were watertight, hence they had become complacent.

Mrs. Wright explained that it was necessary for managers based at the company to take a greater interest in partnership development and suggested that she and Mr. Hargreaves spearhead the discussions with existing partner members. Issues to be talked through included the coordination of business activities, governance, compliance, risk management, crisis management, access to resources (e.g., financial, human and technical) and future stakeholder interaction. It was also important to focus discussions on integrated intelligence systems and CTI and analysis.

In addition to the immediate topics, the discussion also revolved around products in relation to smart living such as autonomous vehicles. Again, issues of connectivity and infrastructure surfaced and were given attention. It was thought that scenario analysis and planning could be used to determine possible smart city cyber risks. But this was for future consideration as there were much more pressing problems to solve.

Mr. Hargreaves and Miss Wright drew up a list of action points. They wanted answers to the flowing questions:

Question 1: How could managers in partner organizations be encouraged to implement a robust biometrics policy?
Question 2: How could the use of blockchain technology be promoted? Think of examples that can be used to make a case for the use of the blockchain concept.
Question 3: What do managers involved in a partnership arrangement need to do to make sure that is it successful in the long term?

References, websites and further reading

Aggarwal, B.A., Gupta, A., Goyal, D., Gupta, P., Bijender, B., and Barak, D.D. (2022). A review on investigating the role of block-chain in cyber security. *Materials Today: Proceedings*, 56, pp. 3312–3316. https://doi.org/10.1016/j.matpr.2021.10.124

Arteche, A., Asher, C., Bull, C., Dare, H., Dately, I., Elshoff, E., and Mahmoud, M. (2022). Data approach to biometrics in cybersecurity with related risks. In: *2022 International Conference on Computational Science and Computational Intelligence (CSCI)*, pp. 1059–1066. Las Vegas, NV.: IEEE. DOI: 10.1109/CSCI58124.2022.00187

Bansal, P., Panchal, R., Bassi, S., and Kumar, A. (2020). Blockchain for cybersecurity: A comprehensive survey. In: *9th IEEE International Conference on Communication Systems and Network Technologies*, pp. 260–265. Gwalior, India: IEEE. 10th to 12th April. DOI: 10.1109/CSNT.2020.48

Carrigan, M., and Kirkup, M. (2001). The ethical responsibilities of marketers in retail observational research: Protecting stakeholders through the ethical 'Research Covenant'. *The International Review of Retail, Distribution and Consumer Research*, 11 (4), pp. 415–435. https://doi.org/10.1080/713770611

Chen, D., Wawrzynski, P., and Lv, Z. (2021). Cyber security in smart cities: A review of deep learning-based applications and case studies. *Sustainable Cities and Society*, 66, pp. 1–12. https://doi.org/10/1016/j.scs.2020.102655

Cho, J., and Lee, J. (2006). An integrated model of risk and risk-reducing strategies. *Journal of Business Research*, 59 (1), pp. 112–120. https://doi.org/10.1016/j.busres.2005.03.006

Fahy, M., Roche, J., and Weiner, A. (2005). *Beyond Governance: Creating Corporate Value Through Performance, Conformance and Responsibility*. Chichester: John Wiley & Sons Ltd.

Glassman, M., and Kang, M.J. (2012). Intelligence in the internet age: The emergence and evolution of Open Source Intelligence (OSINT). *Computers in Human Behavior*, 28 (2), pp. 673–682. Doi:10.1016/j.chb.2011.11.014

Goodman, M. (2016). *Future Crimes: Inside the Digital Underworld and the Battle for our Connected World*. London: Corgi Books.

Hingley, M.K. (2005). Power imbalance in UK agri-food supply channels: Learning to live with the supermarkets? *Journal of Marketing Management*, 21 (1–2), pp. 63–88. https://doi.org/10.1362/0267257053166758

Khan, H.U., Malik, H.Z., Nazir, S., and Khan, A.F. (2023). Utilizing bio metric system for enhancing cyber security in banking sector: A systematic analysis. *IEEE Access*, 11, pp. 80181–80198. DOI: 10.1109/ACCESS.2023.3298824

Konig, L., Unger, S., Kieseberg, P., and Tjoa, S. (2020). The risks of the blockchain: A review on current vulnerabilities and attacks. *Journal of Internet Services and Information Security*, 10 (3), pp. 110–127. DOI: 10.22667/JISIS.2020.08.31.110

Kim, K., Kim, J.S., Jeong, S., Park, J-H., and Kim, H.K. (2021). Cybersecurity for autonomous vehicles: Review of attacks and defense. *Computers & Security*, 103 (102150), pp. 1–27. https://doi.org/10.1016/j.cose.2020.102150

Law, D.M., Shapka, J.D., Domene, J.F., and Gagné, M.H. (2012). Are Cyberbullies really bullies? An investigation of reactive and proactive online aggression. *Computers in Human Behavior*, 28 (2), pp. 664–672. https://doi.org/10.1016/j.chb.2011.11.013

Lee, J.C., Kim, J.H., and Seo, J.T. (2019). Cyber attack scenarios on smart city and their ripple effects. In: *2019 International Conference on Platform Technology and Service (PlatCon)*, pp. 1–5. Jeju, South Korea: IEEE. (28th to 30th January). DOI: 10.1109/PlatCon.2019.8669431

Lim, H.S.M., and Taeihagh, A. (2018). Autonomous vehicles for smart and sustainable cities: An in-depth exploration of privacy and cyber security implications. *Energies*, 11, pp. 1–23. DOI: 10.3390/en11051062

Linkov, V., Zámečník, P., Havlíčková, D., and Pai, C-W. (2019). Human factors in cybersecurity of autonomous vehicles: Trends in current research. *Frontiers in Psychology*, 10, 995. DOI: 10.3389/fpsyg.2019.00995

Makrakis, G.M., Kolias, C., Kambourakis, G., Rieger, C., and Benjamin, J. (2021). Industrial and critical infrastructure security: Technical analysis of real-life security incidents. *IEEE Access*, 9, pp. 165295–165325. https://doi/10.1109/ACCESS.2021.3133348. (Accessed 21st May, 2024).

Madnick, S. (2019). *Blockchain Isn't as Unbreakable as You Think*. MIT Sloan School of Management Working Paper CISL# 2019-21. Cambridge, MA: Massachusetts Institute of Technology. http://dx.doi.org/10.2139/ssrn.3542542

McAuley, A. (2004). Seeking (marketing) virtue in globalisation. *The Marketing Review*, 4 (3), pp. 253–266. https://doi.org/10.1362/1469347042223382

Nardini, G., Bublitz, M.G., Butler, C., Croom-Raley, S., Escalas, J.E., Hansen, J., and Peracchio, L.A. (2022). Scaling social impact: Marketing to grow nonprofit solutions. *Journal of Public Policy & Marketing*, 41 (3), pp. 254–276. DOI: 10.1177/07439156221087997

Odom, W.E. (1997). Chapter 11 National security policymaking: The kinds of things that must be decided for defense. In: Shultz, R.H., Godson, R., and Quester, G.H. (eds.). *Security Studies for the 21ˢᵗ Century*, pp. 403–435. Washington and London: Brassey's, Inc.

Pastor-Galindo, J., Nespoli, P., Mármol, F.G., and Pérez, G.M. (2020). The not yet exploited goldmine of OSINT: Opportunities, open challenges and future trends. *IEEE Access*, 8, pp. 10282–10304. DOI: 10.1109/ACCESS.2020.2965257

Patton, K. (2010). *Sociocultural Intelligence: A New Discipline in Intelligence Studies*. London: The Continuum International Publishing Group.

Raiyn, J. (2018). Data and cyber security in autonomous vehicle networks. *Transport and Telecommunications*, 19 (4), pp. 325–334. DOI: 10.2478/ttj-2018-0027

Rese, M. (2006). Successful and sustainable business partnerships: How to select the right partners. *Industrial Marketing Management*, 35 (1), pp. 72–82. DOI:10.1016/j.indmarman.2005.08.009

Sheffi, Y. (2005). *The Resilient Enterprise: Overcoming Vulnerability for Competitive Advantage*. Cambridge, Massachusetts: The MIT Press.

Sun, C-C., Hahn, A., and Liu, C-C. (2018). Cyber security of a power grid: State-of-the-art. *Electrical Power and Energy Systems*, 99, pp. 45–56. https://doi.org/10.1016/j.ijepes.2017.12.020

Taeihagh, A., and Lim, H.S.M. (2019). Governing autonomous vehicles: Emerging responses for safety, liability, privacy, cybersecurity, and industry risks. *Transport Reviews*, 39 (1), pp. 103–128. DOI: 10.1080/01441647.2018.1494640

Thakhur, K., Qiu, M., Gai, K., and Ali, M.L. (2015). An investigation on cyber security threats and security models. In: *2015 IEEE 2nd International Conference on Cyber Security and Cloud Computing*, pp. 307–311. New York, NY.: IEEE. DOI: 10.1109/CSCloud.2015.71. 3rd to 5th November

Thakhur, K., Tseng, J., and Hayajneh, T. (2019). Cyber security in social media: Challenges and the way forward. *IT Professional* 21 (2), pp. 41–49. IEEE. DOI: 10.1109/MITP.2018.2881373. (Accessed 12th May, 2024).

The Sunday Times. (2019). Deep fake. *The Sunday Times Magazine.* 22nd December, pp. 10–15, & 17.

Thuraisingham, B. (2020). The role of artificial intelligence and cyber security for social media. In: *2020 IEEE International Parallel and Distributed Processing Symposium Workshop (IPDPSW)*, pp. 1116–1118. New Orleans, LA: IEEE. DOI: 10.1109/IPDPSW50202.2020.00184. 18–22, May.

Trim, P.R.J., and Lee, Y-I. (2008). A strategic approach to sustainable partnership development. *European Business Review*, 20 (3), pp. 222–239. DOI: 10.1108/09555340810871428

van der Walk, E., Eloff, J.H.P., and Grobler, J. (2018). Cyber-security: Identity deception detection on social media platforms. *Computers & Society*, pp. 76–89. https://doi.org/10.1016/j.cose.2018.05.015

Vattapparamban, E., Güvenç, I., Yurekli, A.I., Akkaya, K., and Uluağaç, S. (2016). Drones for smart cities: Issues in cybersecurity, privacy, and public safety. In: 2016 International Wireless Communications and Mobile Computing Conference (IWCMC), pp. 216–221. Paphos, Cyprus: IEEE. DOI:10.1109/IWCMC.2016.7577060

Walters, D. (1979). Manufacturer/retailer relationships. *European Journal of Marketing*, 13 (7), pp. 179–222. https://doi.org/10.1108/EUM0000000004955

Williams, H.J., and Blum, I. (2018). *Defining Second Generation Open Source Intelligence (OSINT) for the Defense Enterprise.* Santa Monica, Calif.: RAND Corporation.

Windahl, C., and Lakemond, N. (2006). Developing integrated solutions: The importance of relationships within the network. *Industrial Marketing Management*, 35 (7), pp. 806–818. DOI:10.1016/j.indmarman.2006.05.010

Wonders, B.J., Solop, F.I., and Wonders, N.A. (2012). Information sampling and linking: Reality Hunger and the digital knowledge commons. *Contemporary Social Science*, 7 (3), pp. 247–262. https://doi.org/10.1080/21582041.2012.683447

Wucherer, K. (2006). Business partnering – a driving force for innovation. *Industrial Marketing Management*, 35 (1), pp. 91–102.

Website

Woodward, B. (2024). *Cyber threats will present an ever greater number of risks to international peace and security.* Statement by UK Permanent Representative to the UN Ambassador Barbara Woodward at the UN Security Council meeting on cybersecurity (20th June). New York, United Nations. https://www.gov.uk/government/speeches/cyber-threats-will-present-an-ever-greater-number-of-risks-to-international-peace-and-security-uk-statement-at-the-un-security-council (Accessed 23rd July, 2024).

Further reading

Andersen, P.H., and Kumar, R. (2006). Emotions, trust and relationship development in business relationships: A conceptual model for buyer-seller dyads. *Industrial Marketing Management*, 35, pp. 522–535.

Håkansson, H., and Snehota, I. (2006). No business is an island: The network concept of business strategy. *Scandinavian Journal of Management*, 22, pp. 256–270. DOI: 10.1016/j.scaman.2006.10.005

Hau, Le N., and Evangelista, F. (2007). Acquiring tacit and explicit marketing knowledge from foreign partners in IJVs. *Journal of Business Research*, 60, pp. 1,152–1,165.

Kirca, A.H., and Hult, T.M. (2009). Intra-organizational factors and market orientation: Effects of national culture. *International Marketing Review*, 26 (6), pp. 633–650.

Rosa, L., Freitas, M., Mazo, S., Monteiro, E., Cruz, T., and Simões, P. (2019). A comprehensive security analysis of a SCADA Protocol: From OSINT to mitigation. *IEEE Access*, 7, pp. 42156–42168. 10.1109/ACCESS.2019.2906926

Trim, P.R.J. (2000). The company-intelligence services interface and national security. *International Journal of Intelligence and Counter Intelligence*, 13 (2), pp. 204–214.

7
A COLLECTIVIST ENTERPRISE RISK MANAGEMENT CYBER THREAT MODEL

7.1 Introduction

A collectivist enterprise risk management cyber threat model (Section 7.2) is followed by linking strategic intelligence with cyber security management (Section 7.3). A collectivist cyber threat intelligence policy and strategy framework (Section 7.4) precedes cyber security risk register (Section 7.5), which is followed by risk management (Section 7.6). Reflection and questions (Section 7.7) is followed by a Conclusion (Section 7.8).

7.2 A Collectivist Enterprise Risk Management Cyber Threat Model

A collectivist enterprise risk management cyber threat model can be considered useful in terms of the cyber security manager identifying risks and helping to rectify organizational vulnerabilities. This is achieved partly by devising and implementing organizational structures that can help other managers to interpret the outcome from a formal strategic intelligence analysis. The aim is to establish how an organizational cyber security management system is reinforced by counterintelligence and a strategic organizational monitoring intelligence system. A conceptual model can help the cyber security manager to achieve this task and ensure that a cyber security culture is maintained and is a subset of the organization's security culture. Yamin et al. (2021, p. 3) add to our understanding of the way in which cyber-attacks are evolving and compare classical cyber-attacks with AI-powered cyber-attacks. For example, AI can be considered a game changer because Yamin et al. (2021, p. 3) indicate that current laws are not particularly well suited to deal with AI-powered cyber-attacks. Because of this, managers need to draw more firmly on the strategic intelligence approach and leverage the strengths of the organization so that they are aligned more firmly to take advantage of the opportunities and at the same time deal with the threats in the external environment. Bearing in mind how interconnectivity is helping to reshape business models and at the same time highlight organizational vulnerabilities, it can be suggested that governments should provide more guidance and additional support to ensure that organizations remain compliant and university research

DOI: 10.4324/9781003570905-7

teams have sufficient funding to study evolving patterns of cyber-crime and help devise both technical and human-focused solutions. The objective of a collectivist enterprise risk management cyber threat model is to help managers throughout the organization, and indeed partner organizations, to define cyber attackers in terms of their persistence, their capability to cause immediate and sustainable damage (e.g., an analysis of the resources they deploy) and establish how they are likely to respond to defensive action. In addition, attention needs to be given to how a cyber attacker moves from exploiting a known vulnerability to engaging in cyber warfare. As regards the latter, the cyber security manager needs to be aware of how debilitating and disruptive attacks on critical national infrastructure and critical information infrastructure are and how the government in power is likely/able to respond and repair the facilities that are impacted. Looking to the future and understanding how environmental risk is increasing due to war becoming ideologically embedded, attention needs to focus on what is known as cyber terrorism, which is unpredictable, damaging and linked with the promotion of a political cause. Furthermore, knowing where specific types of cyber security expertise are and how the expertise can be drawn on from international partners (including overseas governments) to counter such actions is a necessity. Government representatives will in the years ahead need to be more proactive in terms of coordinating resources and passing laws that maintain the well-being of society and at the same time guarantee privacy, the rights of the individual and a safe trading environment. However, this can only be achieved through industry–government–academic cooperation because the knowledge and expertise required are dispersed among different audiences and the type of threat is increasing exponentially.

At the centre of the conceptual model outlined in Figure 7.1 are AI and sociocultural intelligence and it is useful to note that the monitoring that occurs to establish the effectiveness of the organizational learning policy that is in place is essentially to ensure that staff are cyber security aware and comply with organizational policy. Staff can only be compliant, however, if the appropriate governance mechanism is in place. Risk

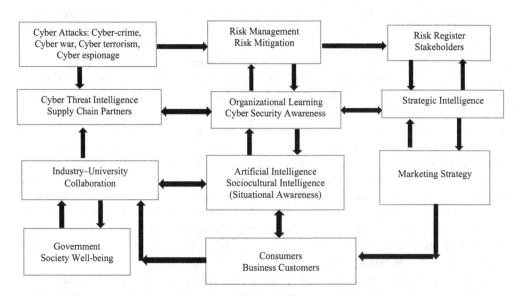

FIGURE 7.1   A collectivist enterprise risk management cyber threat model.

management ensures that the risks identified are listed in the risk register(s). As regards strategic intelligence, continual monitoring of the threat environment by managers ensures that the factors in the organization's internal environment are mapped to the factors in the external environment and there is differentiation between controllable factors and their influence and uncontrollable factors and their influence.

In order to establish if the corporate objectives from a security-related stance are being achieved, it is necessary to divide the risks identified into controllable risks and uncontrollable risks and link them to the vulnerabilities identified. This should, provided that managers are up to date, result in a formal threat detection policy that is collectivist in orientation as the responsibility is distributed among staff in different business functions. It is clear to see from Figure 7.1 that organizational staff place emphasis on intelligence gathering, forming trust-based working relationships with both internal staff and staff based in external organizations and are committed to facilitating data and information sharing and exchange. Emphasis is still placed on devoting time and effort to understanding customer needs (e.g., online feedback that improves customer service and raises concerns relating to customer data handling). Liaising with government representatives is considered necessary because not only are senior staff involved in campaigning for government intervention from time to time but they also help shape international standards and additional laws that protect consumers from the misuse of social media and those behind the development of fake websites. Broadly speaking, senior managers accept that an organization serves the needs of its defined customer group(s) in the most efficient way possible. Understandably, there will be various demands on the organization from its various stakeholders and it is important that the cyber security manager is committed to cyber threat detection because including a new supplier or contractor into the business model may in fact create a new vulnerability.

The conceptual model outlined in Figure 7.1 can be classified as organization specific, but it also mirrors the enterprise as a whole and can be used as a basis for designing a specific enterprise risk management cyber threat model. Accepting that industries differ and that organizations are in different stages of development brings out the point that a new business model configuration requires senior management to view an organization's risk management cyber threat model from the perspective of it being fit for purpose. The meaning of fit for purpose needs to be considered from the organization's ability to defend itself against known threats and evolving threats on a continual basis. This is achieved by senior managers utilizing adequate resources and working with key individuals that have been designated to undertake and assume responsibility for certain cyber security tasks.

The cyber security manager, working with the IT manager, the risk manager, the security manager and the marketing manager, can help promote the organization's cyber security policy by producing a number of outputs that lead to an improvement in the way people throughout the supply chain view cyber security. Consequently, staff are empowered to take responsibility for the different elements of cyber security. The cyber security policy attributes that manifest through management's actions and which are embedded in the structures and mechanisms are designed into the organization's cyber security strategy in a logical and coherent way. Hence, the main advantage of such a model is that it can foster a proactive approach to cyber security management and help managers to identify skill deficiencies that once rectified result in enhanced cyber security awareness and the development of new cyber security knowledge.

Cyber security knowledge needs to be stored within the organization's memory and accessed when needed. Furthermore, the modelling approach can be used to help cyber security specialists develop additional forms of intervention that help improve the lives of those affected (Ebrahim and Rangan, 2014, p. 123) as it takes into account the needs of the community by extending the scope of cyber security provision. This can be considered a somewhat ideal view; however, if an organization does experience a cyber-attack, it is likely that some harm will result and the impact will be felt by the wider community (e.g., suppliers, customers and those buying for resale). A really damaging cyber-attack may cause financial harm to the organization that manifests in the organization closing down, which results in laying staff off. The unemployment that results may have social consequences for people living in the location where the organization operates, and it may be difficult for certain individuals to find employment because there are limited opportunities available. It is because of this that a collectivist view of cyber security can be considered a proactive approach to stakeholder well-being as well as beneficial for society and society's well-being.

A collectivist enterprise risk management cyber threat model will also help managers put in place specific safeguards that counteract the actions of hackers and protect the organization's intellectual property rights. To ensure this is the case, managers need to identify both the formal ties (e.g., contracts in place with suppliers) and informal ties (e.g., verbal agreements with law enforcement personnel) that they have entered into. They also need to classify the two types of ties into: (i) At risk from criminal-oriented threat agents and (ii) at risk from rogue government threat agents, as this form of segmentation will allow them to monitor the company's operations from a particular perspective and provide evidence to the appropriate law enforcement authorities and other stakeholders. If the cyber-attack carried out against the organization is multidimensional (e.g., a ransomware attack combined with a fake news campaign), then it is likely that the risk involved will be assessed as high, but this can only be the case if a risk is rated and ranked in terms of its priority. Hence, the individual components or antecedent conditions of each risk need to be established and further depth can be achieved by linking each risk with each business function (e.g., marketing and sales, finance and accounting, human resource management, purchasing and operations management).

7.3 Linking Strategic Intelligence with Cyber Security Management

The concept of sociocultural intelligence can be used to place in context how innovations in technology such as AI can help senior managers to undertake effective CTI. According to Patton (2010, p. 11), sociocultural intelligence is used by social science researchers to produce situational awareness output that has the advantage of being relevant to a specific operational environment. Sociocultural intelligence can, therefore, be used to define and form CTI policy and strategy (Trim and Lee, 2022); however, in order to enhance its effectiveness, it needs to be used in association with other approaches such as the sequence-of-events model (Trim and Lee, 2014), whereby cyber security analysts identify current and future cyber threats and categorize their expected impacts by identifying specific targets (e.g., a supply chain member that subcontracts out work and has an identified vulnerability). In addition, the T-shaped scaling method (Nardini et al., 2022) has the advantage of allowing a specific topic to be viewed from a community policy perspective that gives rise to innovatory local solutions and helps to "address the circumstances at the root of those challenges" (Nardini et al., 2022, p. 257). These approaches combined prove useful for developing an enterprise risk management cyber threat model that has a collectivist orientation because various participants, known as influential cyber security stakeholders (e.g., highly influential in terms of influencing various communities including both public and private sector organizations, government, universities and professional associations), can be drawn on to help construct such a model.

Cyber security experts are used to identifying and solving complex and evolving problems and possess various aspects of cyber security knowledge that can help the cyber security manager devise a robust model (e.g., once tested it will work in the way expected). Drawing on an insider's view is considered beneficial (Nardini et al., 2022, p. 259) as it allows a scaling wide approach to be adopted. The scaling wide approach advocated by Heimans and Timms (Nardini et al., 2022, p. 263) involves the process of transferring insights so that the common factors and the main themes are in unison. Hence, the scaling approach is useful because it allows the main themes to be identified and linked in a logical order so that the outcome can be depicted in diagrammatic form.

The critical friendship group approach has been used to gain insights into cyber security awareness (Trim and Lee, 2019) and can be described as highly effective as regards providing insights into how cyber security knowledge can be shared and used to develop a cyber security framework that can be used as a foundation for cyber security policy and strategy. In order to fully understand the complexities of security and intelligence work, senior managers need to develop specific types of intelligence and establish a threat intelligence knowledge bank that can be drawn on as necessary. Indeed, intelligence work can be viewed from an environment risk perspective and those that carry out intelligence analysis and solutions can do so knowing that they have a direct input into the collectivist enterprise risk management cyber threat model. They can also assist with the model's development and implementation through time and help integrate it into the structure of the organizational partner(s).

The critical friendship group approach has a number of strengths and can be used by a speaker/author of a research paper or a change agent championing a certain approach to put forward their views/findings to a well-informed and knowledgeable group of people/experts and receive constructive feedback (Golby and Appleby, 1995). The feedback allows them to develop their knowledge of the subject more fully as it is subject specific and current. The group interview method is appropriate for probing and again, making sense of underlying conditions (Patton, 1990) and because of this, it can be argued that various external experts can be used to provide guidance and insights that can help the developer of a collectivist enterprise risk management cyber threat model to identify the inputs of the model.

The members selected and who form the critical friendship group should in order to maximize their contribution be part of a wider stakeholder security group. This is because cyber security incorporates different strands of knowledge and spans different and highly complex subject areas. Furthermore, by attending a range of business functions, organizational staff can extend their own security and intelligence networks and include academic researchers in the discussions. They can also associate with industry members drawn from several industry associations; liaise with personnel from different government departments; attend meetings with staff from government agencies and hire experts from specialist security consultancies. Furthermore, they can monitor consumer interest groups and pay attention to the actions of activists and people in society who are committed to change. This will provide a foundation upon which insights from critical friendship group discussions can be reflected on and used for group interview discussions. It is envisaged that the cyber security manager, the IT manager, the risk manager and the security manager will be involved in such activities.

Ultimately, senior management and their subordinate staff will need to place cyber security threat intelligence in the context of how organizational staff can produce a holistic cyber security framework that is adaptive and supportive of cyber security initiatives and interventions. The interventions (e.g., training and staff development programmes) used to create cyber security awareness can be both technology focused and human "relations" focused, and can be thought of as transformational in nature. Because the threat environment is changing so rapidly, it is imperative that staff manage intelligence proactively as opposed to being reactive and sit back and wait to respond to certain events. The point to be noted is that the organization will face defined threats, and the risks will need to be quantified and itemized in the risk register(s).

Such a strategy will allow organizational staff to work with cyber security researchers and cyber security experts and establish the role that strategic intelligence plays. It will also allow staff involved in cyber security strategic intelligence to devise an enterprise risk management cyber threat model that is flexible and adaptive. The form the model takes will be dependent upon the guidance provided by senior management. The approach adopted should yield benefits as regards helping to determine how impact analysis can help managers to improve external intelligence gathering, which is essential as regards defending against an attack on an organization in real time. To understand the logic of this, it is essential to consider that cyber-attacks are transmuting and becoming more sophisticated; this is increasing an organization's vulnerability, which can in some instances be attributed to organizational delayering. Staff that work via remote means without having adequate security training and support are at risk of making a mistake and this translates into an organizational vulnerability. Employees using their own device (e.g., BYOD – Bring Your Own Device) for work and also using it for leisure are subject to the risk of downloading malware (from a non-company site), which can infect files and cause untold damage. Infected websites are a source of malware, and employees should be informed about avoiding certain types of websites and/or informed as to how to check that the website is legitimate.

The T-shaped scaling approach (Nardini et al., 2022, pp. 257–263) can help staff identify the relationships that exist and establish ways to transfer knowledge among and between community members. By reflecting on this, three interlinked activities can be identified that have a common route: organizational learning (e.g., scaling wide); strategic intelligence (e.g., scaling deep) and marketing strategy formation and implementation (e.g., scaling deep). The relationships identified can also be linked with staff external to the organization as they undertake activities/tasks performed by individuals in the wider community including partner organizations. It is clear that the "buy-in" that Nardini et al. (2022, p. 261) refer to is cyber security awareness and its benefit in terms of creating a security culture. By continually promoting cyber security awareness, individuals in partner organizations and the wider community will become more cyber security aware and the security culture in place will foster a proactive approach to cyber security.

7.4 A Collectivist Cyber Threat Intelligence Policy and Strategy Framework

At this juncture, it is useful to reflect on the question: How can managers create and implement a collectivist CTI policy and strategy framework that eradicates vulnerabilities throughout a networked, partnership arrangement? The approach deployed can be considered fit for purpose because cyber security policy and strategy take into account:

> "(i) the level of risk (high, medium and low) associated with a specific cyber-attack; and (ii) how various stakeholders can be categorized according to their influence/ impact in terms of counteracting/helping to counteract the type of cyber-attack"
>
> *(Trim and Lee, 2023, pp. 42–43).*

To fully understand how an organizational vulnerability will be exploited and how the consequences of the impact should be dealt with, it is necessary to understand that strategic intelligence (Montgomery and Weinberg, 1979) is regarded as providing the context within which the main antecedent conditions for dealing with high-level security threats are interpreted. Indeed, nowadays, the weaponization of AI is resulting in cyber-attacks (Yamin et al., 2021) that are causing much concern, and this is bringing industry and government closer together in terms of the formulation of future cyber security policy and strategy.

Reflecting on the school of strategic marketing (Aaker, 1992), it is possible to propose that managers, especially those working for producers of smart products and services, need to define an unmet customer need from the perspective of providing safe and reliable products that enhance an individual's mobility, standard of living and at the same time keep a customer's data secure (e.g., smart devices used for leisure and home banking). By adhering to governance, the leadership model in place, which underpins the collectivist enterprise risk management cyber threat model, will be viewed as assertive but flexible in the sense that cyber-focused vulnerabilities will emerge and will be addressed through time. Because managers are used to dealing with risk in uncertain and turbulent environments, they will be accustomed to using a range of situational awareness tools, techniques, frameworks and approaches that facilitate the marketing decision-making process (Choi, 2010) and at the same time achieve a balance between meeting customer needs and maintaining the organization's resilience. By drawing on the stakeholder approach (King, 2008) and integrating marketing systems and procedures, throughout the supply chain and marketing channel, CTI will be more specifically defined and organizational staff will be able to deal with various forms of cyber-attack (e.g., those aimed at disrupting the organization's website and/or marketing online activities). By applying the scaling method, managers can widen the scope of cyber security awareness provision and devise interventions for staff in partner organizations so that the systems in place remain up to date. Hence, cyber security and its management can be integrated into other business functions and activities and together, staff can devise and implement a risk mitigation policy and strategy.

Enterprise risk management requires senior managers to identify various types of risks, to establish the probability associated with each risk and understand and estimate the potential impact a risk will have should it become a threat to the organization (Stine et al., 2020, p. 4). The logic of this is that resources are limited and because of this, time and effort have to be put into prioritizing risks and investing in the most likely counter-measures to ensure that if a vulnerability is exploited, then the damage is limited. The point is that the organization does not have sufficient resources to invest in rectifying all the vulnerabilities identified. To ensure that an organization does have the resources nec-essary to invest in an adequate cyber security defence, it is essential that governance is in place and the finance director is supportive.

Guidance in terms of governance is provided by NIST (Stine et al., 2020, p. 6):

> "Senior enterprise executives provide risk guidance (including advice regarding mis-sion priority, risk appetite and tolerance guidance, and capital and operating budgets to manage known risks) to the organizations within their purview. Risk appetite and risk tolerance statements are the usual means for communicating this guidance".

It is important to understand that managers need to both manage and monitor the pro-cesses involved so that there is a balance between the risks identified and the resources allocated owing to the fact that risk tolerance needs to be translated into risk appetite (Stine et al., 2020, p. 6).

Senior managers are charged with defining risk, managing risk and communicating the key points via a risk register. Bearing this in mind, it is possible to understand better the process for putting in place an enterprise risk management model. Stine et al. (2020, p. 8) have provided guidance in terms of this by outlining six steps that senior managers need to undertake to effectively incorporate enterprise risk management, they are: *Identify the context*; identify *the risks*; *analyse the risks*; *prioritize the risks*; *plan and execute risk response strategies* and *monitor, evaluate, and adjust*. The last step is to ensure that the enterprise risk conditions identified are contained within the risk appetite levels previ-ously established because it is important to note that cyber security risks change over time.

It is clear from the above that a risk register is essential as it not only has a description of the different types of risk that the organization is prone to but also requires managers to specify the expected impact associated with each risk that is traced to a specific vulner-ability. A more detailed analysis will include why the risk is expected to remain a risk and this requires a clear understanding of the mitigation of risk and which risk mitigation strategies are in place. By adopting a quantitative approach to the probability that a risk will occur that results in a certain impact, it should be possible for the cyber security manager to work with the risk manager(s) and hold the risk owners accountable. Furthermore, by ranking and prioritizing risks, it should be possible to implement a cyber security risk management and monitoring process that is integrated but independent of the strategic planning cycle. In other words, cyber security risk management is viewed as a process and is undertaken on a continuous basis throughout the year. This suggests that a systematic approach to risk management needs to be adopted.

The National Institute of Standards and Technology (NIST) based in the United States is a forward-looking agency that has done much to promote the use of safe technology. NIST (Stine et al., 2020, p. 11) suggests that: "Many systems upon which agencies and other institutions rely are complex, adaptive 'systems-of-systems' composed of thousands of interdependent components and myriad channels. The systems operate in a rapidly changing socio-political-technological environment that presents threats from individu-als and groups with shifting alliances, attitudes, and agendas". With rapid advances in technology, it is necessary for the cyber security manager to keep up with change. NIST (Stine et al., 2020, p. 11) makes reference to wireless connections, big data, cloud computing as well as the IoT and suggests that new technology provides new systemic risks that can be placed in the context of exploitable vulnerabilities. Bearing this in mind, it is important for senior management to know how to manage risk at the enterprise level and to do this, managers need to know how the interdependence of systems is likely to give rise to risks that need to be identified, tracked and managed (Stine et al., 2020, p. 11).

NIST (Stine et al., 2020, pp. 14–15) makes clear that there are two types of controls in support of enterprise risk management, and they are distinguished as *internal controls* and *security controls*. *Internal controls* are the overarching mechanisms established by the board of directors that are in place and allow managers to both achieve and monitor the enterprise's objectives. Risk management is a key function and is monitored through ICSs. *Security controls* are in fact the safeguards/countermeasures of an information system/an organization that protects the confidentiality, integrity and availability of the system as well as the information therewith (Stine et al., 2020, p. 15). It can be noted that security controls are essential for managing and administering, as well as providing technical methods for responding to cybersecurity risks.

7.5 Cyber Security Risk Register

With reference to what an organization's risk register looks like and what it contains, it can be disclosed that risk registers differ depending on industry circumstances. However, whether the organization is young in age or mature, whether it operates as a market nicher or as a monopolist and whether the industry cyber life cycle is emerging or established, such an approach can be deemed relevant as it reflects senior management's commitment to ensuring that the organization is resilient. Resiliency is, therefore, associated with a formal process that is composed of a number of interlocking cyber security management processes, characterized by formal management structures and systems.

Table 7.1 has been formed as an illustrative example from the guidance provided by NIST (Stine et al., 2020, p. 15) and includes an extra dimension entitled *Critical Thinking Problem Solution*. The *Critical Thinking Problem Solution* dimension has been added to make sure that the cyber security manager and their colleagues reflect on the link between *data*, *process* and *solution* (Butterworth and Thwaites, 2013, p. 82), which are denoted as "D", "P" and "S" in the table. The *Critical Thinking Problem Solution* dimension places added emphasis on identifying the initial problem and making sure that the solution for solving it is robust. By including this dimension, it should be possible for managers to adopt a proactive approach to risk management and include various stakeholders (internal and external to the organization) that have expert knowledge that can be drawn on. The key point to note is that by harnessing expert knowledge and storing it in the organization's memory, the cyber security manager and their colleagues will establish an appropriate knowledge base that feeds into and draws on the organizational learning model that is in place.

One of the outcomes of the approach outlined is a forward-looking approach or the utilization of foresight to solve cyber security–related problems. Furthermore, when constructing Table 7.1, it proved essential to draw on the priority indicators such as likelihood, impact and exposure rating outlined by NIST (Stine et al., 2020, p. 15) as this

TABLE 7.1 Illustrative example of a cyber security risk register

ID	Priority	Risk Description	Risk Category	Likelihood	Impact	Exposure Rating	Risk Response Type	Risk Response Cost	Risk Response Disruption	Risk Owner	Status	Critical Thinking Problem Solution
1	Immediate	IT Based	Information Security Risk Cyber Security Manager Immediate Action	Very High	0.2	Known High	Inter-organizational	US$ 1 Million	Major – Close Down Systems	IT Director IT Manager	Risk Manager Assigned	Replicate Data (D) Integrated Action Plan (P) Collective Ownership (S)
2	Immediate	IT-Based Computer Network	Information Security Risk Cyber Security Manager Immediate Action	High	0.15	Known Moderate	Inter-organizational	US$1 Million	Major – Close Down Systems	IT Director/ IT Manager	Risk Manager Assigned	Replicate Data (D) Integrated Action Plan (P) Collective Ownership (S)
3	High	Financial Control	Financial Risk Cyber Security Manager Immediate Action	High	0.15	Known Low	Inter-organizational	US$0.5 Million	Major – Close Down Systems	Financial Director	Risk Manager Assigned	Replicate Data (D) Integrated Action Plan (P) Collective Ownership (S)
4	Medium	Supplier's database	Network Security Risk Assistant Cyber Security Manager Risk Manager	Moderate	0.08	Known Low	Inter-organizational	US$0.5 Million	Containable	Marketing Director	Monitoring in Progress	Secure Data Systems (D) Link Information Technology and Marketing Systems (P) Collective/joint Business Continuity Planning (S)

| 5 | Low | Marketing Database | Marketing Risk Assistant Cyber Security Manager Risk Manager | 0.07 | Known Low | US$0.2 Million | Intra-organizational | Low | Containable | Marketing Director | Monitoring in Progress | Increase Authentication (D) Link Information Technology and Marketing Systems (P) Joint Management (S) |
| 6 | Low | Human Resource Database | Human Resource Management Risk Assistant Cyber Security Manager Risk Manager | 0.06 | Known Low | US$0.1 Million | Intra-organizational | Very Low | Containable | Personnel Director | Monitoring in Progress | Staff Awareness Campaign (D) Training and Staff Development Programmes (P) Frequent Updating and Reward of Employees (S) |

provided useful in terms of staff making assessments that were logical and robust. For example, the likelihood scale was denoted as very low, low, moderate, high and very high (Stine et al., 2020, p. 29) and the level of impact scale was denoted as (Stine et al., 2020, p. 30): Risk = 0.20 (probability x impact) represents a high risk and lower graded (moderate) risks are rated, it can be argued, between 0.08 and below 0.15. Risk values will be determined by the cyber security manager and the risk manager and their peers, and any decision regarding the determination of risk in association with the risk mitigation strategy will involve other members of the management team and stakeholder representatives.

The illustrative example has been constructed to show what type of information can go into a risk register and is not representative of a particular organization or industry. What is important to note is that the data and information that go into a risk register(s) need to be evidence based. This is so that risk mitigation in the context of each definable risk can be made clear and the individuals responsible for specific actions can be held to account for their actions. Table 7.1 also makes clear the fact that as well as identifying and rating each risk, the staff responsible for mitigating the risk are featured and so too is the process of communication through which the risk is reported and managed. Furthermore, the likely impact of an event is given an impact rating, and the risk response disruption is also disclosed.

NIST (Stine et al., 2020, p. 17) suggests that the contents of a risk detail should include: (i) *Information regarding the risk itself*; (ii) *the roles involved in risk decisions and management*; (iii) *schedule considerations* and (iv) *risk response decisions and follow-up*. As regards *information regarding the risk itself*, detailed risk scenarios can be produced to detail the underlying threats and vulnerabilities, as well as individual assets threatened, the risk category and risk assessment results can be included. With regards to *the roles involved in risk decisions and management*, reference can be made to the risk owner, the risk manager and the action owner for specific activities. Furthermore, it is essential to include the stakeholders involved in risk response decisions and also to cite any contractual agreements relating to supply chain/external partners. The *schedule considerations* need to include the date that the risk was first documented and the date of the last risk assessment. It is important also to refer to completion dates vis-à-vis mitigations and the date that the next assessment will be or is expected to be undertaken. Finally, *risk response decisions and follow-up* can be defined in terms of detailed plans, status and risk indicators.

7.6 Risk Management

In order to place risk and risk management in perspective, it is necessary for the cyber security manager to understand and document what the risk context is. Stine et al. (2020, pp. 17–18) indicate that it is important to consider both the *external context* and the *internal context*. For example, the *external context* can be thought of as the expectations of outside stakeholders. These expectations need to be interpreted from the perspective of how they affect and are affected by the organization. All the stakeholders can be included such as customers, regulators, legislators and also businesses. It is important to take cognizance of the fact that the stakeholders have objectives, perceptions and indeed expectations vis-à-vis risk and how it is to be communicated, managed and indeed monitored over time. As regards the *internal context*, of significance here are the factors and indeed the cyber security considerations that have relevance across the enterprise. A number of factors can be included such as cyber security risk management, which involves knowing what the risk appetite is, as well as risk tolerances, policies and practices; and other factors that can also be included such as the organization's and enterprise's objectives, its governance mechanism and culture.

The risk management process is composed of a framework that is composed of various steps (Stine et al., 2020, p. 20). It is important to establish a risk context by framing risk in such a way that it is logically understood by outlining the environment within which risk-based decisions are made and implemented. The objective is to produce a risk management strategy that outlines how an organization is to assess risk, how it will respond to risk and how managers will monitor risk through time (Stine et al., 2020, p. 20). An interesting point to note is that managers in stakeholder organizations are likely to view risk differently and because of this risk needs to be defined in clear and logical terms. Once this has been done, it is possible to identify a comprehensive set of risks and to record each risk in a way that is appropriate for the risk register use. For example, both inherent and residual risk need to be recorded, and a distinction needs to be made between actual residual risk and target (desired) risk (Stine et al., 2020, p. 21). By outlining the threats in detail, it is possible to provide various levels of risk assessment, quantify the risk accordingly and link each risk with a potential or actual threat actor. A threat actor, known as the instigator of the risk(s) identified is also appraised in terms of their threat capability (Stine et al., 2020, p. 24). By doing this, it should be possible to establish how a threat actor is likely to cause harm to the organization and what action plan or strategy needs to be implemented to ensure that the organization is resilient and can withstand repeated attacks.

Dealing with multiple risks needs care and attention because an unforeseen risk can manifest in a vulnerability being exploited. Should this happen, the cascading effects may dilute management's ability to deal with the incident in a timely and effective manner. As a consequence, further problems may materialize. Should an incident lead to a cascading effect, it is clear that the vulnerability analysis previously undertaken is defective and as a consequence, a new vulnerability analysis needs to be undertaken to detect which possible cyber-attacks will get through the organization's defences and what the consequences will be. NIST (Stine et al., 2020, p. 25) indicates that a vulnerability can be viewed as a condition that allows a threat event to manifest. NIST (Stine et al., 2020, p. 25) provides several examples such as an unpatched software flaw, an error in the system or indeed an individual that has malicious intent. It is possible to identify certain weaknesses (e.g., software flaws, missing patches, misconfigurations and indeed malware) using automated scanners (Stine et al., 2020, p. 25); however, the cyber security manager needs to be able to analyse the risks/potential risks identified, detail them in the risk register and articulate the potential impact associated with each risk. This is so the risk(s) can be mitigated within a short time period. By following such a process, it is hoped that stakeholder organizations will realize the necessity of maintaining their own risk register and integrating their risk register within the organization's risk register. This will help promote cyber security awareness and also help establish a collectivist cyber security culture.

It is useful at this juncture to consider the view of Bromiley et al. (2015) and to reflect on what enterprise risk management involves and how it can be interpreted. This is because some critics suggest that it is not possible to think of placing all the known risks in an organization-specific context. Bearing in mind that there are different approaches to risk management and the categorization of risks, it is possible to suggest that risks can be defined in terms of traditional risks (e.g., product liability) and also strategic risks (e.g., competitor actions) (Bromiley et al., 2015, p. 268). Taking into account that there are many types of risk, it is logical to argue that the transformational approach to management is conducive to establishing an enterprise risk management process to manage risks. For example, Trim and Lee (2022, p. 13) point out that transformational leadership is a precursor to organizational change and make reference to the fact that staff draw on their own social network(s) to gain intelligence regarding cyber-attacks. Another interesting point to emerge from the research of Trim and Lee (2022, p. 14) is that crisis management is deemed necessary because it can be assumed that an organization and its partners will be penetrated at some point in time. Hence, the following question can be posed: How should the cyber security manager equate risk with impact?

NIST (Stine et al., 2020, p. 27) provides advice as regards equating risk with impact. It can be deduced that the cyber security manager needs to think of using risk scenarios to highlight to the finance department certain issues such as the age of the server, the network itself, the reliability of the software in use, the likelihood that it will fail, and how business operations will be reconfigured should an impact occur. If a system fails for any reason, then it is likely to have knock-on effects and these need to be known and considered from a risk communication perspective. If the impact is severe, then possibly trading will cease and the organization will need to close down for a while. Possibly some customers will seek other suppliers and because of this, coupled with the reputational damage sustained, the organization may find that it is unable to regain its lost business.

It is clear that risk embodies a number of factors and the cyber security manager and their colleagues need to be aware that risk perception changes through time as the underlying conditions change. This is, it can be argued of interest because risk is normally associated with a financial cost and although organizational staff have a clear view of what risk is, their interpretation of it may differ depending on their work-related activities and the work-related activities of their colleagues based on different business functions. There is a view that organizational staff involved in a partnership arrangement think of security in the context of a co-owned cyber security strategy (Trim and Lee, 2021, p. 11) and this is useful because it assumes that security-related knowledge has a universal appeal and can be shared with like-minded people.

NIST (Stine et al., 2020, p. 27) provides additional information that can expand our understanding of the topic as it links with crisis/emergency planning. Often, the costs associated with a crisis/emergency are not factored into the relevant budget and senior management is sometimes taken aback by the immediate cost and the ongoing cost associated with rectifying the impact of a cyber-attack. The cyber security manager is well paced to offer advice about this because they can draw on other real-world examples. Working with the risk manager, each potential risk can be identified, quantified in terms of threat and placed in the risk register for future action. Ultimately, the head of finance has to assume responsibility for ensuring that what is defined as an acceptable level of risk, is associated with an appropriate level of resources because each risk identified has also to be linked with potential knock-on effects, should an impact occur. From this, it can be deduced that risk mitigation is ongoing and will require staff to implement solutions by continually monitoring and anticipating how cyber-attacks will be carried out. As well as using humans to undertake the monitoring of the threat environment, it is possible to utilize cyber-attack detection software and deploy it to monitor network intrusions and other types of illegal activity. Sensors in the network can record intrusions, monitor them and send information to appropriate managers who are then required to intervene and establish how the intrusion is developing. Once known, the manager responsible can activate countermeasures to ensure that the intruder is unable to carry out a full-scale attack, which possibly is aimed at extracting data/information or sabotaging the system/files. Indeed, AI-based intruder detection systems may well offer a cost-benefit approach that gives the defender the upper hand, but such a system needs to be managed proactively.

7.7 Reflection and Questions

Figure 7.2 outlines how a collectivist CIT policy and strategy framework is formed. It can be noted that strategic intelligence is incorporated into cyber security management and risk management is undertaken on a continual basis. The risks identified are placed in a risk register(s) and information is provided as to how each risk is to be mitigated. An outcome of the process is a formal approach to CTI, whereby accountability and responsibility are assigned to designated managers.

The strategic intelligence approach should ensure that cyber security staff monitor cyber security threats in the external environment. Organizational learning can be used to make sure staff are cyber security aware and comply with organizational policy. Risk management can be deployed to identify risks and the risks identified can be placed in a risk register(s). A collectivist enterprise risk management cyber threat model can help managers to safeguard an organization's resources and influential cyber security stakeholders can be drawn on to help construct a collectivist enterprise risk management cyber threat model. Cyber security threat intelligence can be placed in the context of a holistic cyber security framework that is adaptive and supportive of cyber security initiatives and interventions. This will provide the basis for cyber security management to be integrated into other business functions and activities, and this should ensure that a holistic approach is adopted by staff and the necessary governance is in being. For cyber security risk management to be effective, it needs to be undertaken on a continuous basis throughout the year. The more comprehensive the risk assessment is, the more specific the information will be in the risk register(s) and organizational staff will develop a comprehensive understanding of risk and how risks are to be mitigated.

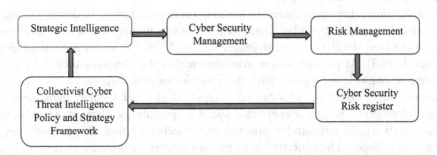

FIGURE 7.2 A collectivist cyber threat intelligence policy and strategy framework.

Question 1: How does strategic intelligence feed into an enterprise risk management cyber threat model?

Question 2: How can cyber security threat intelligence be undertaken?

Question 3: Why is it important for an organization to have a risk register?

7.8 Conclusion

A collectivist enterprise risk management cyber threat model can be considered highly relevant in terms of focusing attention on internal threats (e.g., insider activity) and external threats (e.g., known hacker groups) and can be designed in various stages so that the overall complexity does not overwhelm those responsible for carrying out threat-based activity work. By placing as much relevant information as possible in the risk register(s), it should be possible for senior management to gauge the effectiveness of the governance process in place and ensure that staff are compliant in their actions and are held to account for their actions. In addition, a security culture will be established that incorporates cyber security, which is then adopted by partner organizations.

Case 7: A Collectivist Enterprise Risk Management Cyber Threat Model

Debora Jenkins and Michael Law were strategic management consultants brought in to advise senior management about how to develop a collectivist enterprise risk management cyber threat model. They were well aware of the role of the cyber security manager and had undertaken various risk management assignments in the past. Their latest brief was to advise a medium-sized company on how to devise an appropriate organizational structure in order to facilitate strategic intelligence analysis. Over the years, they had consulted with a number of government representatives on a number of cyber security issues and had sat on both regional and national advisory committees. They were well informed about industry needs and government policy and had a clear view of what risk management involved.

In their work, they deployed the sociocultural intelligence approach as they considered it useful as it allowed them to think more about the human aspects of intelligence work and link with technological applications. Mrs. Jenkins and Mr. Law had advised a number of senior management teams over the years and had developed a reputation for company–industry-specific governance mechanisms. In addition, they had designed risk register frameworks and coached staff about building and maintaining trust-based intelligence and security relationships.

The assignment they were currently working on required them to devise a collectivist enterprise risk management cyber threat model that was managed at several levels: Senior management level (level 1); junior management level (level 2) and a general/administrative level (level 3). At present, senior managers within the company they were involved with were responsible for liaising with the government and ensuring that society's well-being was a main objective. This can be interpreted as cyber security management and strategic intelligence having a corporate social responsibility element whereby skilled company staff liaised with and supported cyber security competitions involving local schools and colleges. The objective is to promote cyber security awareness and ensure that cyber bullying was known about and prevented. Senior managers also took responsibility for the operational aspects of strategic intelligence and security work, providing guidance as regards the future use of AI, risk mitigation, liaising with supply chain partners and marketing strategy formulation and implementation.

Of key interest was the emerging trend for companies to link with university research departments and undertake applied cyber security research. Although universities are well known for blue sky research, it was clear that the government's commitment to innovation and job creation witnessed through funds available for joint industry–university research was essential for the rapid development of AI threat-detection systems that could be installed by companies across industry sectors. It was realized, however, that business–university collaborations needed to be managed effectively because companies had a different organizational cultural value system than a university and staff within companies wanted to know which approach was best and how it could be applied whereas university researchers were more attuned to discovery and explaining why something worked as it did.

It is known that for risk management to be effective, managers have to take responsibility for all aspects of risk management and the risk manager needs to be held accountable for organizing and maintaining the risk register(s). Monitoring the external environment for cyber-attacks, deploying cyber threat intelligence methods, devising cyber security awareness training programmes, framing organizational learning and working on industry–university collaborative projects are key tasks to be assigned to senior managers. General/administrative personnel are responsible for providing customer support and after-sales service to business customers and can provide additional support services if required. Because the company had a flat organizational structure, there was much overlapping of tasks and often, project groups were established to provide in-depth support to existing management teams. For example, the cyber security awareness programme had been established to include all staff within a coordinated training programme that was administered over a number of months and had update sessions. The problem was that some staff refused to attend the training programmes available to them.

Sociocultural intelligence was well regarded because it was used for critical thinking in relation to situational awareness. Other techniques complemented the approach, and the critical friendship group method in particular was ideal for drawing on expert insights that allowed alternative approaches to be identified as regards solving unique problems. The emphasis was on helping staff to develop cyber security initiatives and interventions. During their deliberations with company staff, Debora Jenkins and Michael Law realized that the employees did not know what the term risk appetite meant and needed help to understand how risks could be identified, how they could be analysed and how they could be prioritized.

It was also found that some risk assessments had been undertaken in an illogical way. Data supporting the arguments put forward had been cut and pasted from Internet sources and the depth of the analysis was shallow and at times incomplete. The information contained in the in-house reports often conflicted. For example, staff in the finance department had a different approach to risk assessment than those in other departments and would not share the data, information and their sources with them. They argued that their work was sensitive and could not be shared with other non-finance staff members. This was known to fuel resentment and when it was suggested that data and information could be made available online, various excuses were provided as to why this was not possible.

Debora Jenkins and Michael Law considered that staff would benefit from a critical thinking workshop and had designed a set of exercises that could be undertaken in one-hour sessions. By engaging in critical thinking, staff would be able to be more precise in their judgement and gain confidence to construct and follow through an argument. They would also understand why they had to think "outside the box". Being aware of what constituted the company's ecosystem was considered important. A company's ecosystem can be thought of as all the partner organizations in a company's network, including external influential government agencies (e.g., law enforcement) that combine to allow a strategic intelligence perspective to be adopted. Each node in the network of organizations involved was considered to provide valuable input into the strategic intelligence system and this increased the overall strength of the partnership arrangement in terms of intelligence and intelligence decision-making. The more intelligence that could be drawn on, the more logical the information was that went into the risk register.

Debora Jenkins and Michael Law decided that they would test the knowledge of staff within the organization through a test. The employees were required to answer three questions:

Question 1: How useful is it to define a collectivist enterprise risk management cyber threat model in terms of senior management activities, junior management activities and general/administrative activities?

Question 2: Which factors should be incorporated into a risk register? Think of two contrasting company examples, and devise two separate risk registers.

Question 3: Explain how the critical thinking approach can be used to enhance cyber security management and strategic intelligence.

References and further reading

Aaker, D.A. (1992). *Strategic Market Management*. Chichester: John Wiley & Sons.

Bromiley, P., McShane, M., Nair, A., and Rustambekov, E. (2015). Enterprise risk management: Review, critique, and research directions. *Long Range Planning*, 48, pp. 265–276. https://dx.doi:10.1016/j.lrp. 2014.07.005

Butterworth, J., and Thwaites, G. (2013). *Thinking Skills: Critical Thinking and Problem Solving*. Cambridge: Cambridge University Press.

Choi, Y.K. (2010). Toward developing marketing strategies in turbulent environment. *Journal of Global Academy of Marketing Science*, 20 (4), pp. 279–280. https://doi.org/10.1080/1229711 9.2010.9707432

Ebrahim, A., and Rangan, V.K. (2014). What impact? A framework for measuring the scale and scope of social performance. *California Management Review*, 56 (3), pp. 118–141. https://doi.org/10.1525/cmr.2014.56.3.118

Golby, M., and Appleby, R. (1995). Reflective practice through critical friendship: Some possibilities. *Cambridge Journal of Education*, 25 (2), pp. 149–160. https://doi.org/10.1080/0305764950250203

King, B. (2008). A social movement perspective of stakeholder collective action and influence. *Business & Society*, 47 (1), pp. 21–49. DOI: 10.1177/0007650307306636

Montgomery, D.B., and Weinberg, C.B. (1979). Toward strategic intelligence systems. *Journal of Marketing*, 43, pp. 41–52.

Nardini, G., Bublitz, M.G., Butler, C., Croom-Raley, S., Escalas, J.E., Hansen, J., and Peracchio, L.A. (2022). Scaling social impact: Marketing to grow nonprofit solutions. *Journal of Public Policy & Marketing*, 41 (3), pp. 254–276. DOI: 10.1177/07439156221087997

Patton, M.Q. (1990). *Qualitative Evaluation and Research Methods*. Newbury Park, California: Sage Publications.

Patton, K. (2010). *Sociocultural Intelligence: A New Discipline in Intelligence Studies*. London: The Continuum International Publishing Group.

Stine, K., Quinn, S., Witte, G., and Gardner, R.K. (2020). *Integrating Cybersecurity and Enterprise Risk Management (ERM)*. National Institute of Standards and Technology (NIST). Washington, DC: US Department of Commerce. NISTIR 8286 (October). https://doi.org/10.6028/ NIST.IR.8286

Trim, P.R.J., and Lee, Y-I. (2014). *Cyber Security Management: A Governance, Risk and Compliance Framework*. Farnham: Gower Publishing.

Trim, P.R.J., and Lee, Y-I. (2019). The role of B2B marketers in increasing cyber security awareness and influencing behavioural change. *Industrial Marketing Management*, 83, pp. 224–238. https://doi.org/10.1016/j.indmarman.2019.04.003

Trim, P.R.J., and Lee, Y-I. (2021). The global cyber security model: Counteracting cyber attacks through a resilient partnership arrangement. *Big Data and Cognitive Computing*, 5 (3) (Number 32), pp. 1–17. https://doi.org/10.3390/bdcc5030032

Trim, P.R.J., and Lee, Y-I. (2022). Combining sociocultural intelligence with artificial intelligence to increase organizational cyber security provision through enhanced resilience. *Big Data and Cognitive Computing*, 6 (4) (Number 110), pp. 1–21. https://doi.org/10.3390/bdcc6040110

Trim, P. R.J., and Lee, Y-I. (2023). *Strategic Cyber Security Management*. Oxford: Routledge.

Yamin, M.M., Ullah, M., Ullah, H., and Katt, B. (2021). Weaponized AI for cyber attacks. *Journal of Information Security and Applications*, 57, pp. 1–14. https://doi.org/10.1016/j. jisa.2020.102722

Further reading

Trim, P.R.J. (1999a). The corporate intelligence and national security (CINS) model: A new era in defence management. *Strategic Change*, 8 (3), pp. 163–171.

Trim, P.R.J. (1999b). The corporate intelligence information charter: responsibility and accountability in the defence sector. *Strategic Change*, 8 (6), pp. 359–366.

8

THEORETICAL AND MANAGERIAL IMPLICATIONS

8.1 Introduction

Organizational cyber security interdependency (Section 8.2) is followed by placing a collectivist enterprise risk management approach in context (Section 8.3). Next, marketers and their influence (Section 8.4) is followed by human resource management (Section 8.5) and insights into cyber security education (Section 8.6). Attention is then given to the logic model approach (Section 8.7) and ethical considerations (Section 8.8). Lastly, reflection and questions (Section 8.9) is followed by a conclusion (Section 8.10).

8.2 Organizational Cyber Security Interdependency

There are a number of challenges to be addressed with regard to developing a cyber security policy and strategy and it is important to view cyber security objective setting from several stances. This is because cyber security is part of security but is rapidly becoming the main focus of security. It is for this reason that the cyber security manager and their colleagues need to consider establishing a process by which organizational interdependency is given increased attention. Noting that the complexity of the challenges to be addressed in relation to cyber security provision cannot be dealt with easily, it has to be remembered that the role and influence of government are important as regards helping to determine the skill level of cyber security specialists and setting budgets for cyber security expenditure. The freedom to operate in a market system, with regulatory conditions prevailing, requires the cyber security manager and their colleagues to adopt a proactive approach to managing organizational cyber security interdependency from a stakeholder-centric perspective. The objective of organizational cyber security interdependency is to enable those operating within a partnership arrangement the scope to engage in inter-industry collaboration and at the same time develop online business and marketing initiatives that prove beneficial to stakeholders.

DOI: 10.4324/9781003570905-8

Inter-government involvement can result in more regulation that provides new market opportunities and at the same time gives rise to increased protection to all the parties involved. By drawing on various bodies of knowledge, the cyber security manager can, in tandem with cyber security staff, extend the base of intelligence work within the organization and develop a deeper understanding of CTI work. This means that trust-based intelligence relationships need to be formed both within the organization and with staff in external organizations. In addition, a proactive approach to cyber security will help to expand the body of knowledge in the area of strategic intelligence and also provide more insight into how the cyber security body of knowledge is to be extended, thus establishing a firm base for professional development. Hence, it would seem appropriate to make the case for senior managers to adopt an interdisciplinary/multidisciplinary approach to cyber security problem-solving and also make a distinction between training and staff development. Of key interest is not just how cyber security educational programmes can fulfil skill gaps but also how they can help recruit knowledgeable individuals into the cyber security profession.

Inter-government relationship building can be considered a priority in terms of effective cyber security defence and needs to be viewed from a government level and an organizational level. Government representatives meet at various times throughout the year and are in continual dialogue with other government representatives via a number of institutional arrangements. Senior managers meet government representatives at various functions and arranged meetings throughout the year and both seek and provide CTI and information via various formal and informal communication channels. It is logical to suggest, therefore, that to fully comprehend why a cyber threat manifests and results in an attack being implemented in a certain way, requires staff to have a detailed knowledge of international politics and the way in which nations compete to assert their authority in the world. Because cyber terrorism is expected to be more prominent in the years ahead, it is important that managers understand what terrorism involves.

Collins (2007, p. 292) has explained that terrorism is a tactic, composed of different elements and is undertaken by different kinds of groups. Collins (2007, p. 292) elaborates on this by suggesting that terrorism involves the use of violence/threat of violence; is carried out by an organized group; is achieving political objectives; the violence not only includes a target audience but it also extends beyond the target audience and that a government is either the perpetrator of violence or the target. It is suggested that an act of terrorism is not aimed directly at another government. Collins (2007, p. 292) also draws on the observation of Lutz and Lutz (2005, p. 7) indicating that a sixth point postulates that "terrorism is a weapon of the weak". Some might suggest that the term weak can be interpreted as a terrorist organization being unorganized; however, funding gained can turn a weakness into a strength. Indeed, some terrorist groups are prolific fundraisers and some are funded by individuals and/or organizations. This suggests that they are well organized; however, it is the execution of their acts of violence that can be classified as unorganized as they are known to operate periodically and are not always able to maintain the level of violence that they inflict. Through continual funding, a terrorist group can gain expertise, equipment and other resources and can develop a command-and-control structure.

Baylis et al. (2007, p. 63) enrich our understanding of political economy by outlining the postmodern state of war-making: "Postmodern non-state institutions of violence tend to draw material sustenance not from such formal and centralized national economies and defence industries, but from private production and finance networks organized either locally or on a global scale". The sources referred to include plunder and theft, hostage-taking for ransom and various acts associated with organized crime such as extortion, drug trafficking and money laundering. Baylis et al. (2007, p. 63) also include other sources of funding stemming from remittances and material support from relevant diaspora communities, foreign assistance, the diversion of humanitarian aid and arms trafficking.

By thinking through the concept of environment security and expanding the base of cyber security, it should be possible to enhance the role of cyber security staff within the organization and get them to contribute more directly to the strategic intelligence decision-making process. This would ensure that cyber security staff are guaranteed a higher and more fulfilling role than is the case at present. Cyber security staff are, because of their knowledge and commitment, well able to help expand the organization's business model and at the same time, help formulate cyber security policy. More generally, by embracing organizational learning, it should be possible for senior staff to build a more strategic view of how intelligence work relates to security work and to establish how staff can engage in policy decision-making that strengthens the organization's defences and helps partner organizations to become more resilient. Although resilience is a broad-based term, the key is to place it in the context of reducing vulnerability (Trim and Caravelli, 2009). This means that resilience must be strategized and linked firmly with management processes. One way in which this can be achieved is to adopt a collectivist approach to enterprise risk management.

Viewing resilience from the perspective of it being strategized should help staff to think holistically about cyber security and what cyber security management involves. Cyber security staff should be able to link security activities with intelligence activities and enhance their knowledge through the organizational learning approach. To do this requires the staff to undergo specifically designed training and staff development programmes. Scenarios (Ringland, 2006) can be devised and used in training sessions to get staff to think in terms of not only forecasting future events but also establishing how uncertainties evolve. Scenarios can also be used to identify grey areas that need further attention. Ideally, scenarios are developed for different levels of attainment and can be used to evaluate a situation or future event; identify problems and devise contingency plans and introduce new ways of thinking. It has been suggested that scenario planning and the use of scenario analysis are transformational in the sense that vision can be turned into reality through the use of techniques like the consequence tree approach (Lindgren and Bandhold, 2003, pp. 80–85). A consequence tree is useful for establishing the driving forces affecting a situation and/or giving rise to a specific condition and also for identifying and interpreting clusters of trends and resulting consequences. Lindgren and Bandhold (2003, p. 83) have provided guidance in terms of this and have this to say on the subject of the consequence tree approach:

"The driving forces are the root system and help show why a trend may develop in a particular way. The trend or trend-cluster constitutes the trunk. Height and thickness give us a hint of the development of the trend …. The consequences of the trend are shown as branches".

With regards to the consequences, these are stated in terms of first, second and third-level consequences, and the crown of the tree outlines the complexity in relation to the development and connections (Lindgren and Bandhold, 2003, p. 83).

This type of learning approach is useful as regards setting the scene for the development of simulations, which are increasingly being used to update staff and get them to use technological applications. With respect to a simulation, Aldrich (2004, p. 87) has this to say: "Users express themselves through their *input*; the simulation performs *calculations* and then presents feedback in the form of an *output*. Then the cycle repeats". So, simulations are appropriate for helping a person update their skill/knowledge base and can be used to reinforce a particular organizational policy and help an individual solve a specific type of problem. This can be considered essential bearing in mind that to fully understand why an organization is at risk from a cyber-attack requires the cyber security manager to engage in risk management, which involves the use of appropriate risk analysis tools. By having in place a collectivist enterprise risk management cyber threat model, the cyber security manager can ensure that organizational vulnerabilities are known and rectified before a cyber-attack penetrates the organization's defences and causes harm to the organization.

8.3 Placing a Collectivist Enterprise Risk Management Approach in Context

A collectivist enterprise risk management cyber threat model can help senior managers to devise a cyber security intelligence policy and strategy framework that allows staff to identify with the organization's cyber security objectives and ensure that they are cyber security aware. By establishing a proactive approach to organizational resilience, it should be possible to devise a security culture and maintain an up-to-date risk register, which provides transparency within the industry in which the organization competes. Through managers playing a more visible role in terms of cyber security management, the strategic intelligence school of thought approach can be extended to include corporate intelligence and strategic security. Hence, by adopting a collectivist approach to enterprise risk management cyber threat planning and analysis, the intelligence work of various business functions can be integrated and staff can more easily share information and draw on shared resources with external partners/stakeholders. Consequently, senior managers will be able to devise cyber security training and staff development interventions that enable staff to gain skills and knowledge to counteract the actions of cyber criminals.

It is clear that a collectivist enterprise risk management cyber threat model will help senior managers to contribute to the five pillars outlined by Andreasson (2012, pp. 82–83), which are legal measures; technical and procedural measures; organizational structures; capacity building and international cooperation. Andreasson (2012, pp. 82–83) is right to suggest that national laws that are not in place to prevent acts of cyber-crime need to be put in place and this requires a shared understanding of the problem(s) and continual lobbying of government (Bloom and Chatterji, 2009). It should also result in the provision of globally acceptable standards (e.g., cyber-crime prevention) that are devised to help organizations establish appropriate organizational structures so that they withstand cyber-attacks. Taking these points into consideration, it is possible to make a number of recommendations that are proactive in orientation.

1 Senior managers need to adopt a collectivist approach to cyber security so that cyber security is integrated throughout the partnership arrangement.
2 Senior managers need to promote an in-house security culture through training and staff development programmes so that cyber security measures include the deployment of a collectivist enterprise risk management cyber threat model.
3 Senior managers need to detail the results of a risk assessment in the risk register and outline how risk mitigation will be carried out.
4 Senior managers need to work with staff in partner organizations to utilize organizational learning and ensure that compliance policy and staff behaviour are uniform throughout the partnership arrangement.
5 Senior managers need to be aware that a cyber-attack, even a limited cyber-attack, will have an impact on the organization and possibly its stakeholders.

The recommendations cited add weight to the view that the challenges and opportunities confronting organizational staff need to be placed more within an e-business strategy and the influence of technology; especially, social media has to be aligned with society's changing cultural value system. Marketing managers are aware of the role played by marketing communications, and how social media is likely to increase vis-à-vis business-to-business engagement. However, marketers often have limited input into cyber security policies and this needs to be reviewed. For example, marketers have extensive knowledge of developing and maintaining business relationships and are aware of cultural interactions owing to the fact that they engage with overseas customers and suppliers. Marketers also undertake various forms of analysis (e.g., the market and competitors) and are well placed to make predictions based on the evidence they have collected. An organization will be at risk if it does not update its product range and provide a satisfactory level of customer service; hence, organizational staff need to be confident that the marketing strategies they deploy can withstand the retaliatory actions of competitors.

The sustainability of the organization is high up on senior management's agenda and it is here that a link with business continuity and business continuity planning needs to be made. The cyber security manager is required to give attention to the sustainability of the organization and fully comprehend how an impact needs to be countered but at the same time understand that an impact on an organization is likely to result in some change within it. Aviva (2024, p. 6) provides guidance as regards what managers need to do to have an effective business continuity planning system in place: *Business continuity* refers to the capability of an organization, once it has suffered a disruptive impact, to continue to deliver products/services at acceptable predefined level; *business continuity management* is the process by which management identifies potential threats and their possible impacts on business operations and ensure that there is an effective response that results in the organization maintaining its resiliency. It is important to note that the holistic approach adopted by senior management takes into account the views of key stakeholders, the reputation of all concerned and brand and value-creating activities. With regards to *business continuity policy*, of importance here is the leadership from senior management in terms of the intentions and direction of the organization (Aviva, 2024, p. 6). The *business continuity plan* documents the procedures that guide organizations, and it is crucial that the procedures are classified in terms of response, recovery and restoring business activities to the predefined level of operation that was in existence before the disruption occurred (Aviva, 2024, p. 6). With respect to the *business continuity management programme*, the ongoing management and governance process needs to be outlined that is supported by senior management (Aviva, 2024, p. 6). The objective is to maintain business continuity management.

Aviva (2024, pp. 3–5) has provided advice as regards creating a business continuity plan, which has five steps (*Service Levels; Risk Analysis; Emergency Action Planning; Business Recovery Planning* and *Testing and Maintaining the Business Continuity Plan*). The guidance suggests a business continuity team should be appointed as this will provide focus and coordination and ensure that a business continuity plan is devised that is fit for purpose. The key point is that business continuity is viewed as a continual process. The first step in the planning process is to establish the *Service Levels*. The organization's desired level of service needs to be defined as this will allow an appropriate level of service to be delivered to customers and stakeholders on a day-to-day basis, should an incident occur. A minimum acceptable level of service must be provided in order that organizational staff fulfil primary contractual obligations. Indeed, if an impact does occur, then the organization must be able to provide a minimum level of service during the duration of the period that the impact spans.

Step two, *Risk Analysis*, requires staff to identify the risks that the organization is confronted with, and this requires that each risk is mapped accordingly so that the consequences of a risk occurring are known. This is so that the possible impact on the organization should an impact materialize is known. Hence, business impact analysis needs to be thorough so that each risk can be mitigated. For example, it is important to place a risk in the context of a building, IT equipment and data, machinery and plant and public utility supplies, for example. The assessment needs to be detailed and provide specific details about the key suppliers and what the effect upon the organization would be if a supplier was unfortunate enough to encounter an incident of some kind and have its business disrupted. Contingency plans will possibly identify alternative suppliers because continuity of business operations needs to be maintained. This suggests that thought has gone into how, if an incident occurs, the response will be managed.

As regards Step 3, *Emergency Action Planning*, the business continuity team will be called into action and will manage the incident. Decisions relating to how the organization will deal with specific issues such as personnel, damage limitation, site management and overall management of the emergency as well as the recovery itself need to be documented. Staff will need to communicate with stakeholders, suppliers, customers and possibly the media, so it is essential that they are prepared and can do so in an appropriate manner.

With respect to Step 4, *Business Recovery Planning*, it is essential that the business continuity team has prepared a business recovery plan that can be implemented at the appropriate time. The plan needs to outline how staff will deal with a range of issues including implementing alternative working practices and identifying and equipping temporary premises for example. Maintaining contact with customers is of importance and so is keeping a disaster/incident recovery log up to date. As regards the latter, various actions, losses and expenses incurred will be documented.

Step 5, *Testing and Maintaining the Business Continuity Plan*, is when the plan in being needs to be tested to make sure it is fit for purpose. Testing will make known any deficiencies that need to be rectified and increase awareness within the organization, thus ensuring that staff know what to do in a crisis/emergency. Testing will prepare staff for action and there are various ways this can be achieved. Desktop exercises are useful as they simulate a particular incident and can help staff to ready themselves for action. In addition, discussion-based exercises and live tests can also help staff (denoted as responders) prepare for an incident. An incident may have an impact on business operations, the buildings and/or machinery and processes. Hence, it is clear that staff need to ensure that risk management is undertaken and the results of such an analysis are incorporated into the business continuity plan.

A cyber-attack that impacts an organization may result in various consequences, one of which is reputational damage. Rubrick (2024) acknowledges the importance of business continuity in relation to cyber security strategies and has outlined a number of cyber security strategies (e.g., data replication, disaster recovery and zero trust data security) that incorporate business continuity and disaster recovery. *Data replication*: Data is kept in multiple repositories, and this allows data to be recovered during the recovery period after a disaster. *Disaster recovery*: This needs to be structured so that reinfection is avoided. *Disaster recovery* as a service (DRAAS) exists and can be utilized. *Zero trust data security* does away with the concept of firewalls and perimeter defence and places emphasis on security based on each point of data. *Zero trust data security* is used to verify users and their access to critical functions at each point throughout the network.

At this juncture, it is useful to reflect upon the work of Connolly et al. (2020, p. 13) because these researchers make clear the fact that organizations that possess weak security postures suffer more in terms of harsher outcomes vis-à-vis ransomware attacks compared with organizations that are known to have a strong security posture. Furthermore, organizational staff need to develop their awareness of technical and non-technical controls because they complement each other. Connolly et al. (2020, p. 13) discovered that targeted attacks were aimed at technical shortcomings; however, those carrying out cyber-attacks are well able to exploit human weaknesses, and this brings out the point that attackers are in fact able and prepared to adopt several attack vectors to achieve their objective.

Thinking through the various connotations embedded in the above set of arguments requires the cyber security manager to give some thought to what constitutes a resilient organization. Dupont (2019, p. 7) has this to say on the subject:

> "Resilient organizations not only display adaptive capacities during a crisis but, once basic operations have been restored, are able to learn from their experience and identify improvements in their systems and procedures that will enhance their level of preparedness against future hazards".

In order to develop a clear understanding of what resilience is and what it involves, it is useful to reflect on the UK Government's (2022, p. 19) view that is set out in the National Cyber Strategy 2022 document and understand that cyberspace is composed of three layers: The *virtual layer*, *the logical layer* and *the physical layer*. The *virtual layer* refers to the representations of people and organizations vis-à-vis a virtual identity in a shared virtual space. Hence, it is important to think of email addresses, user identification, or a social media account/an alias. It is complex because "One person or one organisation can have multiple identities online. Conversely, multiple people or organisations could also create just a single, shared identity" (UK Government, 2022, p. 19). The *logical layer* refers to the part of cyberspace that is composed of code or data. For example, operating systems and protocols, applications and software. The *logical layer* is dependent on the *physical layer* because information flows through various wired networks or electromagnetic spectra. It is suggested that the *logical layer* and the *physical layer* allow virtual identities to communicate and act (UK Government, 2022, p. 19). With regard to the *physical layer*, reference is made to the hardware upon which data is transmitted. Of importance are routers, wires and hubs that are found in an individual's home and large telecommunication systems that are operated by companies. Managers need to understand that as well as the physical infrastructure there is also the electromagnetic spectrum, which includes WiFi and radio (UK Government, 2022, p. 19).

Understanding this allows senior management to make a case for employees to be committed to self-learning and updating themselves through in-house cyber security training programmes and staff development programmes, and also, they need to be motivated enough to develop an interest in externally focused environment-related factors. Understanding the role that the government fulfils in terms of its commitment to maintaining critical infrastructure and a safe digital environment brings into focus the need to think more generally about the supply chain and how people in society are engaged in day-to-day activities involving smart living and smart lifestyles. It can be appreciated that resilience is about the environment within which the organization competes, and strategic intelligence requires that each component of that environment (controllable and uncontrollable factors) or ecosystem is broken down into distinct but interlinked parts. Understanding this will help the cyber security manager to devise policies and strategies that are about the survival and sustainability of the organization. For example, by pursuing a proactive cyber security policy, staff can anticipate a cyber-attack(s) and devise countermeasures to protect the data and systems in place. Extending this approach will allow managers to move to the next stage, which is foresight, and identify software developers that are harnessing AI, which can be used for cyber threat detection.

It is clear from the above that the cyber security manager needs to understand what resilience is and work closely with their peers to ensure that the organization becomes resilient. Before giving attention to the concept of resilience, however, it is important to reflect back on what a vulnerability is and how it might materialize. Sheffi (2005, p. 20) has provided guidance regarding this and suggests that in order to fully understand what a vulnerability is, it is important to think in terms of the likelihood that disruption will materialize and also have an understanding of the potential severity of it. When considering what the potential severity may be, it is important to think through the consequences and have some idea of what type of vulnerability is being identified.

Whereas cyber security specialists normally associate a vulnerability with a problem in software, it is relevant to broaden the interpretation because vulnerabilities are not necessarily independent of other vulnerabilities. For example, Sheffi (2005, pp. 24–25) outlines various types of vulnerabilities, defines them in terms of category (e.g., financial, strategic, hazard and operations) and places them in a concentric vulnerability map. If an organization does suffer from an incident of some kind and the impact is severe, then there are likely to be consequences for the stakeholders. This raises the question: How can senior management ensure that the organization is sufficiently resilient to withstand cyber-attacks? Dupont (2019, p. 6) offers useful insights into the way managers should think about this by explaining that it is possible to think of resilience as being networked, which is useful because organizational configurations involve socio-technical systems that are integrated and embedded in complex webs of interdependency. This according to Dupont (2019, p. 6) means that resilience is viewed from the perspective of a dense network of intra-organizational and inter-organizational linkages, which are under-pinned by trust. This implies that strong relationships govern the relationships in place and also, should a threat materialize, it is possible that the stakeholder members will be sympathetic to the needs of the organization affected and offer support and cooperation so that the damage inflicted is less severe than would be the case if no support was forthcoming.

What needs to be understood from this is that resilience relates to an organization's ability to take an impact and continue in business as close as possible to its full function-ing capability. By having an appropriate business continuity plan in place, senior man-agement can maintain the integrity of the organization and it can continue to trade. Unfortunately, in the case of a very severe attack or if the organization has limited resources and is unable to maintain its business operations, then its sustainability is in question. Bearing in mind the full range of cyber-attacks that can be launched on an organization, it is suggested that senior management carry out risk assessments over time, are as transparent as possible in terms of the organization's vulnerabilities and have a fully integrated business continuity planning process in place.

8.4 Marketers and their Influence

Marketers are skilled at assessing issues and challenges and know how to position the firm's products and services to take advantage of the opportunities in the market. They are also skilled at dealing with threats as they monitor the actions of competitors and formulate and implement positioning strategies. Organizational strategists also play an influential role in strategy formulation and implementation, and they participate in tasks that are central to the development and utilization of information systems. By undertak-ing a broad range of research-based activities, marketers and strategists provide business intelligence that can feed directly into the cyber security management process.

Marketing strategists possess unique skills and, those with an understanding of and expertise in high technology products, can help build working relationships with suppliers and marketing channel experts. They can also liaise with staff in partner organizations thus ensuring that transparency between business-to-business and business-to-consumer relationship building occurs. Issues relating to trust and meeting customer expectations are expected to be key considerations in the future because advances in online marketing mean that there is less contact between organizational staff and the end user. Chatbots and virtual influencers are expected to play a more interactive role in company–customer relations, and this has implications for customer service provision.

As regards marketing intelligence and planning and strategy formulation and imple-mentation, it is possible that in the years ahead, much work will be undertaken by AI and this may be logical bearing in mind the prominence of big data and the advancement in marketing analytics. AI allows decisions to be made quickly and is especially effective during periods of rapid market change. It is not clear, however, how AI will link in with organizational learning, but developments in training and staff development programmes will equip staff to use AI software that can map task requirements against skill level requirements. AI will also be used to search for and create content for the development of marketing knowledge and tailor training and educational programmes accordingly to meet human resource skill requirements. Attention will need to be given to what is considered as the process of consumerization and ethical considerations will also need to be addressed.

Buckley and Ghauri (2004) have paid attention to political considerations that widen the base of marketing, and marketers need to note that cyber security not only involves making the organization more resilient but it also indicates that there are market opportunities for new cyber security products and services. Marketers are known to have knowledge and an appreciation of cultural value systems, and this is helpful in terms of segmenting the market for products and services. Working effectively with suppliers and organizations in the marketing channel, marketers can utilize competitive intelligence (Trim and Lee, 2008) that feeds into the marketing strategy process. To contribute fully, however, marketers need to have the skills and expertise to evaluate the marketing department's influence and performance and establish how it can be improved (Verhoef and Leeflang, 2009, p. 29). The logic of this is that marketers, and marketing strategists in particular, need to place online marketing and the use of smart products, within the cyber security domain (Trim and Upton, 2013; Trim and Lee, 2014).

8.5 Human Resource Management

The Internet is providing much scope for new product development and is aiding innovation. Innovativeness can be viewed from two perspectives: (i) The ability of the organization to adapt and implement new structures, mechanisms and processes and (ii) the ability to develop and market new products and services. How is this to be achieved? Salavou (2005, p. 328) indicates that learning orientation is a key factor and staff need to be able to link technology and its usage with cultural value systems so that company–customer relations are placed within the context of consumerization. Human resource management personnel not only monitor the skill level of staff and ensure that cyber security awareness programmes are in being that help to foster a cyber security culture but they also need to take cognizance of the fact that organizational networks are complex entities that require an organizational learning model to be in place. For example, a deeper understanding of connectivity and how the Internet is extending the role of staff through opportunities associated with remote working means that organizational learning can provide staff with insights into how trust-based relationships are formed and maintained; what reporting structures are in place and how a customer service policy and organizational learning are linked (Trim and Lee, 2006). Furthermore, bearing in mind the role played by organizational memory, it can be argued that managers not only need to develop security-based knowledge but they also need to develop and acquire knowledge (Kylaheiko et al., 2011) that can be utilized for the development of a security culture.

As regards the role of intelligence work, it has been suggested that corporate intelligence experts are involved in various public–private partnership initiatives (Trim, 2001a). Indeed, they undertake specific types of work and help establish an Intelligence Unit that is overseen by the Director of Corporate Intelligence and under the auspices of a Corporate

Intelligence Steering Committee and a Corporate Intelligence Advisory Board (Trim, 2001b, pp. 351–353). This is to ensure that the work undertaken is carried out according to set procedures because some of it will be highly sensitive. In addition, it is useful for senior management to put in place an Executive Intelligence Alliance Policy and Strategy Charter (Trim, 2001b, p. 353) that outlines how staff work with stakeholders such as government and industry representatives because it is important to distinguish between company-specific relationship building and government-specific relationship building. Such an approach should ensure that executive integrity prevails, which is composed of system integrity, moral integrity and integrity of vision (Cooperrider and Srivastva, 1987). By defining corporate intelligence in a meaningful way, it is possible to outline what the role of intelligence is. Trim (2001a, pp. 54–55) is of the view that

> "Corporate intelligence is the acquisition of knowledge using human, electronic and other means, and the interpretation of knowledge relating to the environment, both internal and external, in which the organization operates...... It also provides a mechanism for implementing counter-intelligence measures to safeguard corporate data and secrets".

By undertaking corporate intelligence, staff can update their intelligence base over time and develop and implement intelligence policy. One way to achieve this is by deploying the organizational learning approach. Although senior management may demand that staff adopt the learning organization approach, and adhere to the values of the organization, it has to be remembered that people are sometimes resistant to change. Adopting the learning organization approach does not necessarily result in a learning environment where staff take responsibility for their own learning. In order to create a learning environment, the cyber security manager needs to form an emotional attachment with their subordinates (Lee, 2009, p. 190) and manage in a proactive manner. This means being aware of an individual's situation and being sensitive to their needs. Leadership can be viewed as providing advice and support when necessary and ensuring that employees identify with the organization's value system (Lee, 2009, p. 190). Hence, achieving a security culture and having cyber security at the heart of it requires an understanding of how to apply the benefits of transformational leadership. Kakabadse (2000) firmly believes that transformational leadership is about listening and empowering staff, and this can be considered essential during times of change or when change is likely to impact the organization.

8.6 Insights into Cyber Security Education

Although cyber security training programmes are known to help raise awareness in relation to cyber threats, it has to be remembered that cyber security management and strategic intelligence require that an organization build a security knowledge base that provides sustainability of operations. One way in which this can be done is for the human relations management department to establish an in-house educational programme that makes courses available to staff at specific times. The content of the educational programmes can be decided by senior management, but certain subject areas need to be included.

A cyber security management educational programme must include the main topics of *cyber security* which include the types of cyber-attack, threat awareness and threat analysis and the growing influence of AI. *Strategic intelligence* is fundamental and should include CTI, cooperation with government representatives, how to analyse internal and external factors, and how cyber security staff can develop an intelligence mindset. Smart cities and smart products can also be studied.

Corporate security is a key topic for inclusion and can be linked with the cyber security department's security profile and the organization's corporate security objectives. Topics such as scenario analysis and planning, foresight planning and future strategy can be included for the study. As regards *information security*, key topics are the categorization of data, the link between physical security and cyber security, data storage and the role of data centres. Social media networks and platforms can also be incorporated because they include human–technology interaction.

With respect to *human resource management*, leadership can be designated as a main subject and attention can also be given to governance, motivation, personality traits, organizational learning, intelligence policy, team building, modelling and the development of frameworks and managing stakeholder groups.

Law is very much concerned with compliance, regulations and how perpetrators undertake acts of cyber-crime, and should be included because organizations operate in different parts of the world and are subject to different legal impositions. In addition, cyber-attacks emanate from abroad and staff are sometimes required to work with overseas police forces to help track down the people behind the cyber-attack(s).

Project management should be considered essential because staff need to know how to manage projects, how to work in project teams, how to cost projects and work with budgets, as well as how to manage projects over time. *Marketing* needs to be given attention because as well as focusing on relationship building, marketing staff have a clear input into marketing communications, public relations and managing the media. Marketers are also involved in internal marketing programmes and can contribute to establishing cyber security awareness and a cyber security culture.

International relations is not a topic that is considered important, but it is clear that geopolitical factors and inter-government relations are of interest and need to be given attention. Understanding the role that international institutions play can be considered beneficial as some international institutions are well known for their interventionist approach during times of crisis and emergency.

A course on *government policy* can be incorporated with the emphasis being on national security and the protection of critical national infrastructure and critical information infrastructure. Another essential topic for inclusion is *risk management*. Risk management can be broken down into risk analysis, risk assessment, risk communication, business continuity planning and organizational vulnerability. How to compile a risk register can also be given attention.

The above insights into cyber security education represent a guide only and it can be noted that various courses can be developed that help expand the role of people in work and at the same time provide a basis for developing and expanding an organization's cyber security policy and strategy. One way to consolidate the educational provision is to develop a formal process by which it is evaluated through time. The way this can be done is through the use of the logic model approach.

8.7 Logic Model Approach

The logic model approach (Ebrahim and Rangan, 2014) can be used to formulate and evaluate a management framework that has at its core a number of inputs and outputs. The inputs are in fact the resources deployed to achieve the goals agreed and the outputs are what emerge from the activities and services (Gagiu and Rodriguez-Campos, 2007, p. 341). A logic model for cyber security can be constructed and used as a strategic tool, thus enabling the cyber security manager to indicate how a set of objectives are to be achieved. The logic model approach involves mapping out the components that are incorporated into the management decision-making framework. Indeed, the organization's cyber security strategy framework can be used as a basis for determining how senior managers implement governance requirements and how staff respond in terms of compliance.

The logic model approach is useful for formalizing cyber security policy and ensuring that those who have been assigned responsibility are indeed accountable for their actions. This means that the process of evaluation is formally defined and the objectives in place can be evaluated according to strict criteria. A logic model has the advantage of helping senior management focus on specific tasks and relate cyber security to the organization's capability, thus ensuring that organizational vulnerabilities are attended to. This is beneficial in terms of intra-organizational and inter-organization collaboration and the allocation of resources. Through the process of sharing data, information, knowledge and expertise; various stakeholders can effectively integrate the different components of the organization's cyber security policy and strategy into a central focus and framework. This should result in the implementation of a cyber security strategy that makes the best use of the limited resources available.

Another benefit of the logic model approach is its evaluative quality vis-à-vis providing a holistic view of planning generally. For example, business continuity planning can be viewed as a subset of crisis/emergency planning. Indeed, emergency planning is essential with regards to making sure contingencies are in place and can be implemented in times of need. Crisis and emergency planning are called into effect to implement solutions when providers of critical national infrastructure and critical information infrastructure are subject to devastating cyber-attacks that disrupt services and have severe knock-on effects. In addition, emergency planning is considered essential for emergency preparedness and organizational staff often work with emergency service teams (e.g., the police, fire brigade and hospital staff) in order to ensure that they can provide assistance and help to injured people (e.g., a cyber-attack causes power failure and accidents occur); are able to move goods and services to a different location (e.g., computer systems are taken out of service and back-up facilities are activated) and both physical attacks/natural disasters and cyber-attacks render an organization's services inoperable (e.g., subcontracted services are activated and management is handed over to an external provider). Bearing these points in mind, it is useful for the cyber security manager and the risk manager to think of what emergency management services need to focus on because the range of impacts and their consequences can and do have financial implications for the organization. For example, if an organization is no longer able to provide a high level of service, it is possible that business customers may be disadvantaged and penalties embedded in contracts are invoked. As well as financial impositions, there could be additional costs in the form of reputational damage as other customers cancel contracts and seek service provision from an alternative supplier.

Bearing the above in mind, it is useful to reflect on the work of Walker et al. (2010, p. 477) regarding understanding what emergency planning involves. Walker et al. (2010, p. 477) have outlined eight interlinked points that emergency management staff need to consider: (1) The development of comprehensive plans that include possible hazards and outline which managers undertake which actions and how the staff in stakeholder organizations are required to interact with relevant communities; (2) the development of progressive plans aimed at anticipating future emergencies and disasters that outline preventive measures that allow those effected to engage in disaster or emergency management; (3) the development of risk-driven models for use in emergency and disaster situations that indicate the resources needed and assign priorities to designated personnel; (4) the development of integrated plans that bring together the emergency management community; (5) the development of collaborative plans that are aimed at creating communities of practices; (6) the development of coordination plans that integrate and synchronize the activities of community members; (7) the development and implementation of plans that are flexible in orientation and can be adjusted vis-à-vis the environment and (8) the development of a professional community that takes responsibility for integrating technology and science into the various components of emergency planning. As regards the latter, communal values and ethics/ethical systems can be included.

It is clear that situational awareness plays an important role and because of this the cyber security manager needs to consider this from the perspective of cyber situational awareness and place decision-making within a cyber infrastructure resources context so that cyber security abstraction models are developed that can be used to exploit existing knowledge and experience and provide a framework within which discussion relating to and embracing security issues can occur (Walker et al., 2010, p. 477). Walker et al. (2010, p. 478) stated "Emergency management cyber situational awareness requires individuals and organizations to understand and be aware of how digital resources i.e. cyber-infrastructure resources, events, information, and individuals actions impact emergency management tasks both in the near term and future". In order to do this successfully, it is important to view cyber situational awareness as incorporating four dimensions: Mitigation, preparedness, response and recovery (Walker et al., 2010, p. 478).

Emergency exercises are beneficial in the sense that they can be used to prepare designated staff, often referred to as first responders, in ways of coping with a number of tasks that have to be undertaken in real time. Pfeifer (2018, p. 30) is of the view that cyber-attack exercises can be used to get people, often from diverse groups, to share cyber-attack information. It is important, therefore, to get people to connect through various means and in the process identify who they should connect with so that the incident is managed effectively.

Chakraborty et al. (2024, p. 467) are of the view that cyber security specialists need to understand that cybercriminals do take advantage of natural disasters (e.g., hurricanes and wildfires) and natural disasters are increasingly being linked with ransomware attacks. Chakraborty (2024, p. 470) advise cyber security staff to implement a number of recommendations in relation to cyber security provision: (i) Conduct a cyber security audit (e.g., establish the strengths and weaknesses of the security system and identify the key vulnerable areas and prioritize them in relation to security provision); (ii) implement secure data backup plans (e.g., encrypt data and backup the data stored in the cloud); (iii) train employees vis-à-vis best practice and ensure they are cyber security aware and deploy multifactor authentication and strong passwords; (iv) make use of managed IT services (e.g., engage cyber security firms to continuously monitor the organization's computer systems; (v) require background checks on contractors because they have access to the organization's computer systems and ensure that their computer systems are secure; (vi) develop incident response and disaster recovery plans and (vii) test and rehearse incident response and disaster recovery plans. By doing this, the emergency plans in place will be robust and help the organization to remain in business.

8.8 Ethical Considerations

Formosa et al. (2012, p. 2) are of the view that it is necessary to make a distinction between ethical issues associated with state/national cybersecurity and ethical issues related to civil or commercial cybersecurity. This is a logical deduction because the actors and the factors that constitute the cyber threat environment are different. There are a number of overlaps in the sense that an attack on a nation's power grid will affect both individuals and businesses; however, the ethical issues are slightly different.

An attack on a nation's critical infrastructure will result in disruption and it is possible that both cyber-attacks and disruption will occur over a period of time and affect supply chain members in a number of ways. The cyber security manager needs to be aware of how the disruption is likely to affect the organization's customers and how the challenges faced by people in society are dealt with. It could be that there is direct intervention from the government or a competitor, also affected, comes forward to talk about the formation of a strategic alliance that is aimed at making each of the organizations less vulnerable to a future cyber-attack. Should discussion commence regarding the formation of a strategic alliance, then this will raise issues of ethical concern relating to current deals with loyal suppliers and what this may mean for shareholders, as well as transforming market structures through the formation of a monopoly.

As regards a successful cyber-attack on a nation's critical infrastructure, it could be that what occurs is so sensitive the general public are given limited information. The security services may make known certain facts to company representatives either via a communications technology network or an in-person briefing session, but generally, the information provided will be "on a need-to-know basis". Because cyber-attacks are becoming more sophisticated and more targeted, it has to be remembered that eventually, the public will be made more aware of the threat environment and will be asked to be more vigilant. This is important from a community resilience perspective and engagement with the general public.

It is important at this juncture to reflect on why a cyber security manager needs to think about ethical considerations and why they need to focus on legal aspects. Herrmann and Pridöhl (2020, pp. 12–13) state:

"The goal of computer security is to protect assets. Valuable assets can be hardware (e.g., computers and smartphones), software and data. These assets are subject to threats that may result in loss or harm. Computer security consists of information security and systems security".

Herrmann and Pridöhl (2020, pp. 12–13) state that information security relates to the protection of data that is processed by a computer and any information that is derived from its interpretation. This means ensuring that computer systems are secure and those that implement an attack cannot tamper with the system or indeed the data in the system. Herrmann and Pridöhl (2020, pp. 12–13) refer to security measures being designed to address one or more objectives, which include: "*Confidentiality*: prevent unauthorised information gain; *Integrity*: prevent or detect unauthorised modification of data; and *Availability*: prevent unauthorised deletion or disruption".

Formosa et al. (2012, p. 5) reflect on the fact that cybersecurity practices can be viewed from two perspectives: (i) Helping people to avoid harm and (ii) providing positive benefits that manifest in human well-being. As regards the latter, it can be argued that ethical hacking is a useful process for determining possible vulnerabilities and then undertaking actions to make sure that the asset that is likely to be targeted is not viewed as a weakness to be exploited. As people in society embrace advances in technology, it can be assumed that some threats will manifest because of the unknowns involved and the way in which the technology is used, which may be unforeseen. For example, Herrmann and Pridöhl (2020, pp. 20–21) are of the view that data in transit is subject to eavesdropping because the distributed systems are composed of multiple components that "communicate over public networks". If an attacker controls an intermediary system such as a router or Wi-Fi access point, which is used to forward traffic from the sender to a receiver, then it is possible for eavesdropping to occur (Herrmann and Pridöhl, 2020, pp. 20–21). It is also known that eavesdropping can occur regarding wireless communication if an attacker is close to the parties that are communicating with each other (Herrmann and Pridöhl, 2020, pp. 20–21).

Bearing in mind that software security is concerned with vulnerabilities that stem from programming errors (Herrmann and Pridöhl, 2020, p. 30), the ethical issues that surface are clear. If software errors are evident in the code that is widely available then damage caused can be enormous. An attacker may be aware of the vulnerability and carry out an attack before the necessary patching has been completed. If the faulty software was produced by a company and they are aware of the potential risk(s) and do not do anything about it, then they can be considered negligent unless possibly the software is altered in some way and sold on to unsuspecting clients.

If users are tricked or manipulated into accessing a website that is under the control of an attacker, then they are at risk of a "drive-by download" and also, if a user does access a website that has been compromised, then they may fall victim to a "waterholing attack", whereby updates in software are embedded with malware, which when downloaded cause much damage (Herrmann and Pridöhl, 2020, p. 26). So, ethics and law are linked and give rise to a number of inter-related problems. Problems stem from the fact that the legal and ethical practises in countries differ and, in some countries, compensation is viewed as mandatory and in other countries it is not.

Cyber-attacks are increasingly being carried out against networks and security scanners such as Nessus and OpenVAS are used to check infrastructure in order to identify possible vulnerabilities that need to be rectified (Herrmann and Pridöhl, 2020, p. 40). Penetration testing, which is authorized by the cyber security manager, is carried out to identify if a vulnerability is evident and if it is, how it will be exploited (Herrmann and Pridöhl, 2020, p. 40). The cyber security manager has to decide whether to carry out penetration tests in-house or to bring in experts with a known track record. Questions will arise regarding how the penetration tests are to be carried out and whether the results will be made available to cyber security specialists outside the organization. This calls into question the value system of the organization and what senior management allows in the way of public disclosure.

van de Poel (2020, p. 49) is of the view that cyber security staff need to think in terms of a multiplicity of relevant values, and thus the notion of a "value cluster" is advocated. van de Poel (2020, p. 49) stipulates that

"A value cluster is a range of values that express somewhat similar moral concerns. .... values in a value cluster correspond to similar moral reasons for action, or to similar norms. ....the values that are part of one value cluster are typically articulated in response to ....morally problematic situations....".

The value clusters listed by van de Poel (2020, pp. 49–50) are security, privacy, fairness and accountability and fall within the domain of cybersecurity.

The cyber security manager needs to be aware that a number of ethical concerns surface in relation to storing and protecting other people's data and information, and if a data breach occurs, they need to have decided beforehand what information, in the form of a public relations statement, should be made public and when it should be made public. Accountability also suggests liability and, in such a case, a fine may be levied on the organization that has suffered a data breach and if it is serious, for example, the data is highly sensitive, compensation may be necessary. So ethical issues and concerns need to be matched with legal aspects.

If security within an organization is lax, then it is clear that those who have been harmed by a data breach have a case against the organization. In a worst-case scenario, whereby somebody's personal data is hacked and then sold on the Dark Web, it has to be asked if the people whose data has been made public are at personal risk. Their identity may be in jeopardy as the data available for purchase is of a highly sensitive nature and allows another individual to acquire the data, assume their identity and take out a bank loan in their name. Because banks are promoting digital currency and there is a move to online banking, cyber criminals consider there are opportunities to exploit vulnerabilities in the system. Bankers do face an ethical dilemma because banks do not own the money they lend to their customers. It is owned by their depositors or the money is obtained from the inter-bank market and loaned out for a margin/profit. Banks are regulated by the country's central bank and there are international regulations in place also. However, banking practise does vary depending upon the country's banking regulations and how well they adhere to international banking requirements, some of which relate to technology usage and how technology facilitates banking transactions.

Loi and Christen (2020, p. 77) raise a number of interesting points when suggesting: "... cybersecurity technology that aims to protect privacy and confidentiality, such as encryption, is in general aligned with human rights; the threat to human rights is typically not cybersecurity, but inadequate cybersecurity or the lack thereof". Loi and Christen (2020, p. 77) carry forward this argument by suggesting that although cybersecurity technology is used for the protection of privacy and confidentiality, it can also be viewed as a threat. For example, a user supplying information about themselves might be at risk if exposed to privacy infringement.

What is clear is that managers and people generally are putting more and more trust in technology that is used in everyday business. Those who produce and install technology have much knowledge to draw on but still, vulnerabilities can be evident. One way that vulnerabilities can be found is through the process of ethical hacking. Jaquet-Chiffelle and Loi (2020, p. 192) have paid attention to this and state: "Ethical hackers adopt a strict code of conduct that protects their relationship with their clients and their client's interests. Such a code of conduct sets a frame for their attitude. It describes rules that the ethical hacker must abide by". Jaquet-Chiffelle and Loi (2020, p. 192) argue that these rules are to prevent an ethical hacker from taking advantage of the relationship developed with a client and they cite the fact that an ethical hacker may during their work discover trade secrets/sensitive data that relate to the client's activities.

With reference to a vulnerability, Macnish and van der Ham (2020, p. 4) purport that a vulnerability should be reported to the wider community because it will help raise awareness of it. However, raising awareness in this way may prove detrimental because the news may reach an individual who is intent on causing harm and using it to exploit the vulnerability. Kirichenko et al. (2020, p. 305) reaffirm that the European Union's GDPR [General Data Protection Regulation], requires that cyber security service providers operating in the EU are legally obliged to ensure that individuals are protected against "accidental or unlawful destruction, loss, alteration, unauthorised disclosure of, or access to personal data". Those who fail to ensure this are subject to fines. Kirichenko et al. (2020, p. 306) take cognizance of this and list a number of practical considerations that can be drawn on to help managers handle more secure, personal data. Kirichenko et al. (2020, p. 306) suggest that it is important to record all personal data breaches; they also suggest that those investigating a data breach should include the CISO, legal department and executive team; when undertaking a risk assessment in relation to a data breach, a number of factors should be taken into consideration including the number of individuals impacted by the breach; the type of data breach itself should be reported and the data protection mechanisms used also need to be referred to; as regards publishing a Personal Data Breach Notification, it is important to include criteria that identifies the affected parties and the impact that the breach has had on them; a number of other factors including additional time to be spent on the investigation is to be given consideration; and the supervisory authority responsible is to be notified of the breach.

8.9 Reflection and Questions

Figure 8.1 is representative of organizational cyber security interdependency and portrays how a collectivist enterprise risk management approach allows senior managers to implement business continuity plans in time of need and ensure that the organization remains in operation. Resiliency is not a static state and because of this, the systems, mechanisms and procedures in place need to be evaluated over time. Weaknesses identified will be rectified through training and skill enhancement programmes, as well as staff development programmes and the sponsorship of staff to undertake degree programmes and/or a professional qualification.

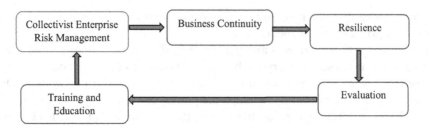

FIGURE 8.1 Organizational cyber security interdependency.

Cyber security management and strategic intelligence are underpinned by a number of theoretical and managerial implications that become evident when cyber security staff are involved in threat analysis. Senior managers are fully aware that cyber security involves different strands of knowledge and integrating these different strands into a single focus is complex and time consuming. The cyber security manager will in the years ahead need to adopt a more open and ambitious approach to cyber security problem solving and display the capability to devise and implement intelligence-based systems and procedures across organizational structures. By doing this, senior management will recognize that cyber security staff can develop higher-level skills and be more strategic in their approach to problem-solving. Furthermore, by paying increased attention to helping to safeguard the organization's IP/trade secrets from cyber-attack, managers will show that they are able to link management theory with management practice and develop a holistic, security intelligence focus to their work.

Question 1: Why is it important for the cyber security management approach and the strategic intelligence approach to be underpinned by theory?
Question 2: Why is it important for the cyber security manager to devise and implement intelligence-based systems and procedures across organizational structures?
Question 3: Why is it important for the cyber security manager to deploy a holistic, security intelligence approach?

8.10 Conclusion

Cyber security management and strategic intelligence require an interdisciplinary approach, if that is a global approach is to fully define the challenges and at the same time create opportunities for confronting the cyber threats that managers are to deal with. The evolving e-business environment has a number of unknowns and technology is going to be used to reshape organizational cultural value systems. Those engaged in cyber security management need to be aware of how to communicate risk and develop business relationships through cultural interaction that ensure that the information systems in place function in the way expected. Hence an understanding of and a commitment to intelligence and cyber security requires relationship building to be placed in a collectivist partnership development context. Furthermore, cyber security management, strategic intelligence and planning and strategy formulation and implementation need to incorporate organizational learning that feeds into training and educational programmes for public, private and not-for-profit organizations.

Case 8: Business continuity and resilience

Sally Fry, head of cyber security policy and strategy at a small high-technology company, had been in protracted discussions with Christopher Russell, the company's financial director, regarding how a proactive approach to managing organizational cyber security interdependency involving stakeholders could be managed. She was aware of the pressure on companies and considered that inter-industry collaboration was essential for outmanoeuvring those behind cyber-attacks. Miss Fry held a firm view as regards what business continuity planning involved but Christopher Russell was less convinced. He considered that business continuity was a normal process and there was no need to invest in additional safeguards as the company was robust enough.

Mr. Russell's view was rooted in the fact that the company had been well able to sustain various types of cyber-attacks in recent years and that investing more in cyber security would take funds away from new product development projects and a planned factory site expansion. Mr. Russell considered that the contingency plans in place, which were three-years old, were sufficient to help the company to continue operating should an impact occur. This view was grounded in the belief that when he helped draw-up the emergency action plan, together with various staff, it was tested via a tabletop exercise. Those participating in the tabletop exercise were mostly in-house staff, but a number of additional external specialists were present and helped guide the activities. With respect to the disaster recovery plan in place, it was assumed that should a crisis turn into an emergency, then staff had the skills and the knowledge to deal with the issues that arose.

Sally Fry explained that a company that was well known to her had experienced a cyber-attack recently and had not been able to undertake its normal business operations for well over a week. The attack appeared to be well coordinated and involved ransomware. During the attack, the company's computer system was locked and it was impossible for staff to receive emails and send emails, and in the process of the attack, a number of files were either destroyed or the data was extracted and made available on the Dark Web. The immediate cost of the attack was thought to be in the region of US$70,000 and the cost of the recovery was expected to be well over US$200,000. In order to help the company recover, an outside consultancy company specializing in disaster recovery had been hired and was expected to work with company representatives for well over a month. This was because it was considered that the company's computer system and network facilities had to be upgraded and also, the software used had to be evaluated for errors and it was suggested that new software should be commissioned. The company's IT manager had been held responsible for the problem and had resigned and walked out the door vowing not to return. This meant that the company had no IT support services because the two other full-time members of staff responsible for IT were away on holiday and could not be contacted.

Sally Fry's view was that more attention needed to be given to the operating systems in place and how they would be affected if an attack got through the company's defences. She considered that a proactive approach was needed for cyber security and suggested that staff should undergo additional training that would make them more aware of how a cyber-attack could impact an organization and knowing this would make them better able to anticipate future cyber-attack(s). This had value she argued because it would place emphasis on linking cyber security management and strategic intelligence with cyber threat detection. To make clear her view, she outlined the company's known vulnerabilities and also highlighted the interdependencies. These were then transformed into intra-organizational and inter-organizational linkages. Next, she identified the individual managers responsible for business continuity and sketched out the tasks to be undertaken. The meeting ended rather abruptly when Mr. Russell was called into another meeting by the managing director. It seemed he was happy to leave the meeting because he considered the topic of discussion somewhat irrelevant.

After returning to her office and thinking through the conversation she had with Mr. Russell, she decided to send him a reflective note highlighting the main points discussed and included also information about a possible scenario that could be developed to help staff relate better to the subject matter discussed. Sally was of the view that a scenario could be devised that contained information relating to how business continuity could be managed and what should go into a business continuity plan. She wanted to include aspects of foresight and assign tasks and responsibilities to key individuals. She also considered that the logic model approach could be used to evaluate the organization's cyber security strategy and make staff aware of why it was important to remain cyber security aware. At the end of the document, she posed three questions:

Question 1: How can cyber security management training provision be made distinct from cyber security management educational provision?

Question 2: How useful is scenario analysis and planning with regards to foresight planning and future cyber security management strategy development?

Question 3: How useful is the logic model approach with regards to evaluating and formalizing cyber security policy?

References, website and further reading

Aldrich, C. (2004). *Simulations and the Future of Learning*. San Francisco, Cal: Pfeiffer.

Andreasson, K. (eds). (2012). *Cybersecurity: Public Sector Threats and Responses*. London: CRC Press.

Aviva. (2024). *Business Continuity*. Pitheavlis, Perth: Aviva Insurance Limited.

Baylis, J., Wirtz, J., Gray, C.S., and Cohen, E. (2007). *Strategy in the Contemporary World*. Oxford: Oxford University Press.

Bloom, P.N., and Chatterji, A.K. (2009). Scaling social entrepreneurial impact. *California Management Review*, 51 (3), pp. 114–133.

Buckley, P.J., and Ghauri, P.N. (2004). Globalisation, economic geography and the strategy of multinational enterprises. *Journal of International Business Studies*, 35, pp. 81–98.

Chakraborty, S., Mombeshora, E.M., Clark, K.P., and Mbavarira, T.S. (2024). Understanding of cyber-attack vulnerabilities during natural disasters and discussing a cyber-attack resiliency framework. In: *SoutheastCon 2024*, pp. 466–471. IEEE (15th to 24th March, 2024), DOI: 10.1109?SouthestCon52093.2024.10500233

Collins, A. (2007). *Contemporary Security Studies*. Oxford: Oxford University Press.

Connolly, L.Y., Wall, D.S., Lang, M., and Oddson, B. (2020). An empirical study of ransomware attacks on organizations: An assessment of severity and salient factors affecting vulnerability. *Journal of Cybersecurity*, pp. 1–18. Doi: 10.1093/cybsec/tyaa023

Cooperrider, D.L., and Srivastva, S. (1987). Appreciative inquiry in organizational life. In: Woodman, R.E., and Pasmore, W.A. (Eds.), *Research in Organizational Change and Development*, pp. 129–169. Greenwich, CT: JAI Press.

Dupont, B. (2019). The cyber-resilience of financial institutions: significance and applicability. *Journal of Cybersecurity*, 5 (1), pp. 1–17. Doi: 10.1093/cybsec/tyz013

Ebrahim, A., and Rangan, V.K. (2014). What impact? A framework for measuring the scale and scope of social performance. *California Management Review*, 56 (3), pp. 118–141. https://doi.org/10.1525/cmr.2014.56.3.118

Formosa, P., Wilson, M., and Richards, D. (2012). A principlist framework for cybersecurity ethics. *Computers & Security*, 109, 102382, pp. 1–15. https://doi.org/10.1016/jcose.2021.102382

Gagiu, P.C., and Rodriguez-Campos, L. (2007). Semi-structured interview protocol for constructing logic models. *Evaluation and Program Planning*, 30 (4), pp. 339–350. Doi:10.1016/j.evalprogplan.2007.08.004

Herrmann, D., and Pridöhl, H. (2020). Chapter 2 Basic Concepts and Models of Cybersecurity. In: Christen, M., Loi, M., and Gordijn, B. (eds.). *The Ethics of Cybersecurity*, pp. 11–44. The International Library of Ethics, Law and Technology Volume 21. Cham, Switzerland: Springer Nature Switzerland AG. https://doi.org/10.1007/978-3-030-29053-5

Jaquet-Chiffelle, D-O., and Loi, M. (2020). Chapter 9 Ethical and Unethical Hacking. In: Christen, M., Loi, M., and Gordijn, B. (eds.). *The Ethics of Cybersecurity*, pp. 179–205. The International Library of Ethics, Law and Technology Volume 21. Cham, Switzerland: Springer Nature Switzerland AG. https://doi.org/10.1007/978-3-030-29053-5

Kakabadse, A. (2000). From individual to team to cadre: Tracking leadership for the Third Millennium. *Strategic Change*, 9 (1), pp. 5–16.

Kirichenko, A., Christen, M., Grunow, F., and Herrman, D. (2020). Chapter 15 Best Practices and Recommendations for Cybersecurity Service Providers. In: Christen, M., Loi, M., and Gordijn, B. (eds.). *The Ethics of Cybersecurity*, pp. 299–316. The International Library of Ethics, Law and Technology Volume 21. Cham, Switzerland: Springer Nature Switzerland AG. https://doi.org/10.1007/978-3-030-29053-5

Kylaheiko, K., Jantunen, A., Puumalainen, K., Saarenketo, S., and Tuppura, A. (2011). Innovation and internationalization as a growth strategy: The role of technological capabilities and appropriability. *International Business Review*, 20 (5), pp. 508–520.

Lee, Y-I. (2009). Strategic transformational management in the context of inter-organizational and intra-organizational partnership development. In: Trim, P.R.J., and Caravelli, J. (eds.). *Strategizing Resilience and Reducing Vulnerability*, pp. 181–196. New York: Nova Science Publishers, Inc.

Lindgren, M., and Bandhold, H. (2003). *Scenario Planning: The Link between Future and Strategy*. Basingstoke: Palgrave.

Loi, M., and Christen, M. (2020). Chapter 4 Ethical Frameworks for Cybersecurity. In: Christen, M., Loi, M., and Gordijn, B. (eds.). *The Ethics of Cybersecurity*, pp. 73–95. The International Library of Ethics, Law and Technology Volume 21. Cham, Switzerland: Springer Nature Switzerland AG. https://doi.org/10.1007/978-3-030-29053-5

Lutz, J.M., and Lutz, B.J. (2005). *Terrorism: Origins and Evolution*. New York: Palgrave.

Macnish, K., and van der Ham, J. (2020). Ethics in cybersecurity research and practice. *Technology in Society*, 63, pp. 1–10, 101382. https://doi.org/10.1016/j.techsoc.2020.101382

Pfeifer, J.W. (2018). Preparing for cyber incidents with physical effects. *The Cyber Defense Review*, 3 (1), pp. 27–34.

Ringland, G. (2006). *Scenario Planning*. Chichester: John Wiley & Sons.

Salavou, H. (2005). Do customer and technology orientations influence product innovativeness in SMEs? Some new evidence from Greece. *Journal of Marketing Management*, 21 (3–4), pp. 307–338.

Sheffi, Y. (2005). *The Resilient Enterprise: Overcoming Vulnerability for Competitive Advantage*. Cambridge, Massachusetts: The MIT Press.

Trim, P.R.J. (2001a). Public-private partnerships in the defence industry and the extended corporate intelligence and national security model. *Strategic Change*, 10 (1), pp. 49–58.

Trim, P.R.J. (2001b). A framework for establishing and implementing corporate intelligence. *Strategic Change*, 10 (6), pp. 349–357.

Trim, P.R.J., and Caravelli, J. (eds.). (2009). *Strategizing Resilience and Reducing Vulnerability*. New York: NOVA Science Publishers, Inc.

Trim, P.R.J., and Lee, Y-I. (2006). Vertically integrated organizational marketing systems: A partnership approach for retailing organizations. *Journal of Business & Industrial Marketing*, 21 (3), pp. 151–163.

Trim, P.R.J., and Lee, Y-I. (2008). A strategic marketing intelligence and multi-organisational resilience model. *European Journal of Marketing*, 42 (7/8), pp. 731–745.

Trim, P.R.J., and Lee, Y-I. (2014). *Cyber Security Management: A Governance, Risk and Compliance Framework*. Farnham: Gower Publishing.

Trim, P.R.J., and Upton, D. (2013). *Cyber Security Culture: Counteracting Cyber Threats through Organizational Learning and Training*. Farnham: Gower Publishing.

UK Government. (2022). *National Cyber Strategy 2022. Pioneering a cyber future with the whole of the UK*. https://assets.publishing.service.gov.uk/media/620131fdd3bf7f78e469ce00/national-cyber-strategy-amend.pdf (Accessed 11th June, 2024).

van de Poel, I. (2020). Chapter 3 Core Values and Value Conflicts in Cybersecurity: Beyond Privacy Versus Security. In: Christen, M., Loi, M., and Gordijn, B. (eds.). *The Ethics of Cybersecurity*, pp. 45–71. The International Library of Ethics, Law and Technology Volume 21. Cham, Switzerland: Springer Nature Switzerland AG. https://doi.org/10.1007/978-3-030-29053-5

Verhoef, P.C., and Leeflang, P.S.H. (2009). Understanding the marketing department's influence within the firm. *Journal of Marketing*, 73 (2), pp. 14–37.

Walker, J., Williams, B.J., and Skelton, G.W. (2010). Cyber security for emergency management. In: *2010 IEEE International Conference on Technologies for Homeland Security (HST)*, pp. 476–480. Waltham, MA: IEEE. DOI: 10.1109/THS.2010.5654965 (8th to 10 December).

Website

Rubrick. (2024). *Business Continuity and Cybersecurity*. https://www.rubrik.com/insights/business-continuity-and-cybersecurity (Accessed 7th June, 2024).

Further reading

Christen, M., Loi, M., and Gordijn, B. (eds.). (2020). *The Ethics of Cybersecurity*. The International Library of Ethics, Law and Technology Volume 21. Cham, Switzerland: Springer Nature Switzerland AG. https://doi.org/10.1007/978-3-030-29053-5

Chung, M., Ko, E., Joung, H., and Kim, S.J. (2020). Chatbot e-service and customer satisfaction regarding luxury brands. *Journal of Business Research*, 117, pp. 587–595. https://doi.org/10.1016/j.busres.2018.10.004

Fisher, A. (2011). *Critical Thinking: An Introduction*. Cambridge: Cambridge University Press.

Paliwoda, S.J. (2011). Critically evaluating the IMP research contribution. *Industrial Marketing Management*, 40, pp. 1,055–1,056.

van der Merwe, R., Bentley, P.B., Pitt, L., and Barness, B. (2007). Analyzing 'theory networks': identifying the pivotal theories in marketing and their characteristics. *Journal of Marketing Management*, 23 (3–4), pp. 181–206.

Wright, L.T., Millman, C., and Martin, L.M. (2007). Research issues in building brand equity and global brands in the PC market. *Journal of Marketing Management*, 23(1–2), pp. 137–155.

INDEX

Pages followed by "n" refer to notes.

Aaker, D. A. 98–99
academic articles and conference papers
    55, 56–58
advanced persistent threat (APT) 26, 74,
    75, 78, 100
Ahmad, A. 99
Aldrich, C. 147
Al-Mohannadi, H. 34
Americas Partnership for Economic Prosperity
    (APEP) 29
analytical skills 9
Andreasson, K. 147
Anonymous 24–25
Arteche, A. 110
artificial intelligence (AI) 58–60, 69–84, 125;
    awareness 73–74; balancing opportunities
    with risk 72–73; case study 83–84; Dark
    Web 74–76; see also Dark Web; marketing
    and 152–153; threats 76–82
artificial neural networks (ANN) 59
autonomous vehicles 116–117
availability 159
avatars 80
Aviva 148–149
awareness see cyber security awareness

backdoor attack 26
Bandhold, H. 146–147
Barney, J. B. 49
Baylis, J. 145–146
BBC 99–100
big data 29
big data analytics 9
bioeconomy 78

bioindustry 78
BlackEnergy (BE) 107
blockchain-based supply-chain management
    (BC-SCM) 18
Bloom, P. N. 87
Bonfanti, M. E. 80
Boukherouaa, E.B. 70, 71
Bresniker, K. 80
British Library 92–93
Brockhoff, K. 97
Bromiley, P. 137–138
Buckley, P. J. 153
business continuity 148
business continuity management 148
business continuity management
    programme 149
business continuity plan 148–149; business
    recovery planning 149; emergency action
    planning 149; risk analysis 149; service
    levels 149; testing and maintaining
    149–150
business continuity policy 148

Cambridge University Press & Assessment
    (CUPA) 93
Camrose, Viscount 58
Capital One 71
Carnegie Mellon University 94–95
categorization of data 47–49
Cavelty, M.D. 50, 80–81
CCTV 119
Center for Strategic and International Studies
    (US) 9, 13
Chakraborty, S. 157–158

ChatGPT (Chat Generative Pre-Trained Transformer) 70, 80
Chatterji, A. K. 87
Chen, D. 118
Chertoff, M. 74–75
Chief Information Officer (CIO) 21
Chief Information Security Officer (CISO) 21
Chief Security Officer (CSO) 21
Christen, M. 160–161
collectivist approach 2, 4, 7, 19, 20, 28, 36; case study 65–66; logic underpinning 46–47
collectivist enterprise risk management approach 62, 147–152; case study 140–142; intellectual property rights 128; objective 126; risk management 136–139
Collins, A. 145
Colonial Pipeline 107
common ground 35–36
Conference on Cyberspace 52
confidentiality 159
Connolly, L.Y. 150
controls: internal 133; security 133
cooperative partnership 114; see also partnership
Corbin, J. 35
corporate security 155
corporate social responsibility 79
criminal entrepreneur 23
critical friendship group 129–130, 141
critical infrastructure 106–108; challenges and issues 106–108
Critical Thinking Problem Solution 133
culture (cyber security) 91–94
Cuntz, A. 51
CWT 16
Cyber Attack Modeling and Impact Assessment Component (CAMIAC) 34
cyber attacks 9–14, 99–100; categorization 9–13, **11–12**, 76; changing nature 18; interpretation 10; risk rating 10, **11–12**; Ukrainian power system 107–108; variation 14; see also threat actor(s)/agent(s)
cyber bullying 113, 140
cyber criminals 4, 19, 22, 23–24, 25, 27, 28, 31, 35, 48, 50, 81–82, 100, 101, 108–109, 110, 116
cyber espionage 4, 13, 24, 50, 77, 79, 81
cyberpsychology 96–97
cyber security see collectivist approach; culture 91–94; defined 14–15; developing appreciation 17–19; incidents see cyber attacks; knowledge 128; risk register 133–136, **134–135**; situational awareness and analysis 94–96; vulnerabilities 15–16
cyber security awareness 19, 130; academic articles and conference papers **55**, 56–58;

organizational learning and 96–99; threat 110–112; training videos 53–55
cyber security education 154–155
cybersecurity management 4, 15
cyber security managers 1–4, 9, 10, 13–14; course of action 36; fear appeal(s) 19; organizing intelligence function 14; solutions to evolving situations 34–35; see also artificial intelligence (AI); cyber attacks; cyber security
"Cyber security strategy of the European Union: An open, safe and secure cyberspace" 51–52
cyberterrorists 25
cyber threat intelligence (CTI) 19–27; policy and strategy framework 131–133; sociocultural intelligence 128
cyber warfare/conflict 13

DarkSide ransomware 107
Dark Web 19, 23, 61, 74–76, 77, 83, 87, 92, 99, 160
data: breach 16; categorization 30, 47–49
data challenges 29
datafication 9
data replication 150
Davis, B. J. 88–89
DeBerry-Spence, B. 20
Declaration for the Future of the Internet (DFI) 28
deepfakes 71, 81, 84, 109
Deep Learning (DL) 59, 81, 118
defensive intelligence 9
delivery 87
detailed knowledge 9
digital footprint 22, 41
digital risk and intelligence 22
disaster recovery 150
disaster recovery as a service (DRAAS) 150
distributed denial-of-service (DDoS) attacks 26, 100
DNA-based exploit 77
DoS attacks 26, 107
drones 87, 117
Dupont, B. 150, 151–152
Duqu 107
dynamic capabilities theory 86

emergency planning 156–158
espionage see cyber espionage
ethical considerations 158–161
European Commission 17, 51–52
European Cybercrime Centre 29
European Union 161
European Union Agency for Cybersecurity (ENISA) 79–80, 100

Fahy, M. 115
fake news 59, 76, 80, 109, 128
fear appeals 19
Ferdinand, J. 15
financial terrorism 81
formal ties 128
Formosa, P. 158, 159
Four-Pillar Model of Critical Information
    Infrastructure Protection 98
four-step operation cycle approach 113
Freeman, R. E. 49

GDPR (General Data Protection
    Regulation) 161
GenAI (Generative AI) 70, 71–72
Ghauri, P. N. 153
Glassman, M. 113
Global Positioning System (GPS) 117
Goodman, M. 108–109
Google Street View 108–109
government and institutional commitment to
    societal well-being 60
Government Communications Headquarters
    (GCHQ) 27
government policy 155
Grove, G. D. 9

hackers-for-hire 100
hacking 24, 26, 48–49, 100, 159
hacktivists 24, 72–73, 74, 100; groups 100
Han, S-L. 94
Harrison, J. S. 49
Haunschild, J. 50
Haveman, H. A. 36
Havex 107
Herrmann, D. 158–159
Hidden Wiki 74
hospitals 99–100
Hossain, S. K. T. 76
Huang, M-H. 80
human machine interface (HMI) 107
human resource management 153–154;
    leadership and 155

IBM 24, 26
IIP (identity, ideological and political)
    factors 10
Independent 99
Indonesia 26
Indo-Pacific Economic Framework for
    Prosperity (IPEF) 29
Industrial Control System (ICS) 106–107
Industroyer/CrashOverride 107
inference 59
informal ties 128
information breach 16

information security 155
Informatization White Paper (Korea Internet
    and Security Agency) 52
insider threat 25, 97
integrity 159
intelligence service (MI6) 27
internal controls 133
international agreements 27–29
International Counter-Ransomware
    Initiative 29
International Monetary Fund (IMF) 15
international relations 155
Internet-of-Medical-Things (IoMT) 18
Internet of Things (IoT) 117–118
inter-organization collaboration 156
intra-government and inter-government
    cooperation 27–29
intra-organizational collaboration 156

Jaquet-Chiffelle, D-O. 161
Jenab, K. 15
Jones, N. A. 62–63
JPMorgan Chase 71

Kakabadse, A. 154
Kang, M. J. 113
Karmini, N. 26
Kauppi, M. V. 10
Kill Chain Attack modelling technique 34
Kirichenko, A. 161
Konig, L. 111
Kracher, B. 48–49
Kujala, J. 49
Kumar, A. 75–76
Kwon, I-W. G. 94

Lange, D. 35
law 155
Lawrence, T. B. 90
leadership: human resource management and
    155; stakeholder theory 49; strategic
    intelligence 9
learning approach 147
"Learning Lessons from the Cyber-attack"
    (British Library) 92
learning organization 98
Lee, Y-I. 90, 94, 98, 138
Leicester City Council 99
Lim, H.S.M. 115–117
Lim, K. 9
Lindgren, M. 146–147
logical layer 151
logic model approach 156–158
Loi, M. 160–161
Lutz, B. J. 145
Lutz, J. M. 145

machine learning (ML) 58, 70, 79–80, 81; *see also* artificial intelligence (AI)
Macnish, K. 161
Madnick, S. 111
Makrakis, G. M. 106–107
malicious actors *see* overseas-based threat actors
malware 15, 16, 24, 25–26, 34, 59, 74, 76, 80, 84, 93, 100, 107, 115, 118, 130, 137, 159
management challenges 29
Maness, R. C. 13
marketers 152–153; internal marketing programmes 155
marketing 155; strategic 131
Martin, K. D. 48–49
mathematical frameworks 89
Mathur, M. 86
McAuley, A. 115
McLoughlin, D. 98–99
Microsoft 13
modelling approach 89–91
Montgomery, D.B. 9
Morris, D. 14–15
Moslehpour, S. 15
multifactor authentication (MFA) 93, 158
Murch, R. S. 78
mutual market responsibility 115

Nardini, G. 87, 130
National Cyber Security Centre (NCSC) 16, 20–21, 27
National Health Service (NHS) 17
National Institute of Standards and Technology (NIST) 132–134, 136, 137, 138
National Protective Security Authority (NPSA) 27
national security 112
National Technical Authority 27
natural sciences 35
Ney, P. 77
Northern Lincolnshire and Goole NHS Foundation Trust 92
NotPetya 107

Odom, W. E. 112
Ofcom (Office of Communications, UK) 75
offensive intelligence 9
The Onion Router 74
Online Safety Act (UK) 75
OpenAI 71
Open-Source Intelligence (OSINT) 112–113, 119
organizational cyber security 60, 88–89; culture 91–94; interdependency 144–147; inter-government relationship 145; learning and awareness 60, 96–99; modelling

frameworks 89–91; recent attacks 99–100; situational awareness 94–96
organizational interventions 47
organizational learning 60, 89, 96–99
overseas-based threat actors 28

Paiuc, D. 8
partnership 113–115; arrangements 28–29, 119; case study 121–122; cooperative 114; international 27–29; need for 113–115; sustainable, strategic approach to 119
passive intelligence 9
Pastor-Galindo, J. 112
Patton, K. 113, 128
Pearce, F. T. 97
Pelosi, Nancy 109
penetration test/testing 159–160
Pfarrer, M. D. 35
Pfeifer, J. W. 157
phishing emails 16, 19, 22, 24, 25, 61, 71, 76, 79, 88, 93, 95, 100, 107, 110
physical layer 151
power outage 107–108
Pridöhl, H. 158–159
Privileged Access Management (PAM) 93
process challenges 29
project management 155

Qian, Y. 51
Quadrilateral Security Dialogue 29

Radoynovska, N. 49
Raiyn, J. 116
RAND 113
ransomware 16, 24, 41, 52, **53**, 76, 77, 99–100, 101, 111, 128, 150, 157, 163; British Library 92; cyber criminals 35; DarkSide 107; defined 25; Essex school 99; INC 93; Indonesia 26; Leicester City Council 99; LockBit 26; software 96; WannaCry 92, 107
Ransomware-as-a-Service (RaaS) 100
relationship-building process 49
risk context 136–137; external 136; internal 136–137
risk management 95, 136–139, 155
Risk Management Solutions, Inc. 47–48
risk rating system 9, 10
risk register 133–136, **134–135**
Rosenbach, E. 75–76
Rubrick 150
Rust, R. T. 80, 89

Salavou, H. 153
SCADA (Supervisory Control and Data Acquisition) 106, 120, 121
scaling out 87

scaling up 87
scenario analysis and planning 9, 21, 61, 62, 99, 117, 119, 122, 146, 155
Schünemann, W. J. 50
Schweidel, D. A. 89
security controls 133
security service (MI5) 27
Senge, P. M. 98
sequence-of-events model 128
SG (security and geographic) factors 10
Shabsigh, G. 70, 71
Shamoon 107
Shaping Tomorrow 8–9
Sheffi, Y. 115, 151
situational awareness and analysis 94–96
Sivarajah, U. 17, 29
smart cities 115–119
social engineering attacks 16, 22, 25–26, 61, 65, 76, 77, 88–89, 100, 109, 116, 117, 120
social media networks and platforms 108–110
social network theory 86
sociocultural intelligence 128, 140, 141
South Korea 51, 52
spear phishing attacks 16, 25, 76, 79
spoofing 76, 110, 117
stakeholder approach 4, 49
state-nexus threat groups 100
Stine, K. 132, 136–137
strategic intelligence 155; defined 8–9; geopolitical events 9; leadership 9; objective 8
strategic intelligence approach 60
strategic marketing 131
Strauss, A. 35
Stuxnet 107
Suh, T. 94
Sun, C-C. 107
The Sunday Times 109
supply chain partners 60
Synnovis 100

Taeihagh, A. 115–117
Thakhur, K. 109
theft of intellectual property 16
theoretical insights 33–36
threat actors/agent(s) 15, 18, 19–27, 63; common ground 35–36; ENISA categorising 100; interpreting actions 10

threat awareness see cyber security awareness
threat detection software 77
thrill seekers 25
Thuraisingham, B. 108
TM (technological and military) factors 10
training videos 53–55
trilateral security and technology pact 29
Trilateral Security Dialogue (TSD) 29
Trim, P. R. J. 62–63, 90, 94, 98, 138
tripartite cyber-criminal entity 23–24
Triton/Trisis/HatMan 107
T-shaped scaling framework 87, 128–129, 130

Ukraine 107
United Nations (UN) 13, 115; Framework for Responsible State Behaviour 111
Unites Staes (US) 27–29; bioeconomy 78
universities 93
unmanned aerial vehicles (UAV) see drones
US–EU Trade and Technology Council (TTC) 29

Valeriano, B. 13
van de Poel, I. 160
van der Ham, J. 161
Vattapparamban, E. 117
Viotti, P. R. 10
virtual layer 150–151
VPNFilter 107
vulnerabilities 15–16

Walker, J. 157
Walters, R. 74–75
WannaCry 92, 107
Web-based platforms see social media networks and platforms
Weinberg, C.B. 9
Wells Fargo 71
Wenger, A. 50, 80–81
Westley, F. 87
Woodward, B. 111

Yamin, M. M. 125

Zahorik, A. J. 89
zero trust data security 150

Printed in the United States
by Baker & Taylor Publisher Services